Quantum Ready

Are you ready for the day your encryption fails silently?

Quantum Ready is not just a warning; it's a field guide for the era of quantum disruption. As quantum computing accelerates toward the threshold where today's encryption becomes obsolete, organizations must prepare now or risk a catastrophic breakdown in digital trust.

Written by one of the world's first Field CISOs, this book delivers a strategic, vendor-neutral roadmap for CISOs, security architects, and IT leaders responsible for protecting long-term data and infrastructure. It introduces the Q-Ready Framework, a comprehensive five-phase approach to discovering, prioritizing, migrating, validating, and sustaining quantum-safe cryptography across the enterprise.

In this hands-on guide, you'll learn how to:

- Identify where vulnerable cryptography lives in your environment
- Evaluate business impact using real-world risk models like Mosca's equation
- Design migration and testing plans tailored to your infrastructure
- Replace RSA, ECC, and other algorithms with NIST-approved quantum-safe alternatives
- Apply post-quantum cryptography to TLS, VPNs, code signing, and IoT
- Build crypto-agility into your systems, teams, and governance

With practical checklists, actionable advice, and insights from hundreds of field engagements, *Quantum Ready* goes beyond theory and into the trenches. Whether you're already on your migration journey or just beginning to assess the threat, this book will prepare you to lead with confidence through one of the biggest shifts in cybersecurity history.

The clock is ticking. Read now, and be the reason your organization is still trusted tomorrow.

Walt Powell, an experienced Executive Coach and CISO Advisor, has extensive experience working with countless CISOs and developing cybersecurity programs. Walt helped pioneer the role of Field CISO and is a Founding Member of the Global Security Strategy Office at CDW. Walt now leads a team of Field CISOs, composed entirely of former executives, who bring a wealth of experience and knowledge to their clients, underpinned by unique insights gained from contributing to and learning from the strategies of hundreds of CISOs and CIOs across every size of organization and vertical. Walt and his team leverage this wealth of knowledge and experience to provide executive coaching, support, and mentorship to elevate other CISOs, their programs, and organizations, sharing lessons and providing strategic guidance that would typically take several careers to acquire.

Quantum Ready

The Enterprise Guide to Post-Quantum Cryptographic Readiness

Walt Powell

CRC Press
Taylor & Francis Group
Boca Raton London New York

CRC Press is an imprint of the
Taylor & Francis Group, an **informa** business

Designed cover image: Shutterstock ID: 2228719455

First edition published 2026
by CRC Press
2385 NW Executive Center Drive, Suite 320, Boca Raton FL 33431

and by CRC Press
4 Park Square, Milton Park, Abingdon, Oxon, OX14 4RN

CRC Press is an imprint of Taylor & Francis Group, LLC

ISBN: 9781041166689 (hbk)
ISBN: 9781041166696 (pbk)
ISBN: 9781003685760 (ebk)

DOI: 10.1201/9781003685760

Typeset in Sabon
by Deanta Global Publishing Services, Chennai, India

Dedicated to my family – Lindsay, Rivers, and Axel

Thanks for all the love and support

Contents

Foreword

As a cybersecurity scientist, standards leader, and advisor on critical infrastructure protection, I have spent the last few years of my career helping organizations prepare for emerging technological threats, especially those posed by quantum computing. My work includes serving as Chair of Quantum Technologies and Cybersecurity for the InfraGard National Members Alliance Cross-Sector Council, leading the IEEE P1947 Working Group to develop a Quantum Cybersecurity Framework, chairing SC10 for IEEE Industry Connections on Next-Generation Cybersecurity in Quantum Computing, and co-founding the Quantum Economic Development Consortium's Quantum Use Cases Technical Advisory Committee. Through these roles, I have collaborated with industry, government, and academic stakeholders to translate quantum science into practical, actionable strategies for security and resilience.

The quantum threat is no longer an academic curiosity or distant concern; it is a systemic risk to the very foundations of digital trust on which our economy, government, and society rely. As someone who has spent years working at the intersection of quantum science, cybersecurity policy, and critical infrastructure protection, I have seen firsthand both the unprecedented opportunities quantum technologies offer and the serious obligations they impose on us as stewards of secure systems.

Quantum computing promises remarkable advances in materials science, logistics, finance, and medicine. Yet it also threatens to undermine the cryptographic safeguards that enable everything from online banking and secure communications to the integrity of software updates and industrial control systems. This is not a hypothetical risk set decades in the future. Adversaries are already executing "Harvest Now, Decrypt Later" strategies, collecting encrypted data today in anticipation of decrypting it when sufficiently powerful quantum systems become available.

Over the past several years, I have had the privilege of working with a wide range of stakeholders in industry, government, and academia to confront this challenge directly. As Chair of Quantum Technologies and Cybersecurity on the InfraGard National Members Alliance Cross-Sector Council, I help critical infrastructure owners and operators understand both the quantum threat and the promise of quantum technologies for enhanced resilience. At the IEEE Standards Association, I chair the P1947 Working Group, developing a Quantum Cybersecurity Framework that will provide much-needed guidance and standardization for enterprises navigating this shift.

Previously, as Chair of SC10 within the IEEE Industry Connections initiative on Next-Generation Cybersecurity in Quantum Computing, I worked with experts to define the core principles of quantum cybersecurity as a practice, highlighting the importance of threat modeling, risk-based decision-making, governance, and standards development. These efforts underscored that post-quantum readiness is not simply a technical migration project but an enterprise-wide transformation that demands leadership, collaboration, and sustained commitment.

I am also a co-founding member of the Quantum Economic Development Consortium's (QED-C) Quantum Use Cases Technical Advisory Committee. In this role, I have collaborated with industry leaders, technologists, and government partners to identify and evaluate real-world quantum security use cases across sectors. Notably, I helped organize and lead workshops such as the QED-C Financial Messaging Security Workshop, which brought together financial institutions, technology providers, and policy experts to analyze the impact of post-quantum cryptography (PQC) and quantum key distribution (QKD) on securing cross-border payments, infrastructure, and communications. These workshops did not just advance theoretical understanding; they produced concrete recommendations and frameworks for transitioning entire sectors toward quantum-resilient security architectures.

This experience has reinforced for me that readiness is not just about technical adoption but about strategic foresight, governance, and communication across entire organizations and industries. That is exactly the perspective this book embraces. In *Quantum Ready*, Walt Powell provides one of the most clear-eyed, practical, and actionable guides available for enterprises preparing for the post-quantum era. Rather than leaning on hype or abstract theory, he offers a phased, operational framework, the Q-Ready model, that organizations of any size or industry can adopt. This approach aligns with the guidance emerging from NIST, CISA, and standards bodies worldwide, yet it is presented in accessible language that empowers CISOs, engineers, architects, and executives alike to plan and act.

It is especially important to recognize that the urgency here is real. As Walt rightly emphasizes, remediation is not a switch to be flipped on "Q-Day". It is a multi-year effort requiring discovery of cryptographic assets, risk assessments, vendor coordination, crypto-agile architectures, workforce training, and staged remediation. Early planning reduces cost, complexity, and business disruption while helping to maintain customer trust, compliance readiness, and operational resilience.

This book is not just for cybersecurity practitioners. It is for board members, policymakers, technology leaders, and business executives who must treat quantum readiness as an enterprise risk management imperative. Walt's emphasis on governance, accountability, and cross-functional collaboration reflects exactly the kind of mindset organizations will need to navigate the post-quantum transition successfully.

I commend Walt Powell for writing this timely and important book. It is a necessary call to action and a practical guide for anyone responsible for safeguarding systems, data, and critical infrastructure in the decade to come. *Quantum Ready* belongs on the shelf of every security leader preparing their organization to weather one of the most consequential technological shifts of our time.

We cannot afford to wait. The time to act is now. This book is a great resource to take this next step!

Dr. Keeper L. Sharkey, PhD
Chair, Quantum Technologies and Cybersecurity, InfraGard National Members Alliance Chair, IEEE P1947 Standards Working Group for Quantum Cybersecurity Former Chair, SC10, IEEE Industry Connections Next-Generation Cybersecurity in Quantum Computing Co-Founding Member, Quantum Use Cases Technical Advisory Committee, Quantum Economic Development Consortium (QED-C) Founder and CEO, ODE, L3C

Acknowledgments

To my Field CISO team, John Candillo, Aaron McCray, Justin MacDonald, Steve Allison, Tom Sinnott, and our director, Buck Bell, thank you for your insights, for reviewing chapters, and for being a phenomenal group of collaborators. Your collective knowledge and experience have added depth and richness to every page.

My gratitude also goes to Dan Swanson, whose willingness to share knowledge and resources has been invaluable. Your perspective and support have been a guiding force throughout the development of this book.

Thank you to Casey Kochey for your help in drafting the original whitepaper and for creating the Q-Ready Framework graphics. Your early work shaped the foundation of what this book became.

Thank you to Jeffrey C. Thompson, MS CS, JD, for the thoughtful peer review and the many insightful notes and suggestions along the way. Your feedback sharpened the manuscript and helped surface new angles and ideas that made this book stronger.

To my family, Lindsay, Rivers, and Axel, thank you for your constant love and encouragement. This book is for you, and it would not exist without your patience and support.

I would also like to recognize Michele Mosca, a Canadian mathematician whose contributions to the field of quantum computing have had a lasting impact. As a professor at the University of Waterloo and co-founder of the Institute for Quantum Computing, he has dedicated his career to bridging the gap between theoretical research and practical application. His early work helped bring clarity to the quantum threat at a time when few were paying attention. I am especially grateful for his development of a clear and actionable threat model, which has shaped how many of us approach quantum risk today.

A special thanks to Dr. Keeper L. Sharkey for writing the foreword to this book and for her thought leadership in the quantum cybersecurity community. As Chair of the IEEE P1947 Working Group, her efforts to establish a Quantum Cybersecurity Framework have been instrumental in guiding industry readiness. Her deep commitment to translating quantum science into practical, actionable security strategies continues to shape how critical infrastructure, government, and enterprise stakeholders prepare for the quantum era. I am honored to include her voice in this work.

To everyone who contributed ideas, time, or guidance during this project, I am truly grateful. Your involvement gave this work its strength and its purpose.

About the author

Walt Powell, an experienced Executive Coach and CISO Advisor, has extensive experience working with countless CISOs and developing cybersecurity programs. Walt helped pioneer the role of Field CISO and is a Founding Member of the Global Security Strategy Office at CDW. Walt now leads a team of Field CISOs, composed entirely of former executives, who bring a wealth of experience and knowledge to their clients, underpinned by unique insights gained from contributing to and learning from the strategies of hundreds of CISOs and CIOs across every size of organization and vertical. Walt and his team leverage this wealth of knowledge and experience to provide executive coaching, support, and mentorship to elevate other CISOs, their programs, and organizations, sharing lessons and providing strategic guidance that would typically take several careers to acquire.

Prior to his role at CDW, Walt was the owner and vCISO at Left Brain Security, which is now Left Brain Security Media. He has served as an award-winning cybersecurity leader, advisor, architect, and pre-sales engineer, and has also served as a professor of networking and security at Wright College. Walt firmly believes in the importance of giving back to the industry, which is why he taught CISSP and CISM boot camps and contributes as a certification exam development committee member for numerous organizations. He holds an impressive array of professional certifications, including CISSP, CISM, C|CISO, Carnegie Mellon CISO, the Stanford Advanced Cybersecurity Certificate, and numerous technical and sales certifications from leading cybersecurity firms. Walt also leads a cybersecurity book club, which is being launched as a podcast.

Walt Powell is also the author of *The CISO 3.0: A Guide to Next-Generation Cybersecurity Leadership*, which is a practical guide for cybersecurity leaders looking to evolve into strategic business partners, offering tools, insights, and real-world examples to align security with enterprise goals and board-level priorities, reflecting Walt's mission to elevate the role of the CISO beyond technical execution.

A proud Mensa member and futurist, Walt is deeply invested in exploring the implications of emerging technologies on cybersecurity. He actively contributes to the cybersecurity community by writing and speaking at industry conferences such as BSides, CypherCon, and Crowdstrike Fal.con, sharing white papers, and authoring articles on critical security topics. Beyond his professional life, Walt is a former professional musician and multi-instrumentalist who cherishes spending quality time with his children, traveling, and learning new languages.

AI usage

For *Quantum Ready*, the author used OpenAI's ChatGPT (GPT-4) to assist with outlining and refining select sections of the manuscript, particularly for formatting and summarization. Version GPT-4 was employed throughout the development process to improve consistency and generate Alt Text for figures. Additionally, the book cover was generated using OpenAI's ChatGPT with image generation capabilities.

Preface

We live in a moment of technological transition. What has long been theoretical, the idea that quantum computers could one day undermine the cryptographic foundations of modern systems, is quickly becoming real. The purpose of this book is to help organizations navigate that transition. Not with vague warnings or overhyped predictions, but with clear, practical guidance on what to do, when to do it, and how to do it well.

This book is written for technical leaders responsible for making and sustaining long-term cryptographic decisions. That includes CISOs, security architects, PKI engineers, DevSecOps leads, and anyone responsible for the cryptographic health of an enterprise. You may already be deep into the weeds of key management and certificate lifecycle tooling. Or you may be just starting to ask whether your infrastructure will be ready when the day comes. Either way, this book is designed to meet you where you are.

My goal is to turn an abstract threat into a concrete plan. Each chapter focuses on a different part of the migration journey, from discovery and inventory, through algorithm replacement and certificate renewal, all the way to ongoing maintenance and operational readiness. Along the way, we emphasize the role of crypto-agility, hybrid deployments, and shared accountability across teams.

If you're confident in your understanding of cryptography, certificates, and public key infrastructure, feel free to skip ahead. However, if you need a refresher or want to bring a colleague up to speed, the following primer provides the high-level context you require.

P.1 A BRIEF PRIMER ON CRYPTOGRAPHY AND ITS BUILDING BLOCKS

At its core, cryptography is the science of protecting information. It ensures that messages, data, or transactions remain confidential, unaltered, and attributable to a trusted source. Cryptography gives us privacy, integrity, and authenticity, all without requiring physical locks or face-to-face conversations.

To accomplish this, modern cryptography relies on several foundational concepts:

P.1.1 Symmetric and asymmetric cryptography

Most systems use a combination of two main types of cryptography: symmetric and asymmetric.

Symmetric encryption uses a single key to encrypt and decrypt data. Both parties must have the same secret key, which makes it fast but also harder to manage securely at scale. AES (Advanced Encryption Standard) is the most common symmetric algorithm. When you encrypt a file or a hard drive, you're probably using AES.

Asymmetric encryption, also known as public key cryptography, uses a pair of keys: one public, one private. You can share your public key freely, but only your private key can unlock messages encrypted with it. This allows for secure communication without the need to share a secret in advance. Rivest-Shamir-Adleman (RSA) and elliptic curve cryptography (ECC) are classic examples. Asymmetric algorithms are often used for key exchange, digital signatures, and establishing trust between machines.

P.1.2 Algorithms and their vulnerabilities

Every cryptographic function relies on an algorithm, a defined sequence of steps used to transform information in a predictable yet secure way. These algorithms do the heavy lifting behind the scenes, whether it's scrambling data so it can't be read, verifying the identity of a message sender, or ensuring that a file hasn't been tampered with. Depending on the goal, different types of algorithms are used.

Some algorithms are designed for *encryption*, which is the process of hiding information from unauthorized access. Others are used for *digital signatures*, which don't hide data, but instead prove who created it and whether it's been changed since. You can think of encryption as sealing a letter inside an envelope, and signing as scrawling your name across the flap so others can confirm you were the sender.

Encryption relies on *keys*, which are essentially very large numbers that act as instructions for locking and unlocking the data. When you encrypt something, the algorithm takes your message and combines it with the key in a way that makes the result look like gibberish to anyone who doesn't have the right key to reverse the process. Imagine turning a document into an unreadable block of noise. Without the key, it stays that way. With the right key, the algorithm knows how to turn the noise back into the original message.

Key generation is handled by algorithms designed to create unpredictable values. These often utilize random number generators and employ complex mathematical algorithms to ensure that no one can guess the output. For example, RSA key generation depends on selecting large prime numbers and multiplying them together. The math involved makes it easy to encrypt the message if you have the key, but extremely hard to decrypt it without one.

Some algorithms, such as SHA-1, are used for hashing, a one-way process. Hashing takes a piece of data, like a password, document, or file, and creates a short, fixed-size "digest" that represents it. You can think of it like creating a fingerprint. Even a tiny change in the original data will produce a completely different fingerprint. This makes hashing useful for checking integrity. If two files produce the same hash, they're almost certainly identical. If the hashes don't match, something has been altered.

Hashes are also commonly used in digital signatures and password verification. In a digital signature, a sender might hash a document and sign that hash, proving both authorship and that the contents haven't changed. In password storage, instead of saving the actual password, systems store its hash. When you log in, your password is hashed again, and the system compares it to the stored version. This means the actual password is never stored or transmitted in clear text.

Some algorithms, such as RSA or ECDSA, are used for signing or encryption. Each type serves a different purpose, and often they are used in combination. For instance, a file might be encrypted with *AES* (a symmetric algorithm), signed with *RSA* (an asymmetric algorithm), and hashed with *SHA-384* to verify integrity.

Over time, some of these algorithms have become vulnerable. SHA-1 can now be broken with affordable computing power. RSA with small key sizes can be brute-forced. Even elliptic curve cryptography, once considered efficient and secure, is expected to fall to quantum attacks. In contrast, algorithms like AES-256 and SHA-384 remain solid defenses, at least against classical computers.

P.1.3 Keys

A *key* is simply a long string of numbers, but in cryptography, it serves as a passcode or identity badge. A *private key* is kept secret and used to decrypt data or create digital signatures. A *public key* is shared and used to encrypt data or verify a signature.

Behind every cryptographic operation is a key. Managing those keys, how they're generated, stored, rotated, revoked, and eventually retired, is the foundation of secure cryptographic systems. This discipline is known as *key management*.

Key management covers the entire lifecycle of cryptographic keys, including:

- *Generation*: Creating strong, unique keys using secure random number generation.
- *Storage*: Ensuring keys are safely stored in a way that prevents unauthorized access.
- *Distribution*: Safely transmitting keys to the right users or systems.
- *Rotation*: Regularly replacing old keys with new ones to reduce exposure if a key is compromised.
- *Revocation and Destruction*: Retiring keys when they are no longer needed or when trust is lost.

To do this securely at scale, most organizations rely on dedicated technologies.

P.1.3.1 Hardware Security Modules (HSMs)

An *HSM* is a physical device built specifically to generate, store, and manage cryptographic keys. It's designed to resist tampering and provides secure environments for key operations. When a key is stored in an HSM, it never leaves the device in plaintext. All cryptographic operations, such as signing or encryption, happen inside the HSM itself. This makes it extremely difficult for attackers to extract or misuse private keys, even if they gain access to the surrounding systems.

HSMs are commonly used by banks, government agencies, and cloud providers where key protection is non-negotiable. They are also used to protect the private keys of root and intermediate certificate authorities.

P.1.3.2 Key Management Services (KMS)

A *Key Management Service* is a cloud-based or on-premises solution that handles key lifecycle tasks, generation, rotation, permissions, and auditing. AWS KMS, Azure Key Vault, and Google Cloud KMS are common examples. These systems often integrate with other cloud services, making it easier to encrypt storage, databases, or messages without manually handling keys.

KMSs abstract away much of the operational complexity while still allowing control over who can use what key and when. Policies and access controls help prevent misuse, while audit logs track key usage for compliance purposes.

P.1.3.3 Secrets Management Systems

While KMS handles keys used for cryptographic operations, **secrets management systems** focus on credentials like API keys, tokens, passwords, and database credentials. Tools like HashiCorp Vault, CyberArk, and Azure

Key Vault (in its secret mode) help store these sensitive values securely, manage access, and ensure they are rotated regularly. They can also inject secrets into applications at runtime, avoiding hardcoded credentials in code or config files.

P.1.3.4 Key Rotation and Physical Vaulting

Key rotation is the practice of replacing keys at regular intervals. This limits the damage if a key is ever compromised. For example, symmetric keys used in encrypted backups might be rotated monthly, while TLS certificates are often renewed annually. Automated rotation policies enforced by KMS or secrets managers reduce the risk of human error.

In high-security environments, *master keys*, such as the root keys used by internal CAs or to encrypt key-encrypting keys, may be stored offline in a *physical vault*. These master keys might exist only on secure USB tokens, smart cards, or paper backups, stored in safety deposit boxes or physically split across multiple locations. This approach, called "air gapping", minimizes exposure and ensures that even a full network compromise won't expose the most sensitive keys.

P.1.4 Certificates and trust

A *digital certificate* binds a public key to a specific identity. For example, when you visit a secure website, your browser checks its certificate to ensure the site really is who it claims to be. That certificate includes the public key, the domain name, and metadata, all signed by a trusted third party called a *Certificate Authority (CA)*.

In many enterprise environments, organizations choose to operate their own internal Certificate Authority rather than relying solely on commercial third parties. This is especially common for internal services, identity systems, and development environments. By standing up your own CA, you gain control over issuance policies, validity periods, naming conventions, and automation workflows.

Setting up a CA involves generating a private key and a self-signed root certificate. That root certificate becomes the trust anchor for everything below it. From there, you can issue intermediate certificates, which in turn sign end-entity (or leaf) certificates used by servers, devices, or users. Most enterprise deployments use intermediate CAs for day-to-day operations, while keeping the root CA offline to maximize security.

A root CA is the single most critical trust anchor in your certificate hierarchy. If it's compromised, all certificates signed by it (directly or indirectly) lose their integrity. For this reason, many organizations keep their root CA offline. This means the private key is stored in a secure, air-gapped environment that is not connected to any network. Signing events happen manually, often in highly controlled ceremonies that include audit trails, witness validation, and physical security measures.

Using an offline root CA minimizes the attack surface and ensures the long-term trustworthiness of the hierarchy. Intermediate CAs handle the operational workload, including issuing certificates for servers and users. At the same time, the root CA is reserved for rare, high-priority actions, such as renewing or creating a new intermediate.

Sometimes a certificate must be revoked before its expiration date. This could happen if the associated private key is lost or compromised, if the certificate was issued in error, or if the identity bound to the certificate is no longer valid (e.g., an employee leaves or a system is decommissioned).

Revocation is handled through two primary mechanisms:

- *Certificate Revocation Lists (CRLs)*: A CA periodically publishes a signed list of serial numbers for certificates that are no longer valid. Clients download the list and check whether the certificate in question is on it.
- *Online Certificate Status Protocol (OCSP)*: Instead of downloading a full list, clients can ask an OCSP responder whether a specific certificate is valid. This allows for more efficient, real-time validation.

Not all systems consistently check for revocation, and availability issues with CRL or OCSP endpoints can cause unintended failures. As such, designing for revocation resilience, including short certificate lifetimes and redundant responders, is a best practice.

P.1.5 Public Key Infrastructure (PKI)

Certificates are issued, validated, and revoked through a system known as *Public Key Infrastructure*, or PKI. PKI helps machines trust each other without needing to know one another in advance. It achieves this by establishing a chain of trust that links certificates to a root CA that everyone agrees to trust.

Here's how PKI works in practice:

An organization generates a key pair and creates a Certificate Signing Request, or CSR. This is a formal way of saying, "Here's my public key, and here's who I claim to be". That CSR is sent to a Certificate Authority, which verifies the requester's identity. If the request checks out, the CA signs the public key and issues a certificate that includes the requester's identity and their public key.

Now that the certificate has been signed by a trusted authority, anyone receiving it can check the signature using the CA's public key. If the signature is valid, they can trust that the certificate and its public key belong to the named party.

This is where certificate chaining comes in. Not everyone has the public key of every CA already stored. So PKI uses a chain of certificates that lead back to a known, trusted root. For example, a web server might present its own certificate (called a leaf certificate), which is signed by an intermediate certificate, which itself is signed by a root certificate. The root certificate is already trusted and stored in your browser or operating system.

Here's a simple way to think about it: imagine you meet someone new, and they say they're trustworthy because a mutual friend says so. You trust your friend, so you extend that trust. If that mutual friend heard it from someone you also trust, that trust extends further. Certificate chaining works the same way. Trust moves upward through the chain until it reaches a certificate your system already knows and trusts.

In a functioning PKI, this chain of trust enables secure and transparent encrypted communications, digital signatures, and authentication to occur. Without it, modern digital life, everything from secure websites to VPN connections to signed software updates, simply wouldn't work.

P.1.6 Key exchange, IPsec, and TLS

One of the trickiest problems in cryptography is how to exchange keys securely. If you're using symmetric encryption, both parties need to know the same secret key, but you can't just send it over the internet like a plaintext message. That would defeat the purpose. To solve this, cryptographers developed key exchange protocols that let two systems agree on a shared key without ever actually transmitting it. This is the basic idea behind Diffie-Hellman and its more modern cousin, Elliptic Curve Diffie-Hellman (ECDH).

Here's how it works, in simple terms. Imagine two people want to mix a secret color of paint. They each start with a shared base color (like yellow) and privately mix in their own secret color (say, red or blue). They then send the mixed paint to each other. Even if someone intercepts that mixed color, they can't tell what the secret ingredients were. Each person then mixes the received color with their own secret again. Both now end up with the same final blend, even though they never shared their secret ingredients directly with each other. In cryptography, this "color" is just a really large number, and the math ensures that both parties can arrive at the same secret key without exposing it.

Now let's look at IPsec, or Internet Protocol Security, which is a widely used method for securing communications between systems, especially over a VPN. IPsec actually uses both symmetric and asymmetric encryption. It starts with asymmetric encryption to handle the secure key exchange, using something like Diffie-Hellman. Once the two systems have established a shared secret, they switch to symmetric encryption, which is faster and more efficient for transmitting large amounts of data.

Here's what that looks like in action. Say you connect your laptop to your company's VPN. First, your laptop and the VPN server use IKEv2, a negotiation protocol, to authenticate each other and agree on what algorithms to use. They exchange public information using Diffie-Hellman or ECDH, which lets them both calculate the same encryption key without sending it directly. This becomes the key for symmetric encryption, typically using a cipher like AES. From that point on, all of your data, emails, file transfers, and remote desktop sessions are encrypted with this shared key, keeping your traffic secure.

This blend of asymmetric key exchange and symmetric encryption is what makes IPsec both secure and practical. You get the security benefits of public key cryptography where it's needed, and the speed of symmetric encryption once the connection is established.

TLS, or Transport Layer Security, works in a similar way. It's the protocol used to secure your browser when you visit websites with HTTPS. TLS replaced SSL, or Secure Sockets Layer, which was the original protocol for securing internet traffic but is now considered outdated and insecure. TLS improved upon SSL by fixing vulnerabilities and supporting stronger encryption and more flexible negotiation during handshakes.

When you connect to a secure website, your browser and the server perform a handshake that agrees on a set of cryptographic algorithms and securely exchanges keys. Like IPsec, TLS uses asymmetric encryption for the key exchange and then switches to symmetric encryption for the rest of the session. The handshake also verifies the server's identity using digital certificates, so you know you're talking to the right site and not an imposter. Once the handshake is complete, all communication between your browser and the site is encrypted, ensuring both privacy and authenticity.

Technically, the TLS handshake begins when your browser sends a message to the server that includes a list of supported cryptographic algorithms and a randomly generated number. The server responds with its digital certificate and another random number. If the certificate checks out, the browser uses the server's public key to exchange key material, often through a key encapsulation mechanism like ECDHE. Both the browser and the server use the exchanged data to independently compute the same symmetric key. Once they confirm that they've derived the same key, they use it to encrypt the rest of the session. The whole process happens in just a fraction of a second every time you open a secure connection.

P.2 LET'S BEGIN

This book does not assume you are a cryptographer, and it won't bury you in the math behind lattices, polynomials, or quantum gates. However, it does assume that you are someone responsible for systems that rely on cryptography and are committed to making those systems more resilient. If that sounds like you, congratulations. You've already taken the most important step: choosing to understand and prepare rather than wait and react. The road to quantum readiness may seem technical, but it's not just about encryption. It's about leadership, stewardship, and adaptability. In the coming chapters, you'll be introduced to a practical framework that will help you guide your organization through the transition. Whether you're protecting customer data, critical infrastructure, or your company's reputation, the journey starts here. Let's begin.

Introduction

Executive summary and overview

Quantum computing is no longer theoretical. Over the past decade, advances in quantum hardware have moved it from academic speculation into a strategic concern for enterprise security. The reason is simple: quantum computers are uniquely capable of breaking the cryptographic systems that underpin digital trust across every sector. Unlike traditional computers, which process information in binary (ones and zeros), quantum computers utilize quantum bits, or qubits, that can represent multiple states simultaneously. This allows them to solve certain mathematical problems exponentially faster, including the kinds of problems that protect our data today.

This chapter is written specifically for board directors and executive leaders who need to understand the risks, challenges, and opportunities of post-quantum cryptography without having to read the entire book. It is also designed to help CISOs and other security leaders who need to brief their boards or executive teams with a clear, concise overview of what matters, why it matters now, and what decisions lie ahead.

This book as a whole provides a roadmap for organizations to prepare, but this chapter stands alone as a strategic primer. It is not about science fiction or hypothetical threats. It is about a predictable disruption to how we protect sensitive data, ensure system integrity, and maintain the trustworthiness of software, communications, and transactions.

The book outlines a five-phase framework for achieving quantum readiness. It is built around practical action: discover, plan, implement, validate, and maintain. Each phase includes clear guidance, real-world examples, and business-aligned insights to help leaders support and fund the journey ahead.

While the technical details are available to those who need them, the overall message is clear and strategic. Quantum readiness is not optional. It is not just a cybersecurity issue. It is an enterprise risk issue that affects everyone, from legal to engineering to finance, and the boardroom.

If you are already familiar with the strategic context or prefer to dive straight into the practical roadmap, you can skip ahead to Chapter 1.

DOI: 10.1201/9781003685760-1

1.1 WHY THIS MATTERS TO EXECUTIVES

Every organization today relies on encryption to secure its digital operations. Encryption is what protects customer information, confirms the legitimacy of transactions, secures communications, and supports compliance with regulations. But much of the encryption in use today is based on mathematical methods that quantum computers will be able to break. When that happens, the systems we depend on to protect data and verify trust will no longer be reliable.

The moment when a quantum computer becomes powerful enough to break these algorithms is known as "Q-Day". When that day arrives, attackers will be able to decrypt communications, forge digital signatures, and impersonate trusted systems. This not only compromises confidentiality but also undermines the ability to prove identity and verify the integrity of systems. In other words, it breaks trust.

Even worse, threat actors do not need to wait for Q-Day to act. Many are already harvesting encrypted data today with the goal of decrypting it later. This tactic, called "Harvest Now, Decrypt Later", means that the data your business transmits or stores now could be exposed years from now if it isn't quantum-safe. The primary actors behind this threat include nation-state intelligence agencies and highly resourced cyber operations teams. These groups are systematically collecting sensitive data from governments, enterprises, and infrastructure providers, especially data with long-term strategic, economic, or military value. Their goal is to stockpile encrypted content today and break it once the necessary quantum computing power becomes available.

This is not a routine security upgrade. It is a massive global infrastructure challenge – comparable in scope and urgency to the Y2K crisis. Much like Y2K, avoiding the most serious impacts will depend on years of proactive preparation and coordinated technical effort across both public and private sectors. Organizations that prepare early will navigate the transition smoothly. Those who wait may find themselves scrambling to retrofit critical systems under pressure, with limited options and rising costs.

1.2 UNDERSTANDING THE RISK IN BUSINESS TERMS

At the board level, the quantum threat should be framed as a matter of revenue protection, cost control, and enterprise risk management. This is not just a cybersecurity issue; it is a strategic concern that impacts operations, compliance, customer trust, and long-term competitiveness.

Every organization today relies on encryption to secure its digital operations. Encryption protects customer information, validates transactions, secures communications, and ensures regulatory compliance. If these protections fail, the consequences extend far beyond the IT sector. They affect how the business generates revenue, manages costs, and maintains trust in the market.

1.2.1 Revenue

Trust drives revenue. Customers expect their data to be protected, transactions to be authentic, and digital services to function without interruption. If that trust is lost due to a breach, fraud, or service failure caused by a cryptographic compromise, customers leave, contracts dissolve, and brand equity erodes. But there is also a positive case: early adoption of post-quantum cryptography (PQC) can serve as a competitive differentiator. Organizations that lead in this space can build trust with government clients, compliance-sensitive industries, and global partners who are actively assessing quantum risk. Proactively investing in quantum-safe infrastructure may become a key value proposition in RFPs, audits, and due diligence processes. Demonstrating leadership in this area can open doors to new markets, attract forward-looking customers, and reinforce your organization's commitment to long-term digital security.

1.2.2 Cost

The cost of delay can be substantial. Late-stage quantum remediation may require unplanned capital investments, the early replacement of long-lived systems, and compressed implementation timelines, which can drive up labor and consulting costs. For example, operational technology, industrial controls, and embedded systems that were expected to last 10 to 20 years may need to be replaced sooner than planned, which can impact capital depreciation schedules and long-term budgeting.

Long-lived systems, such as industrial control equipment, embedded devices, and IoT endpoints, often cannot be updated with a software patch. These systems may require full replacement or complete architectural redesign to accommodate post-quantum cryptography. The planning horizon for these changes may span five to ten years, so early identification and budgeting are critical to avoid costly surprises.

For most organizations, a complete post-quantum cryptography (PQC) migration is expected to cost between *$2 million and $30 million*, depending on size, complexity, and regulatory exposure. Smaller organizations may spend far less, while highly regulated global enterprises could invest *$30 million to $50 million or more over* a *three- to six-year period*. These costs include asset discovery, risk assessments, vendor coordination, cryptographic updates, testing, policy changes, and workforce readiness.

However, organizations that build *crypto-agility* into their infrastructure by designing systems to switch out cryptographic components easily can significantly reduce future costs. Crypto-agility means that your systems can adapt quickly and affordably when algorithms are deprecated or standards evolve. Investing in agility now enables future cryptographic changes to become routine upgrades rather than expensive overhauls.

1.2.3 Risk

The risk is already active. Many threat actors are collecting encrypted data today with the intention of decrypting it once quantum tools mature. The Harvest Now, Decrypt Later tactic targets sensitive data with long shelf lives, such as medical records, trade secrets, financial agreements, and source code. The risks affect three critical areas:

1. *Long-term confidentiality*: Sensitive data, such as intellectual property, medical records, and legal contracts, must remain secure for decades. If exposed, the financial, legal, and competitive fallout could be substantial.
2. *Integrity and authenticity*: Cryptographic signatures are what tell us a software update is legitimate, that an email came from a known sender, or that a transaction hasn't been altered. Once quantum computers can forge these signatures, attackers can bypass detection and operate as trusted insiders.
3. *Operational reliability*: Critical infrastructure, cloud platforms, and connected devices rely on encryption to function safely. If these cryptographic protections fail, service outages or systemic compromise become real possibilities.

The impact of inaction is measurable. For a typical mid-to-large enterprise, the estimated cost of a cryptographically driven breach, caused by quantum-capable adversaries, could range from *$50 million to $300 million*, depending on the scope of the exposed data, regulatory penalties, loss of customer trust, and remediation costs. In regulated sectors, failure to address foreseeable encryption risks may also trigger enforcement action or lawsuits, thereby compounding financial exposure.

1.3 WHY NOW?

To help organizations understand the urgency of this issue, a simple model known as the *Mosca Model* is used. It asks you to consider three variables:

1. How long does your data needs to stay secure
2. How long will it take your organization to fully migrate to quantum-safe systems

3. How long experts believe it will take before quantum computers can break today's encryption (about 2035)

If the first two numbers, data lifespan and migration time, add up to more than the third, which is about 10 years, then your organization is already in the danger zone. Many companies are surprised to find that they are closer to that tipping point than they thought. Even if Q-Day is 10 years away, data that needs to stay secure for 15 years and systems that will take 5 years to upgrade are already at risk.

This is why quantum readiness must be treated as a business priority today. The earlier the leadership engages, the more options are available. Early planning lowers costs, reduces exposure, and protects both the continuity and credibility of the business.

PQC is not just an internal concern. Many vendors, suppliers, and cloud platforms that your business depends on may still be using vulnerable cryptographic libraries or outdated standards. As part of quantum readiness, organizations will need to evaluate and reassess third-party dependencies, update contract language to include cryptographic accountability, and ensure that external partners can demonstrate their own migration timelines.

Post-quantum readiness will not go unnoticed by regulators or audit teams. Organizations should expect that crypto-inventory management, algorithm migration progress, and cryptographic risk assessments will become standard components of audit scopes. Board members and senior leaders should prepare for their oversight responsibilities and request regular updates from security and compliance teams on quantum preparedness milestones.

Regulatory bodies and standards organizations are already moving. The U.S. National Institute of Standards and Technology (NIST) has selected new post-quantum cryptographic algorithms for standardization, and supporting frameworks such as FIPS 203 through 206 are being finalized. These will shape future audit expectations and compliance benchmarks. Enterprises that begin aligning now with these emerging standards will reduce future rework and gain favor in regulatory reviews and procurement processes.

1.4 WHAT NEEDS TO BE DONE

Responding to this threat is not a purely technical project. It is a strategic transformation that requires sustained leadership, capital investment, and cross-functional coordination. Quantum readiness must be approached with the same seriousness as digital transformation or enterprise risk management.

Key actions that businesses must plan for include:

- *Inventorying cryptographic assets*: Understand what algorithms, keys, certificates, and protocols are in use across your infrastructure. Many organizations are unaware of where their vulnerable encryption resides. This includes discovering cryptographic libraries in use, mapping dependencies in applications and third-party components, and creating a cryptographic bill of materials (CBOM) to guide remediation.
- *Assessing business exposure*: Align cryptographic risk with the value and shelf life of your data. If your data needs to stay secure longer than the world needs to build a quantum computer, you are already exposed. Prioritize systems based on their sensitivity, criticality, and the duration they will remain in service.
- *Planning for migration*: Begin identifying and testing quantum-resistant algorithms recommended by NIST, such as ML-KEM and Dilithium. Evaluate compatibility with existing systems and pilot hybrid implementations that run both classical and quantum-safe algorithms in parallel. Update APIs, protocols (like TLS and VPNs), and software that rely on vulnerable public key infrastructure. Replace digital signatures, key exchange mechanisms, and certificates that depend on RSA or ECC. For embedded or long-lived systems, assess hardware constraints early and collaborate with vendors to determine upgrade timelines.
- *Building crypto-agility*: Redesign systems to support modular cryptographic frameworks, allowing algorithms to be replaced without requiring the rewriting of large portions of code. This includes adopting abstraction layers, using cryptographic libraries that support post-quantum standards, and avoiding hard-coded algorithms.
- *Updating policies and controls*: Refresh governance, compliance, and lifecycle policies to align with the post-quantum transition. This includes certificate lifecycle management, incident response plans that account for cryptographic compromise, and revised audit checklists that include quantum readiness.
- *Training and resourcing*: Prepare your workforce. Ensure engineers, developers, architects, legal counsel, procurement teams, and risk managers understand their responsibilities and the roadmap ahead. Provide role-based training, create playbooks, and assign ownership for post-quantum migration within each functional area.
- *Executing staged remediation*: Begin phased deployment of quantum-resistant algorithms across high-priority systems. Test functionality, performance, and interoperability in controlled environments before rolling out to production. Validate results, measure against key performance indicators, and refine based on lessons learned.

- *Building board visibility*: This is not a problem that can be entirely delegated to IT. It touches business continuity, reputational risk, and legal liability. Directors must expect regular updates and clear progress metrics. Establish a governance model that includes executive oversight, milestone tracking, and alignment with enterprise risk frameworks.

1.5 EXECUTIVE COMMUNICATION TOOLKIT

To help CISOs and security leaders engage executive stakeholders, this section introduces a reusable toolkit for boardroom and leadership communication. Clear messaging is critical to securing buy-in, budget, and cross-functional alignment for a PQC migration effort. While technical teams may understand the cryptographic implications, executives need context that maps directly to business value, financial risk, and strategic positioning.

1.5.1 Sample board slide: framing the quantum risk

Title: "Quantum Computing and the Future of Trust"

- Quantum computers will break today's encryption. The systems that protect our data, identities, and transactions will fail unless we modernize them.
- Sensitive data is already being harvested for future decryption.
- Data with a long shelf life, such as contracts, medical records, and financials, is the highest risk.
- The global response is underway. Standards are being finalized.
- Migration will take three to seven years. Waiting shrinks your margin for success.
- This is a business continuity issue, not just a cybersecurity concern.
- Organizations that prepare early reduce costs, avoid disruption, and gain trust.

1.5.2 Executive elevator pitch (30 seconds)

"Quantum computing is about to break the encryption that keeps our data and systems secure. It's not science fiction. Nation-states are already collecting encrypted data to decrypt later. This creates a business risk for any organization with sensitive data that needs to stay private for years. We have a limited window to get ahead of this. The organizations that act early will avoid disruption, reduce long-term costs, and strengthen trust".

1.5.3 Executive FAQs

Q: Is this really urgent? How far off is quantum decryption?
A: Experts estimate that quantum computers could break RSA and ECC encryption in the early to mid-2030s. But attackers are collecting data now to decrypt later. The clock is ticking, and migration takes years. Early action is not optional – it's a strategic necessity.

Q: What's the potential financial impact?
A: The cost of a quantum-driven breach varies by business size, sector, and the sensitivity of the compromised data:

- *Small businesses* may face *$500,000 to $5 million* in direct and indirect costs. This includes incident response, customer notification, legal fees, contract losses, and potential regulatory penalties. For smaller healthcare or financial services providers, the cost may skew higher due to compliance exposure.
- *Midsize enterprises* typically face *$10 million to $75 million* in impact. These costs stem from legal exposure, breach containment, system overhauls, vendor renegotiations, regulatory fines, and reputational damage. Organizations in regulated industries or with long-lived sensitive data – such as trade secrets, medical records, or intellectual property – will incur costs at the higher end of the range.
- *Large global enterprises*, especially in sectors such as *finance, healthcare, energy, government contracting, and defense*, may see impacts of *$100 million to $500 million* or more. These costs reflect the complex and distributed nature of cryptographic systems across global operations. They include breach remediation, legal settlements, contract renegotiations, loss of government certifications or clearances, investor lawsuits, audit sanctions, and sustained brand erosion.

In addition to breach costs, remediation alone, without an incident, will still be substantial:

- Small businesses: *$250,000 to $2 million*
- Midsize organizations: *$2 million to $20 million*
- Large enterprises: *$30 million to $100 million*, depending on system scope and compliance demands

Prevention costs a fraction of crisis response. Investing in crypto-agility and early migration provides significant cost avoidance and preserves strategic optionality. However, PQ readiness will still be a substantial investment that will likely require planning and budgeting.

Q: What if we just wait until the standards are final?
A: NIST has already selected primary algorithms. Finalization of FIPS 203–206 is expected soon. Migration requires updating systems, vendors, policies, and staff. Waiting means compressing a multi-year project into a crisis response. Early pilots give you leverage and flexibility.

Q: What are our competitors doing?
A: Many large financial institutions, defense contractors, critical infrastructure, and global tech firms have already launched quantum-readiness programs. Regulatory bodies and supply chain auditors are starting to assess PQC preparedness as part of compliance reviews. This shift is gaining momentum.

Q: How does this affect our cloud providers and vendors?
A: If your vendors use vulnerable cryptography, your systems may still be at risk. PQC must be validated across your supply chain. Expect to review contract language, service-level agreements, and vendor roadmaps.

Q: What role does the board play?
A: Oversight. The board is responsible for fiduciary governance of foreseeable risk. PQC is a predictable disruption. Expect this topic to be part of enterprise risk, audit, and compliance reviews.

I.5.4 Messaging templates

I.5.4.1 Executive email template (from the CISO)

Subject: Preparing Our Business for the Quantum Era

Over the next decade, quantum computing will change how we secure data and systems. Nation-state actors are already collecting encrypted data with the intent to decrypt it once quantum tools mature. This presents a real and predictable risk to our most sensitive data.

We are launching a program to inventory our cryptographic assets, align with new NIST standards, and prepare our infrastructure for post-quantum resilience. This is not a theoretical threat; it is a strategic shift. We will keep you informed as we progress. Thank you for your continued leadership in supporting long-term trust and business continuity.

I.5.5 Department leader talking points

"This is not just a cybersecurity issue. It's about how we protect our customers, comply with regulations, and avoid having to make rushed, expensive upgrades later. We're joining a global transition. Our job is to make sure we're not playing catch-up".

1.5.6 Procurement message

"Our contracts and SLAs must now account for cryptographic sustainability. We'll be asking vendors to share their post-quantum migration timelines, and we may revise agreements to include crypto-agility and PQC compliance requirements. Procurement plays a critical role in protecting the trust we extend to third parties".

1.5.7 Q-ready executive overview

This one-page summary is designed to support board-level conversations about quantum readiness. It provides a concise, business-focused overview of the Q-Ready Framework, a five-phase model for preparing your organization for post-quantum cryptography. The goal is to equip directors with clear, actionable insights ahead of formal presentations or discussions. It highlights strategic priorities, expected timelines, and key performance indicators (KPIs) that align quantum risk management with enterprise resilience and governance expectations. Include this overview in your board packet to promote alignment, foster engagement, and support executive decision-making.

1.6 PREPARING FOR THE POST-QUANTUM CRYPTOGRAPHY TRANSITION

1.6.1 Why this matters

Quantum computing is expected to break today's encryption standards within the next decade. The systems that protect customer data, secure transactions, and verify trust will no longer be reliable. Threat actors are already harvesting encrypted data for future decryption. This is a strategic risk with financial, operational, and reputational implications.

The Q-Ready Framework helps organizations prepare in five phases. It enables security and technology leaders to identify where encryption is used, assess risk, and migrate safely to post-quantum cryptographic (PQC) standards.

1.6.1.1 Q-ready five-phase model

Table 1.1 5 Phases

Phase	*Objective*	*Timeline*	*Key Board-Level KPIs*
1. Discover	Inventory cryptographic assets, systems, and third-party dependencies.	Year 1	"CBOM (Crypto Bill of Materials) coverage rate % of assets with known cryptographic dependencies"
2. Plan	Prioritize risks, define use cases, select vendors, and build the business case.	Year 1–2	"Migration budget approved % of high-risk systems mapped to remediation plan"
3. Implement	Deploy PQC controls, update certificates, test hybrid configurations.	Year 2–5	"% of PQC algorithm deployments completed % of systems crypto-agile"
4. Validate	Test, audit, and simulate failures to ensure integrity and compliance.	Year 3–6	"Audit readiness score % of PQC controls tested in production"
5. Maintain	Monitor new standards, rotate algorithms, manage crypto-lifecycle at scale.	Year 5–7 and beyond	"% of workforce PQC-trained % of systems under cryptographic lifecycle management"

1.6.1.2 Executive considerations

- *Cost avoidance*: Early preparation reduces future breach and remediation costs.
- *Regulatory alignment*: Upcoming standards (FIPS 203–206) will be enforced.
- *Third-party exposure*: Vendor and cloud dependencies must be evaluated.
- *Reputational risk*: Trust failures affect market perception and revenue.

1.6.2 What board members should ask the CISO

- Have you completed an inventory of our cryptographic assets and mapped them to the sensitive or long-lived data they protect?
- What is your timeline and budget for migrating to post-quantum cryptography, and where are we on that roadmap today?
- Are you holding our vendors accountable for their quantum readiness, and have contractual requirements been updated to reflect that?
- How are you measuring and reporting our progress toward quantum readiness to the executive team and board?

- Which systems or business functions are most at risk due to long data retention periods or limited crypto-agility?
- What is your estimate of the total remediation cost over the next five to seven years, and how does that compare to the potential risk exposure?
- Have you integrated PQC considerations into our procurement, architecture, and third-party risk management processes?
- Are new systems being designed to support crypto-agility, so we can avoid costly rework as algorithms evolve?
- How are you preparing our teams to respond to quantum-era cryptographic failures or compromise scenarios?
- What training and awareness efforts are underway to prepare technical teams, vendor managers, and compliance staff?
- Are we aligned with evolving standards such as FIPS 203–206, and are we tracking relevant regulatory developments?
- What role are audit, legal, and compliance teams playing in validating and supporting our quantum migration strategy?

I.6.3 Board priorities

- *Protect long-lived data*: Focus on systems where data must remain confidential for 10+ years.
- *Audit third parties*: Require vendors to disclose quantum migration plans and cryptographic roadmaps.
- *Build crypto-agility*: Ensure new systems can adapt to evolving algorithms and compliance standards.
- *Embed governance*: Integrate PQC readiness into risk frameworks, board reports, and capital planning.

I.6.4 Key message for the board

This is not a routine upgrade. It is a multi-year risk transformation effort with financial, operational, and reputational implications. Boards must oversee and fund quantum readiness with the same rigor as digital transformation or cloud migration initiatives.

For more information: Contact your CISO or review the attached Quantum Readiness Board Briefing materials.

I.6.5 Additional supplemental materials for board packets

CISOs can include these attachments in their board briefings:

1. *Sample Board Dashboard* (see **Figure I.1**)
    - % of cryptographic assets discovered
    - % of systems tested for PQC compatibility

- Number of critical vendors PQC-assessed
- Staff quantum training coverage

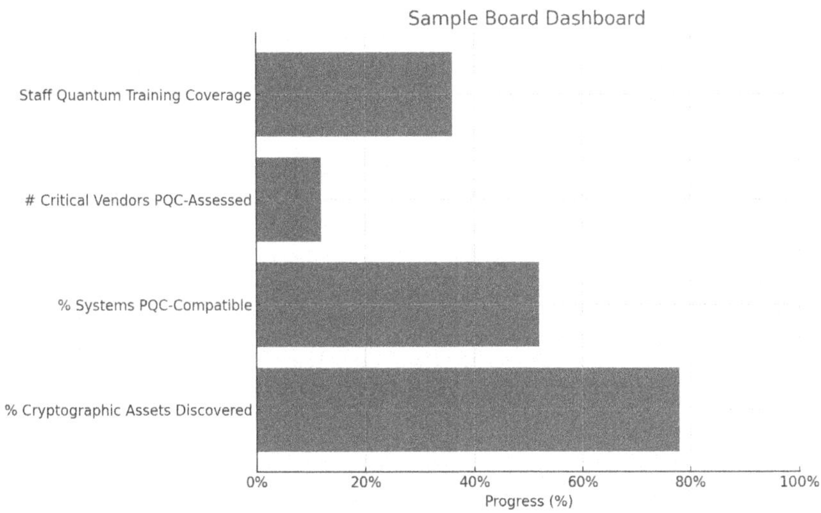

Figure I.1 Board dashboard.

2. Mosca Model Risk Heatmap (see Figure I.2)
   A visual matrix showing which data classes exceed the safe threshold for migration, helping illustrate urgency.

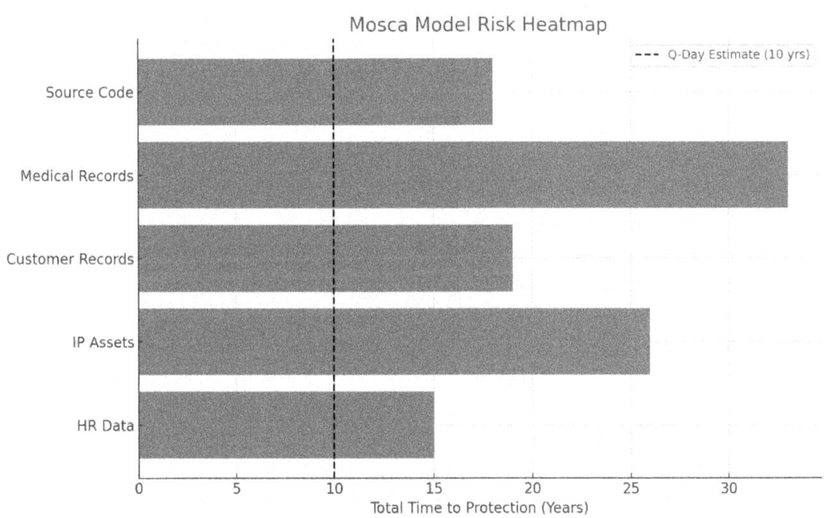

Figure I.2 Mosca heatmap.

3. *Cost Curve Comparison Sheet*
   Chart showing estimated costs for proactive vs. reactive migration by organization size and system lifespan.
4. *Vendor Readiness Assessment Checklist*
   A checklist procurement teams can use to vet vendors on PQC preparedness (key management, hybrid TLS, algorithm roadmaps, etc.).
5. *Draft Contract Language Examples*
   Including SLAs requiring quantum-safe algorithms by a target date, crypto-agility clauses, and PQC compliance declarations.
6. *Boardroom FAQ Handout*
   A page with top questions and plain-English answers possibly based on the FAQ and questions presented above to reinforce executive alignment.

1.7 FINAL THOUGHT FOR THE BOARDROOM

You do not need to understand how quantum computing works to lead your organization through this shift. But you do need to ask the right questions. You need to know whether your teams have a plan, whether your cryptographic assets have been inventoried, whether your contracts and suppliers are aligned, and whether your organization is treating this as the systemic risk it is.

Quantum computing is not a problem for tomorrow. It is a readiness issue today. Like cloud migration or digital transformation, quantum readiness will reshape how we conduct our business. Preparing now puts your organization on the front foot. You will reduce risk, protect trust, and demonstrate leadership in a world where digital assurance is a competitive advantage. This is a moment to lead, not wait. Your data, your systems, and your brand's trust depend on it.

Section I

Intro to quantum readiness

Chapter 1

Why quantum threats can't be ignored

1.1 WHAT THIS BOOK WILL AND WON'T COVER

This book is not a physics textbook, nor is it a comprehensive exploration of the theoretical foundations of quantum computing. You will not find discussions of Hilbert spaces, complex vector fields, or Euler's theorem. There are no detailed derivations of quantum algorithms or visualizations of Bloch spheres. You won't need to understand the geometry of qubit state vectors or the use of ket notation to follow along. Those subjects are important, but they are not the focus here.

You will also not find walkthroughs of quantum programming or tutorials for simulating quantum states using Qiskit or IBM Q Experience. You will not be asked to grasp the mathematical underpinnings of Shor's algorithm or Grover's search algorithm. If you're looking to explore how complex numbers map onto circular polarization states or how vector spaces apply to quantum bit manipulation, there are excellent academic books that go deep into that material. This is not one of them.

This book does not aim to make you a quantum physicist or cryptographer. It assumes that you have a working knowledge of cybersecurity, risk management, or enterprise IT, and that you are looking for clear, actionable guidance on how to prepare your organization for a shift that is already underway.

What this book does offer is a roadmap. It will help you understand the operational risks posed by quantum computing and walk you through the steps to reduce your exposure. You will learn how to identify vulnerable cryptography in your systems, assess the risks, and begin transitioning to quantum-resistant solutions. You will receive practical strategies for implementing, testing, validating, and maintaining quantum-safe infrastructure in the long term.

The approach is grounded in the Q-Ready Framework, a five-phase model designed specifically to help cybersecurity and IT leaders take meaningful steps toward readiness. The focus is on protecting trust, your systems, certificates, communications, and business operations. You don't need to

DOI: 10.1201/9781003685760-3

know how quantum computers are built. You need to know what they will break and what to do about it.

This book is for the practitioner. It is for the person responsible for maintaining security in a constantly evolving threat landscape. It does not promise to answer every theoretical question. Still, it will help you ask the right operational ones, and it will guide you in making informed, strategic decisions that safeguard the future of your organization's digital trust.

1.2 A NEW KIND OF COMPUTING

In cybersecurity, most threats are accompanied by clear warning signs: a phishing link, an open port, a known vulnerability. However, the quantum threat doesn't work that way. It's a slow burn, hiding in plain sight. You won't get an alert when it hits. There won't be a zero-day exploit to patch. There will be a moment when cryptography quietly fails, and with it, the digital trust your organization depends on. This book is about preparing for that moment before it arrives.

Understanding the quantum shift isn't about chasing hype. It's about recognizing a very real, very practical risk to the systems we use every day. This chapter aims to clarify the concept of risk and provide the necessary context before we begin solving for it. You don't need to understand quantum mechanics. You need to understand what's at stake and what to do about it.

If you're like most technology professionals, you've seen headlines about quantum computing over the years. Most make it sound like science fiction, but here's the truth: the fundamentals of quantum computing are not that complicated, at least not at the level we need to understand in cybersecurity. To understand the urgency of post-quantum cryptography, you don't need a physics degree. You only need to understand that quantum computers don't process information the way traditional computers do.

You can think of classical computing as a camera and quantum computing as a kaleidoscope. Imagine a digital camera taking a photo. Each image is a snapshot of one clear outcome. It's either this or that, a one or a zero, true or false. Classical computers work in that same way. They process information in fixed states, flipping binary switches one after another at high speed.

Now, imagine looking through a kaleidoscope instead. What you see isn't one picture. It's a swirl of possibilities. The shapes are all there at once until you choose to focus and freeze the pattern. That moment of focus is like a measurement in quantum computing. Until that point, the system holds multiple potential outcomes. Only when it's observed do those possibilities collapse into a single answer.

That's the power of quantum computing. It doesn't just try one path at a time. It can explore multiple paths simultaneously. And that changes everything when it comes to the kinds of problems computers can solve, especially, problems like breaking encryption.

We'll explore how quantum computers do that in Chapter 2. For now, what matters is that quantum computing is real and it's advancing faster than expected. When it hits certain milestones, it will render most of today's encryption insecure.

1.3 WHAT IS Q-DAY?

Q-Day is the name given to the moment when a quantum computer becomes powerful enough to break widely used cryptographic systems. This includes the public key algorithms that underpin nearly every secure transaction on the internet. These algorithms are embedded in almost everything, including secure websites, financial transactions, software updates, VPNs, digital signatures, smart contracts, and email systems. When that day arrives, encrypted data that was once considered safe could be exposed almost instantly. The issue isn't whether quantum computing will reach that threshold. The question is when.

Some forecasts suggest Q-Day could arrive as early as 2030. Others believe we may have a little longer, but that debate misses the point. Most sensitive data, whether it's health records, patent files, contracts, or legal archives, needs to remain protected for far longer than five or ten years. If you are securing data with a shelf life of a decade or more, then you are already within the risk window. This is not just a future concern. It's a current crisis in slow motion, and the moment it hits, we won't just lose privacy, we'll lose trust.

Digital trust is built on the integrity of systems, ensuring that a document is genuine, a transaction is verified, and a certificate is valid. When those guarantees can be broken, it doesn't just expose data; it opens the door to impersonation, sabotage, and fraud at a systemic level. This isn't about identity theft; it's about wealth theft; it's about unauthorized transfers, forged signatures, and compromised firmware. It's about losing the ability to know what's real in a digital world.

1.4 HARVEST NOW, DECRYPT LATER

The risk, however, isn't limited to what might happen in the future. It has already begun. That's because encrypted data can be stored today and decrypted later. Attackers don't have to wait for a working quantum computer to start collecting valuable information. They are already capturing traffic, stealing certificates, and harvesting cryptographic assets with the intention of breaking them once the right tools are available.

This attack method is known as Harvest Now, Decrypt Later (HNDL). It's already being used by well-resourced adversaries, especially state-sponsored threat actors. Their goal is simple; they want to collect as much encrypted data as possible and store it until quantum tools become available.

In traditional security models, encryption is often viewed as a "fix-it-and-forget-it" measure. Once encrypted, data is assumed to be safe. But HNDL turns encryption into a delayed liability. If that data hasn't been protected with quantum-resistant algorithms, it's a breach waiting to happen. The data they target is not random. It includes items that retain their value over time, such as private medical records, intellectual property, bank credentials, and legal contracts. The longer this information remains valid, the more attractive it becomes to harvest and decrypt in the future.

This tactic has implications across industries and use cases:

- *Finance*: Encrypted payment transaction logs, investment histories, or SWIFT messaging traffic can be harvested now and decrypted later to reveal patterns or credentials.
- *Healthcare*: Patient histories, genomic records, and insurance claims have long-term value and are often transmitted or stored in encrypted formats vulnerable to future quantum attacks.
- *Legal and government archives*: Diplomatic cables, litigation files, land records, and intellectual property documents may sit in encrypted archives for decades, and all of them are targets for retrospective decryption.
- *Authentication systems*: TLS session recordings, VPN tunnels, SSH keys, and encrypted login traffic are being harvested today. Once broken, these reveal credentials, access patterns, and user behaviors.
- *Software integrity*: Code-signing certificates, encrypted build pipelines, and firmware verification systems can be compromised retroactively, allowing malicious updates or backdoors to be silently accepted.

One of the biggest targets is public key infrastructure, or PKI. This includes the digital certificates that verify websites, sign software, and authenticate users. If a quantum computer breaks a certificate chain, the attacker can impersonate trusted entities, decrypt private traffic, or insert malicious updates into systems that appear legitimate. HNDL attacks also thrive on existing weaknesses. Misconfigured certificate chains, expired or weak public keys, and improper use of legacy protocols provide attackers with more opportunities to exploit vulnerabilities. DNS spoofing and cache poisoning can help redirect encrypted traffic through points of surveillance, where it can be silently collected and stored. Even organizations that believe their current infrastructure is sound may be exposing valuable information without realizing it. Cloud backups, archive storage, and encrypted application data may be passively collected, awaiting a day when encryption is no longer a barrier to access. The threat isn't just that someone could read what you send today. It's that someone already has a copy of it and is just waiting to read it tomorrow.

1.5 REFRAMING THE RISK: IT'S NOT JUST DATA, IT'S TRUST

To fully appreciate the scope of the quantum threat, it helps to move beyond the word "data". This is not just about files or records. It is about the fragile web of trust that holds digital infrastructure together. Certificates, signatures, and encryption protocols are not just security tools. They are what prove identity, authorize access, validate software, and preserve the integrity of everything from financial transactions to national records.

Quantum computing poses a direct threat to these trust mechanisms. Q-Day will not look like a new malware campaign or a wave of ransomware. It will feel like the foundations of digital authentication and verification have quietly come undone. Transactions may be forged without detection. Encrypted channels might be silently compromised. Trusted software updates could deliver malicious payloads, which can be verified by certificates that attackers can now counterfeit. The most unsettling part is that much of the data needed to carry out these attacks may already be in the hands of adversaries, collected through "Harvest Now, Decrypt Later" strategies. This isn't about someone reading your old emails. This involves someone forging digital signatures to access your treasury systems, hijacking firmware updates that allow attackers to control hardware, or tampering with legal documents and falsifying financial records. These are not theoretical risks. They are real outcomes that become possible when public key cryptography is no longer reliable.

Even before quantum computing becomes mainstream, attackers are already exploiting the weaknesses in our current cryptographic systems. DNS spoofing and cache poisoning allow malicious redirection. Downgrade attacks coerce servers into using outdated and less secure cipher suites. Misconfigured or expired certificates create opportunities for impersonation. These tactics show just how brittle the status quo has become, even without quantum tools. Some threat actors are already building the foundation for future attacks. They are harvesting certificate chains from public sources and using them to build databases for later use. Others are scraping public repositories or capturing traffic through man-in-the-middle attacks on unsecured networks.

What this ultimately threatens is not just privacy, but also legitimacy, the ability to verify identity, the authenticity of documents, and code integrity. The reliability of updates and transactions is at stake. This is not simply a data breach scenario. It is a scenario where digital signatures lose their authority, cryptographic assurances collapse, and the systems we trust to run commerce, government, and society become unreliable.

This is why the quantum threat must be treated as a matter of strategic urgency, because when trust breaks, value follows. For organizations that rely on digital infrastructure, which is nearly everyone, the consequences reach far beyond compliance. They touch sovereign wealth, national security, and the stability of global systems. Imagine your organization's most critical systems, authentication, code signing, and transaction validation, suddenly becoming untrustworthy. Now, imagine that adversaries already have the data they need to make that happen. That's the Q-Day scenario. Not a hacker in a hoodie, but a silent unraveling of everything digital trust is built on. This is a threat to the value layer of the internet, not just the information layer.

> *Q-Day is not just the moment an algorithm is cracked;*
> *it is the moment trust can no longer be assumed.*

1.6 CONCLUSION

Quantum computing is no longer a distant frontier. It is here, it is evolving, and it is pushing past research labs into the real world. For the security and IT professional, this is not a time to watch and wait. It is time to take stock of what you're protecting, how you're protecting it, and how long you expect that protection to last.

The chapters ahead will provide a practical path forward. But before we move on, it is worth being clear about what this threat really means. This is about trust, not just encryption, and knowing that a software update came from the right source, that a transaction was indeed completed, and that a system has not been compromised beneath the surface. When quantum tools reach the threshold of breaking public key cryptography, the systems that guarantee those truths begin to fail. And that failure does not look like a flashy cyberattack. It looks like silence and forged credentials are passing through unchanged. It appears that malicious code is signed with a trusted certificate, and no alarm is raised.

And the worst of it is already underway. Attackers are not waiting for the technology to mature before acting. They are collecting encrypted data today. They are building databases, scraping public certificates, and capturing traffic in hopes of unlocking it tomorrow. The Harvest Now, Decrypt Later tactic is not hypothetical; it is operational, targeted, and happening right now.

What comes next is not about learning quantum computing. It's about understanding where your systems are vulnerable, what actions are worth taking now, and how to position your organization to maintain its footing when the ground begins to shift. In the next chapter, we will explore how quantum computers actually break encryption. We will explain the specific vulnerabilities in today's most common cryptographic systems and how quantum algorithms exploit them. For now, here's what matters: the threat is real, it is active, and it is growing. Your data is already valuable to those preparing for Q-Day. What you do next determines whether it stays safe or becomes part of the next great breach.

This is not about fear. It is about readiness, and readiness starts here.

Chapter 2

How quantum breaks encryption

If Chapter 1 was about understanding the threat, this chapter is about understanding why it works, not in terms of physics textbooks or university lectures, but in terms of what quantum computers actually do differently, and how that difference changes the rules for encryption.

We will walk through three key ideas: how quantum computers handle information, how they break the systems we use today, and what we have learned so far from real-world experiments.

2.1 CLASSICAL VS. QUANTUM: THE BASICS

Let's start with something familiar. Classical computers, the kind we use every day, process information in binary. That means each bit is either a zero or a one. These bits are like tiny switches inside your computer that are either off or on. Billions of them flipping in rapid succession power everything from search engines to banking systems.

Quantum computers, on the other hand, use qubits. A qubit is not just a switch that's off or on. It can be both at once. This is due to a property known as superposition. A good way to picture this is with a coin.

In classical computing, the coin has already landed. It is either heads or tails. In quantum computing, the coin is spinning in the air. It is both heads and tails until someone catches it and looks. That moment of observation forces it to land on one side.

In Chapter 1, we used another analogy to help visualize this difference. We compared classical computing to a digital camera and quantum computing to a kaleidoscope. A camera captures one fixed frame at a time. A kaleidoscope, on the other hand, holds many patterns and shapes at once, all shifting until you choose to focus. That focus point is like measuring a quantum state. Until then, the system holds multiple possible outcomes at once.

This is what makes quantum computing powerful; it is not just faster, but fundamentally different. Quantum computers can hold many possible answers in their memory at the same time and evaluate them in parallel. When programmed correctly, they can work through complex problems far

 DOI: 10.1201/9781003685760-4

more efficiently than any traditional system. That is the breakthrough, but it is also the danger, because much of modern encryption is built around the idea that some problems are simply too hard or too time-consuming to solve. Quantum computing changes that assumption.

2.2 UNDERSTANDING SYMMETRIC AND ASYMMETRIC ENCRYPTION

Before we get into how quantum computers break encryption, it is helpful to understand the two main types of encryption in use today: symmetric and asymmetric. They solve different problems, work in different ways, and are impacted by quantum computing in various ways as well. If you read the Preface, some of this will be review.

2.2.1 Symmetric encryption

In symmetric encryption, the same key is used for both encryption and decryption of data. Think of it like a locked box. You use the same key to lock and unlock it. Both the sender and the recipient need to have the same key in advance.

This method is fast and efficient, which makes it ideal for securing large volumes of data. Symmetric encryption is commonly used to protect data at rest, such as files on a hard drive, or data in transit, such as the content of an encrypted email or file transfer.

Examples of symmetric encryption algorithms:

- AES (Advanced Encryption Standard)
- 3DES (Data Encryption Standard) – now considered obsolete
- ChaCha20

2.2.2 Asymmetric encryption

Asymmetric encryption, also known as public-key encryption, uses two different keys: a public key for encryption and a private key for decryption. You can share your public key with anyone, but your private key must be kept secret.

This approach allows secure communication between people or systems that have never met or exchanged keys before. It is also used for digital signatures, where you can prove that a message or file came from you by signing it with your private key.

Examples of asymmetric encryption algorithms:

- RSA (Rivest–Shamir–Adleman)
- ECC (Elliptic Curve Cryptography)
- DSA (Digital Signature Algorithm)

2.2.3 How Public Key Infrastructure (PKI) works

Most online trust today is built on something called Public Key Infrastructure, or PKI. PKI is what allows you to securely connect to websites, install software updates, and send encrypted messages. It works by using digital certificates, which are issued by trusted organizations called certificate authorities.

Here's a simplified version of how PKI functions:

1. A website or service generates a pair of keys: a public key and a private key.
2. The public key is included in a certificate, along with identity information about the site.
3. A certificate authority (CA) digitally signs this certificate to vouch for its authenticity.
4. When you visit the site, your browser verifies that the certificate is signed by a trusted Certificate Authority (CA) and hasn't been altered.
5. If everything checks out, your browser uses the public key to initiate a secure connection.

The private key is never shared and is used by the website to decrypt messages or sign responses. The entire model depends on the assumption that no one can derive the private key from the public key. That assumption breaks down with quantum computing.

If Shor's Algorithm can factor large numbers quickly, then an attacker could compute the private key from the public key, impersonate the site, and decrypt all secure traffic. That would collapse the trust model at the heart of the internet.

2.2.4 How Diffie-Hellman key exchange works

Another building block of online encryption is the Diffie-Hellman key exchange, which allows two parties to securely agree on a shared secret key, even over an insecure connection.

Here's how it works in plain terms:

1. Both parties agree on some basic mathematical values to use in their calculations.
2. Each party picks a secret number and uses it in a formula to create a public number.
3. They exchange public numbers over the network.
4. Each side then uses its own secret number and the other party's public number to compute the same shared secret.

What's clever is that even if someone intercepts the public numbers in transit, they cannot easily figure out the secret key without solving a very hard math problem. That problem is called the discrete logarithm, and it is what gives Diffie-Hellman its security. This is exactly the type of problem that can be quickly solved with a quantum computer. An attacker could observe a Diffie-Hellman exchange and then compute the shared secret, effectively allowing them to decrypt what was supposed to be secure.

This also applies to Elliptic Curve Diffie-Hellman (ECDH), a faster and more efficient version of the same idea, which is widely used in mobile apps and modern web services. It too is vulnerable.

The next section of the chapter will cover how Shor's Algorithm works in more detail and how it directly threatens these systems. For now, it is important to understand the key takeaways from what we have just explored.

Symmetric encryption is vulnerable to quantum computing, but it is not completely broken. Algorithms like AES can still offer strong protection, especially when longer key lengths are used, but they will need to be reassessed to ensure they hold up under quantum attack methods like Grover's Algorithm.

Asymmetric encryption, on the other hand, is fundamentally compromised. Public key systems like RSA and Elliptic Curve Cryptography are based on mathematical problems that quantum computers are well-suited to solve. Once Shor's Algorithm becomes practically usable on a large enough quantum system, these algorithms will no longer provide meaningful security. This matters because most of the internet's trust infrastructure depends on asymmetric encryption. Technologies like RSA, Diffie-Hellman, and ECDH are used in everything from establishing secure website connections to digitally signing software updates and verifying email integrity. When these systems fail, the consequences will be broad. Website security, digital identity, software authenticity, and secure messaging will all be at risk. The systems that rely on these cryptographic tools will no longer be able to guarantee the authenticity or confidentiality of the information they protect. Understanding these building blocks helps make sense of why quantum readiness is not just a future-facing initiative or a compliance checkbox. It is a necessary shift to preserve trust in the systems we rely on every day.

2.3 SHOR'S ALGORITHM: BREAKING RSA AND ECC

Asymmetric encryption is critically vulnerable to Shor's Algorithm. Quantum computers using Shor's approach can break RSA, ECC, and other public key systems by solving the hard math problems they rely on, such as factoring large numbers or computing discrete logarithms. Once these systems fall, anything protected by public key cryptography is at risk.

For RSA, the security comes from the challenge of factoring large numbers. If you take two very large prime numbers and multiply them, the result is easy to compute. However, if all you have is the result, figuring out what two primes were used is incredibly hard. It can take classical computers thousands of years to solve.

Quantum computers, using an approach called Shor's Algorithm, can solve this problem in a fraction of the time. Shor's Algorithm uses quantum principles to find patterns in numbers that are invisible to classical methods. With enough stable qubits and low enough error rates, it becomes possible to break RSA encryption in hours or even minutes. The same is true for ECC. Elliptic curve systems rely on a different kind of hard math problem, called the discrete logarithm. Shor's Algorithm breaks this as well, which means that both of the most widely used forms of public key cryptography are vulnerable. This is not a theoretical weakness; it is a structural one. If and when quantum computers reach a certain level of capability, these algorithms will no longer protect anything.

2.4 GROVER'S ALGORITHM: WEAKENING SYMMETRIC ENCRYPTION

Symmetric encryption is different. Systems like AES use the same key for both encryption and decryption of data. They are faster and more efficient for large volumes of information. Fortunately, symmetric systems are more resistant to quantum attacks than public key systems.

But they are not immune.

Quantum computers can use Grover's Algorithm to perform a brute-force search more efficiently than classical machines. In simple terms, Grover's method reduces the number of guesses needed to find a key, basically cutting the effective length of the key in half. For example, with AES-128, a quantum computer would only need to search through 2^{64} possible keys instead of 2^{128}. While 2^{64} is still a large number, quantum systems may eventually reach the capability to process that many key guesses in a relatively short period, potentially within a day. This means that while AES-128 may be considered secure against classical attacks, it is no longer strong enough in a post-quantum world. Security experts now recommend using AES-256, which still provides strong resistance even under Grover's more efficient search model. So, while symmetric encryption survives, it will need to be strengthened. The same principle applies to hashing algorithms. Some, like SHA-2, may hold up longer. Others may need to be replaced or reinforced.

Grover's Algorithm provides quantum computers a materially better attack against symmetric encryption than classical brute-force methods by effectively halving the key length. For example, with AES-128, a quantum computer would only need to search through 2^{64} possible keys instead of 2^{128}.

While 2^{64} is still a large number, quantum systems may eventually reach the capability to process that many key guesses in a relatively short period, potentially within a day, making AES-128 insufficient for long-term protection. This is why security experts recommend using AES-256 or higher to maintain post-quantum resilience.

2.5 REAL EXPERIMENTS: DEMONSTRATING THE TRAJECTORY TOWARD Q-DAY

It is one thing to understand theory. It is another to test the boundaries of what's practically achievable.

The Q-Day Prize, a challenge intended to incentivize the first successful quantum attack against widely used public-key systems like RSA or ECC, remains unclaimed. But each experiment brings us a step closer, underscoring the urgency for organizations to begin quantum readiness planning today.

While no quantum computer has yet broken real-world cryptographic systems like RSA, ECC, or Diffie-Hellman at practical key sizes, researchers have begun to demonstrate the building blocks of such attacks on a small scale. In 2023, a team from Tsinghua University published a controversial paper claiming to break RSA-2048 using a combination of quantum techniques and a hybrid classical-quantum algorithm. However, the cryptographic community largely dismissed this as infeasible with current technology and flawed in its assumptions.

More realistically, controlled experiments have successfully demonstrated Shor's Algorithm on actual quantum hardware, albeit for very small numbers. For instance, IBM, Google, and IonQ have all used their quantum platforms to factor small integers like 15 or 21, showing that the theoretical foundation for breaking RSA is valid, but not yet scalable.

Similarly, simulations of quantum attacks against cryptographic primitives have been performed using emulators or limited qubit systems to explore how algorithms like Shor's or Grover's would behave under ideal conditions. These proof-of-concept experiments confirm that quantum attacks are not merely hypothetical. They're technically sound and await only the hardware maturity, specifically, large-scale, fault-tolerant quantum systems, to become a real threat.

In May 2025, a Google Quantum AI researcher published a study revealing a dramatic reduction in the estimated resources needed to attack RSA-2048 using quantum systems. The team found that breaking RSA-2048 could take under a week with fewer than one million noisy qubits, which represents a significant drop from earlier estimates that required ~20 million error-corrected qubits.

Google's Willow quantum processor represents a significant leap in the evolution of quantum hardware. Designed by Google's Quantum AI team,

Willow is a superconducting quantum processor built to demonstrate error mitigation at scale and sustain longer, more stable quantum operations. Unlike earlier prototypes, Willow's architecture emphasizes fault-tolerant design principles and showcases tangible improvements in coherence time, gate fidelity, and noise suppression. It isn't just a lab experiment, it's a step toward practical quantum computing.

Some, including Hartmut Neven from Google's Quantum AI team, interpreted Willow's performance as consistent with the multiverse interpretation of quantum mechanics. This view suggests that quantum computations may occur across multiple parallel universes. Others pushed back, arguing that the result can be explained using traditional interpretations of quantum theory without invoking parallel dimensions.

Whether or not Willow tells us something about the nature of reality, it clearly tells us something about the pace of progress. The chip is faster, more precise, and more robust in handling errors than its predecessors. It proves that quantum hardware is no longer experimental in name only. These machines are rapidly advancing toward capabilities that will soon begin to impact real-world systems.

Meanwhile, on the other side of the globe, researchers in China have made major advances with a system called Zuchongzhi 3.0. This machine was developed by a team at the University of Science and Technology of China and represents one of the most powerful quantum processors built to date. Zuchongzhi 3.0 has demonstrated the ability to handle high-complexity quantum tasks with over 370 qubits, showing strong error control and performance that rivals or surpasses Western benchmarks in several areas.

Like Google's Willow, Zuchongzhi 3.0 has been used to perform random circuit sampling and other benchmark tasks designed to test the outer limits of quantum speed. While the technical details differ, the larger picture is the same. Quantum computing is no longer a race between theory and engineering. It is a race between time and readiness.

Together, these developments show a trend that can't be ignored. Quantum systems are becoming faster, more stable, and capable of solving harder problems, and they are closing in on the kinds of cryptographic systems that protect the digital world today. These advancements do not mean the internet is broken or that cryptography has failed. They do mean that the assumptions we have depended on for decades are beginning to shift. The timeline is tightening. Planning for quantum-safe infrastructure is no longer optional. It is becoming a basic requirement for protecting trust in the years ahead.

2.6 CONCLUSION

This chapter has focused on what makes quantum computing a real and immediate threat to modern encryption. We began by looking at how quantum computers process information in fundamentally different ways from classical machines. These systems are not just faster; they work on a different set of rules entirely. That shift in how information is handled is what gives quantum its power and what makes it so dangerous to today's cryptographic systems.

We then explored the two main types of encryption: symmetric and asymmetric. Symmetric systems like AES can still hold up, especially with longer key lengths, although they will need to be reassessed. Asymmetric systems such as RSA and ECC are in a much more fragile position. Shor's Algorithm will eventually allow quantum computers to break these systems completely, undermining the security of everything from websites and emails to software updates and digital identities.

The examples from IBM, Google, and China demonstrate that this is no longer just a theory. IBM's Q-Day Prize experiments, Google's Willow chip, and the Zuchongzhi 3.0 processor built in China have all demonstrated real progress in quantum performance. They have successfully modeled attacks on encryption protocols that are still in widespread use today. These systems did not compromise the internet overnight, but they did prove that the tools to do so are beginning to take shape. This is the warning signal. The tools are becoming more powerful, timelines are getting shorter, and the assumptions we have relied on for decades are starting to fall apart.

In the next chapter, we will introduce a framework known as the Mosca Model. This model will help you determine the urgency of your quantum readiness efforts. It will help you assess how long your data needs to stay secure and how long your systems will take to upgrade. By combining these timelines, you will be able to answer the most important question: how soon do you need to act?

For now, the takeaway is simple. Quantum computing changes what is possible, and that change is already in motion. What we thought was safe for decades may not be safe for the next five years. Which means it is time to start planning accordingly.

Chapter 3

The Mosca Model and why time is not on your side

One of the most pressing challenges in cybersecurity today is knowing when to act. Quantum threats can sometimes feel abstract, but the timeline for responding is not. Waiting until quantum computers reach maturity is not a safe option. Some organizations are already exposed without realizing it. So, how do you measure your risk? How do you know when your window to act is closing?

That is where the Mosca Model comes in.

3.1 UNDERSTANDING THE MODEL

The Mosca Model is named after Michele Mosca, a Canadian mathematician and one of the leading voices in quantum computing. He is a professor at the University of Waterloo and co-founder of the Institute for Quantum Computing. Over the last two decades, he has worked to translate quantum research into practical, real-world insight for governments, businesses, and the broader cybersecurity community (Figure 3.1).

His model helps organizations answer a simple but urgent question: Are we already out of time?

At the heart of the model is a basic inequality:

$$X + Y > Z$$

Each of these letters represents a variable in your organization's exposure to the quantum threat.

- X is how long it will take you to implement a quantum-safe solution. This includes time to plan, budget, test, migrate, validate, and train your teams.
- Y is how long you need your data to remain secure. In other words, how many years into the future must this data stay confidential or trustworthy?

 DOI: 10.1201/9781003685760-5

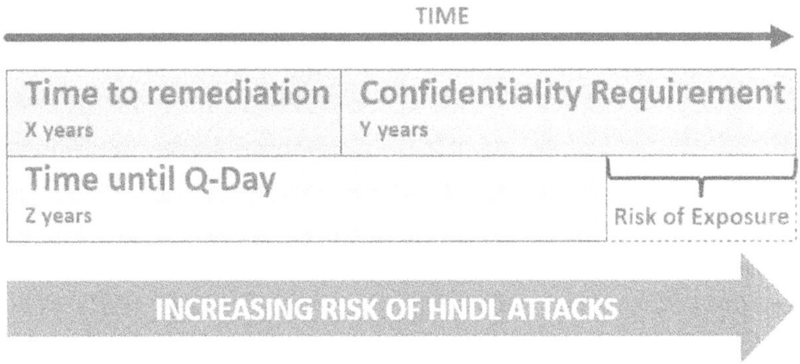

Figure 3.1 Mosca Model.

- *Z* is how long experts estimate it will take before a large enough quantum computer exists to break today's encryption.

If the combined value of X and Y is greater than Z, your organization is already vulnerable. It means that by the time you finish your migration, it will already be too late for the data you are protecting today.

This model turns abstract risk into something measurable. It provides a formula to work with, rather than relying on vague guesses, and helps you shift the conversation with stakeholders from speculation to timelines and planning.

3.2 APPLYING THE MODEL IN PRACTICE

Let's say your organization has trade secrets, and those records need to be protected for at least 15 years. That is your Y value. Now, estimate how long it would take to assess your environment, replace all vulnerable cryptographic components, test your systems, and ensure operational readiness. Maybe that's five years, depending on your current maturity. That gives you an X value of 5.

Now, consider the best estimates for quantum decryption capability. Many experts believe that a cryptographically relevant quantum computer could exist by 2030 to 2035. Let's be conservative and use 2035. If it's currently 2028, you have a Z value of 7 years.

So:

$X\ (5) + Y\ (15) = 20$

$Z = 7$

Your result is 20 > 7. According to the Mosca Model, your data is already at risk. Even if you start your migration now, your encrypted records may remain vulnerable until you complete the transition.

This situation is critical because of Harvest Now, Decrypt Later, which we covered in Chapter 1. If attackers are capturing encrypted data today, they may be able to unlock it in the future once quantum systems reach sufficient strength. The longer your migration takes, and the longer your data needs to stay protected, the greater the chance that data will be compromised after the fact.

Determining how long data needs to remain protected seems straightforward until you consider the numerous unknowns that are still in play. While Z is the only variable outside your control, it is not the hardest to estimate. That distinction belongs to X, your remediation time. Many of the remediation tools and quantum-safe replacements are still being finalized or have not yet reached full commercial maturity. Even if you know what needs to be protected, you may not yet know how to protect it. That makes it extremely difficult to define a clear and realistic X value.

To understand what that means in practice, think back to previous major cryptographic shifts, such as when the industry moved from DES to 3DES. That transition took the better part of a decade, and at the time, most cryptographic operations were hardware-based. Now, cryptography is everywhere. It lives in software, firmware, APIs, embedded systems, and authentication protocols. It touches cloud platforms, endpoints, mobile devices, and workloads that most organizations never fully inventory. Replacing DES was hard. Replacing today's encryption will be harder.

The challenge becomes even greater when we consider long-lived hardware environments, such as industrial control systems (ICS), operational technology (OT), and Internet of Things (IoT) devices. These systems are often built on hardware that is expected to run for 10, 15, or even 20 years. Some are difficult to access, expensive to update, or unsupported by modern patching cycles. They often include cryptographic components that cannot be swapped out with a software update. In many cases, post-quantum options may not even exist for them yet.

That leaves organizations with two difficult options. The first is to replace hardware early, before its expected service life has ended. That can create significant capital expenditure (CAPEX) impacts and disrupt carefully planned replacement schedules. The second option is to wait and replace these devices on their normal timeline; however, doing so may extend X well beyond Z, which would expose those systems and the secrets they protect, long before a fix is in place. This is why many organizations are likely underestimating both X and Y. It is not just about how long you want to keep your data safe. It is about how long it will actually take to replace the cryptography that surrounds it, much of which may be hidden deep inside systems that were never built to support change.

So, when you apply the Mosca Model, give each number the scrutiny it deserves. Take a conservative view of how long data must stay protected. Be honest about how long it will take to complete the migration. Consider legacy systems, unsupported devices, third-party dependencies, and vendor timelines. These are not theoretical challenges. They are real-world constraints that could define the moment your organization becomes exposed.

3.2.1 Why this model matters

The strength of the Mosca Model lies in its clarity. In a landscape saturated with buzzwords, theoretical papers, and complex threat forecasts, the model offers a practical, grounded way to assess urgency. It distills the quantum risk timeline into three variables: how long your data needs to remain secure, how long your current systems will be in place, and how long it will take to replace them. Simple as that may sound, it forces a fundamental shift in how organizations think about cryptographic transition. It replaces vague notions of "someday" with a pointed question: will you finish in time?

Understanding this model matters because it reframes quantum readiness as a race against three moving clocks. If your systems are expected to run for another 15 years, and it takes five years to fully migrate your cryptographic stack, you are already living inside the risk window. The model shows that delay is not a neutral choice. The longer you wait to begin, the more you compress your migration timeline and the more risk you assume by default.

Michele Mosca did not develop this model to cause alarm. He created it to break the cycle of inaction. His work has helped elevate post-quantum cryptography from obscure academic research into a strategic business and policy priority. By laying out a non-theoretical, time-based rationale for early preparation, the model makes quantum risk tangible in ways that boardrooms, policymakers, and engineers can all understand. It replaces fear with focus.

This kind of focus is fundamental in sectors where long-term confidentiality and infrastructure lifespans are measured in decades, not years. For example, in the financial sector, data confidentiality isn't just a best practice; it's a legal requirement that often extends decades into the future. Encrypted records from a trade, transaction, or client onboarding process may need to remain secure well into the 2040s and beyond. This is why banks, payment networks, and financial services firms should be among the earliest adopters of post-quantum cryptography. Financial institutions should be piloting hybrid key exchange mechanisms in their VPN infrastructure and exploring the integration of PQC algorithms into digital signature workflows for SWIFT and ISO 20022 transactions.

But the model applies far beyond finance. Healthcare organizations must preserve patient records indefinitely. Government agencies are bound by national security classification timelines. Critical infrastructure operators manage hardware lifecycles that can outlast entire IT generations. In each of these cases, the Mosca Model offers a clear, customizable framework for answering the only question that matters: how soon must we begin?

In post-quantum planning, the danger isn't just that quantum computers will arrive faster than expected. The deeper risk is that migration takes longer than anyone wants to admit. The Mosca Model makes that reality unavoidable. It shows that this is not a wait-and-see problem. It is a start-early-or-finish-late problem, and finishing late may mean failing altogether.

Organizations that understand this model have a strategic advantage. They are able to look past marketing timelines and vendor promises to make their own readiness decisions. They can build rational migration roadmaps, secure executive buy-in, and set realistic expectations with regulators and stakeholders. They don't overreact, but they don't underprepare either. By rooting quantum readiness in a simple equation of time, the Mosca Model helps organizations move from vague concern to specific, actionable planning. That clarity is its true power.

3.3 ARE YOU ALREADY VULNERABLE?

If your data has a long shelf life or if your systems take years to upgrade, the answer might be yes. Many organizations are already closer to their risk threshold than they realize. Some operate with long procurement cycles and infrastructure timelines that make quick changes nearly impossible. Others rely on legacy systems that are difficult to patch, reconfigure, or replace, and some manage highly sensitive information, such as medical records, financial data, or government documents, which must remain protected for decades.

These are exactly the kinds of environments where the Mosca Model proves useful. It gives structure to what might otherwise be a gut feeling or vague concern. It helps you measure and communicate how much time you really have. So, how do you begin assessing whether you are vulnerable and, more importantly, how much that vulnerability matters?

The first step is understanding the scope of exposure. Even without a comprehensive cryptographic inventory, you can begin to identify likely areas of concern by examining the systems that support key business processes and contain long-lived or high-value data. Think in terms of functions and roles rather than individual devices. If a system is responsible for authentication, transaction signing, regulatory reporting, or protecting sensitive communications, it likely relies on cryptographic tools that require evaluation.

Once you have a sense of potential exposure, the next step is to assess risk in measurable terms. In traditional cybersecurity, this is done by evaluating three key factors: likelihood, impact, and exploitability. Quantum exposure adheres to the same structure, even if the threat vector differs.

- *Likelihood* in this context is about timing. Based on current research and expert consensus, when might a quantum computer capable of breaking current encryption actually arrive? Combine this with how long your data needs to remain secure and how long your migration might take to get a sense of whether your window is closing.
- *Impact* is about consequence. What happens if the cryptography used to secure a system is broken? Would it result in the loss of confidentiality, the failure of a service, or the compromise of system integrity? Would it expose sensitive customer data or undermine regulatory compliance?
- *Exploitability* refers to whether the data is attractive and accessible to attackers today. If encrypted traffic can be intercepted now and decrypted later, the exposure may already exist. If the system is connected to the internet, dependent on outdated encryption, or handling sensitive information, the risk is likely higher.

Several existing risk frameworks can be adapted to evaluate post-quantum exposure:

- *FAIR (Factor Analysis of Information Risk)* helps quantify risk in financial terms by assessing threat frequency and probable loss. This model can help express quantum exposure in business language that resonates with executive teams.
- *The NIST Risk Management Framework (RMF) and ISO 27005 provide structured approaches for* evaluating information security risks. These can be used to document the quantum threat alongside traditional risks, allowing for consistent prioritization.
- *DoCRA (Duty of Care Risk Analysis)* emphasizes reasonable and appropriate protections based on the sensitivity of the data, the likelihood of harm, and the duty of the organization to prevent it. This model is particularly useful for compliance-sensitive industries.

Another consideration is the cascading impact of trust failure. Even if a single system seems isolated, breaking its encryption could create a ripple effect. For example, if a certificate authority is compromised, attackers may be able to spoof entire branches of an organization's digital identity. If cryptographic integrity is lost in a supply chain, the consequences may affect customers, vendors, and regulators.

While the value of data can sometimes be estimated in terms of revenue, contracts, or liability, the value of trust is harder to define. Yet it is often the most critical. Suppose your systems can no longer verify their identity or confirm the validity of the data they send. In that case, it becomes very difficult to continue operations, let alone maintain customer or stakeholder confidence. That loss is difficult to price, but easy to feel.

Ultimately, the question is not just whether you are vulnerable, but how much risk that vulnerability introduces into your environment. Not every exposure is equal, but the ones that matter most are often the ones with the longest timelines, the greatest access, and the deepest connections to trust.

In the next chapter, we will introduce the Q-Ready Framework, which provides a clear structure for preparing your organization. It will guide you through identifying where cryptography exists, prioritizing what to fix, and building a roadmap for readiness. Inventory, planning, and implementation come next.

For now, the focus is simple: determine whether you are already exposed, and if so, begin quantifying the potential cost of that exposure. Understanding the risk is the first step to addressing it.

To get started, ask yourself a few key questions:

- How long must the information we store remain confidential or trustworthy?
- What systems in our environment contain or depend on cryptography?
- How long would it take to complete a full migration to post-quantum cryptographic standards across those systems?
- How many of our systems rely on third-party vendors for cryptographic functions or security updates?
- Are any of our critical systems built on embedded hardware with long replacement cycles?
- Do we manage any devices in OT, ICS, or IoT environments that are difficult or expensive to upgrade?
- Have we inventoried our cryptographic assets and protocols recently?
- How soon could quantum computers realistically compromise the cryptographic tools we use today?

If your answers indicate that you are cutting it close or worse, that you are already behind, it's time to act. The good news is that you do not have to solve this all at once. The Mosca Model is not about forecasting the exact day of risk. It is about recognizing when the window for action is closing faster than we think.

3.4 CONCLUSION

The Mosca Model makes one thing painfully clear. If the time it takes to prepare your systems and the time your data needs to remain secure are together longer than the time left before quantum computing becomes a real threat, then you are already behind. Many organizations are, and most do not yet realize it.

This chapter has focused on helping you measure that gap. The equation is simple, but the implications are not. Quantum readiness requires more than just identifying vulnerable systems. It requires you to understand the business risk that comes from inaction. Trust in digital systems is built on cryptographic assurance. Once that trust is broken, it does not just lead to lost data; it leads to lost confidence, lost continuity, and potentially lost customers.

The Mosca Model gives you a starting point. It shifts the conversation away from theory and toward timelines. It helps you see the risk in practical terms and puts you in a better position to explain that risk to executive leadership, boards, regulators, and partners. It also forces a more honest look at operational timelines, procurement delays, hardware dependencies, and the kinds of embedded systems that are difficult or expensive to touch. These are the realities that extend X, and if you are not accounting for them, your estimates may be dangerously optimistic.

Understanding the risk is only the first step. The next step is preparing to act. In the following chapter, we will introduce the Q-Ready Framework. It is designed to help organizations take practical steps toward quantum readiness, starting with visibility, moving through prioritization, planning, and ending with implementation and long-term maintenance. The path forward will take time, coordination, and investment. It begins with clarity. If you are already exposed, the cost of delay is greater than the cost of action, and if you are not sure yet, now is the time to find out.

Chapter 4

Overview of the Q-Ready Framework and how to use this book

4.1 WHY A FRAMEWORK IS NEEDED NOW

As we've seen throughout the last few chapters, quantum computing is no longer confined to academic research or government-funded labs. It is advancing steadily through private investment, international competition, and accelerated development in both hardware and software. This progress is pushing quantum technology toward practical capabilities faster than many organizations are prepared to manage. The urgency is not hypothetical; it is practical.

While this is not solely a federal government concern, the US government has already provided considerable guidance that every type of organization can leverage. The White House formalized the urgency in National Security Memorandum 10 (NSM-10), which requires federal agencies to prepare for a post-quantum future by performing cryptographic discovery, documenting risks, and migrating to quantum-resistant algorithms. NIST, CISA, and the NSA have followed with their own detailed roadmaps, encouraging public and private sector organizations alike to begin immediate planning.

NIST Special Publication 1800-38 outlines a practical approach to post-quantum migration, grounded in risk management. NIST IR 8547 provides a phased transition plan, and the draft FIPS standards 203, 204, 205, and 206 specify the first approved quantum-resistant algorithms. Together, these resources define a shift that is expected instead of optional. CISA has repeatedly echoed this message in its alerts and guidance, emphasizing the importance of discovery, agility, and early implementation to mitigate long-term risk. This guidance has made one thing clear: organizations must begin preparing for quantum today, even if they plan to adopt later.

4.2 INTRODUCING THE Q-READY FRAMEWORK

The Q-Ready Framework is built to translate these national and industry requirements into an actionable, enterprise-level strategy. It is designed to

DOI: 10.1201/9781003685760-6

help organizations move through quantum readiness with structure, clarity, and accountability.

I developed the Q-Ready Framework as part of my role as Lead Field CISO at CDW. In that position, I have the opportunity to work directly with hundreds of organizations across industries. I speak regularly with CIOs, CISOs, and their teams. I get to see what works, what fails, and what gets stuck somewhere in between. Those conversations have shaped my perspective on how cybersecurity programs succeed and how they often struggle when faced with complex, long-term challenges.

Quantum readiness is one of those challenges. The risk is clear and the timelines are tightening, but for many teams, it is not obvious how to begin or what to prioritize. The Q-Ready Framework was created to fill that gap. It is a practical model designed to help organizations make progress even when the path ahead is uncertain.

The purpose of the Q-Ready Framework is to help make this transition manageable. It provides organizations with a structured approach to identify vulnerabilities, plan a response, implement changes, and maintain trust in the face of uncertainty. It is built for real-world use and designed to meet the needs of both technical and non-technical decision-makers.

The framework's purpose is to provide:

- A repeatable process for discovering and managing cryptographic risk
- A method for aligning security, operations, and compliance teams around a shared plan
- A practical model that supports progress without requiring perfection
- A guide that organizations of any size or maturity level can adapt to their environment

Without a framework, organizations risk either doing too little or starting too late. This is not a threat that can be solved with a single tool or product; it will require a comprehensive program. The Q-Ready Framework is here to help you build that program, tailored to your current situation and your desired outcome.

The framework is divided into five phases. Each phase contains three steps. These steps are based on federal guidance, industry best practices, and real-world lessons learned from organizations that are already in the process of transitioning. Together, they provide a roadmap for navigating the transition to post-quantum cryptography in a structured, measurable, and sustainable manner. Whether you are leading a mature cybersecurity program or just beginning to plan your approach to quantum risk, this framework is built to meet you where you are.

4.2.1 The five phases of the Q-Ready Framework

The framework is organized into five phases, each with three distinct steps (see Figure 4.1):

Phase 1: Discovery

Understand what cryptographic assets you have, where they reside, and what they protect.

1. Identify cryptographic assets and protocols
2. Assess data sensitivity and system dependencies
3. Prioritize systems based on exposure and business impact

Phase 2: Planning

Develop a strategy that aligns with your risk profile and operational capacity.

1. Define program scope and governance
2. Engage stakeholders and align timelines
3. Map dependencies and establish success metrics

Phase 3: Implementation

Deploy solutions and harden cryptographic infrastructure.

1. Replace vulnerable algorithms with approved post-quantum alternatives
2. Upgrade key management systems
3. Update applications, certificates, credentials, and interfaces

Phase 4: Validation

Test and verify readiness at scale.

1. Validate cryptographic performance and resilience
2. Conduct audits and compliance checks
3. Simulate failure scenarios and operational impact

Phase 5: Maintenance

Sustain your progress and remain agile as standards evolve.

1. Monitor the algorithm and key lifecycle
2. Track policy updates and vendor alignment
3. Train personnel and refine incident response plans

Figure 4.1 Q-Ready Framework.

Each phase builds upon the one before it, progressing from initial discovery to long-term sustainment. While the model is sequential in structure, it is flexible in practice. Some organizations will linearly progress through these phases. Others may iterate or parallelize tasks based on resources, priorities, or external requirements.

4.3 ALIGNMENT WITH NATIONAL STANDARDS AND BEST PRACTICES

The Q-Ready Framework aligns directly with the cybersecurity guidance outlined by NIST and other federal agencies. See Figure 4.2 for the NIST PQC Lifecycle. It mirrors the Identify, Assess, Select Controls, Remediate, and Monitor structure used in federal cyber risk programs, including the NIST Cybersecurity Framework (CSF) and Risk Management Framework (RMF). These guidelines form the foundation of most government and regulated industry security standards.

- *Discovery* corresponds with NIST's *Identify* and *Assess* steps.
- *Planning* and *Implementation* align with *Control* Selection and *Remediation.*
- *Validation* and *Maintenance* fall under *Monitoring* and Continuous Improvement.

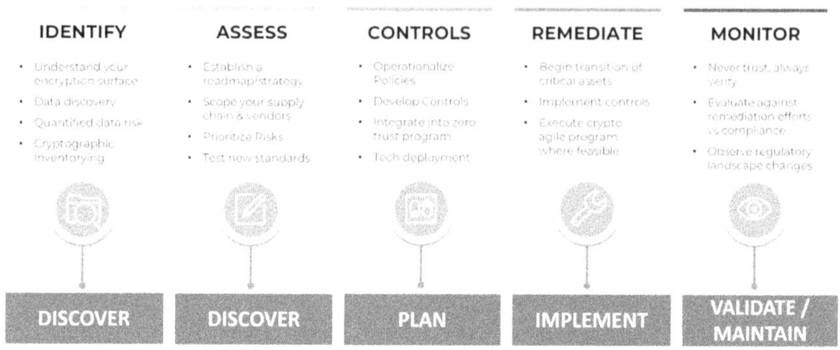

Figure 4.2 NIST guidance.

This alignment is intentional. It ensures that organizations using the Q-Ready Framework not only build effective defenses but also do so in a manner that meets audit, reporting, and oversight expectations.

In addition to federal guidance, the framework incorporates lessons from real-world transitions. Cryptographic migrations are not new, but what makes this one different is the scale, complexity, and uncertainty around timing. The Q-Ready Framework was designed to support those conditions.

4.4 HOW TO USE THIS BOOK

This book is structured to follow the Q-Ready Framework, one phase at a time. Each phase of the framework is explored in its own dedicated section. Within each section, you'll find three chapters, one for each of that phase's key steps. The chapters are intentionally concise and practical, offering field-tested guidance, common pitfalls, and proven strategies for implementation. From governance planning to integration patterns and tooling options, each chapter is designed to move you from theory to execution.

The structure of this book is intentionally modular. You do not need to read the entire book before getting started. It is not a narrative with a fixed beginning and end; it's a toolkit. If you already know your organization is in the early stages of inventory and discovery, start with the Discovery section. If you're further along and facing architecture or integration decisions, jump to the Planning or Implementation phases. If you're operationalizing your controls, you might begin with Validation or Maintenance. You can use the chapters in sequence or dive into specific topics as needed. Each section is self-contained, yet aligned with the broader roadmap.

The Q-Ready Framework is designed not as a checklist, but as a maturity model. While each phase is distinct, they are interdependent. You may revisit previous phases as new systems come online, regulations change, or cryptographic policies mature. Quantum readiness will not happen overnight, and it cannot be solved with a single product, vendor, or policy. It requires strategic alignment across teams, technical coordination across infrastructure, and operational discipline across business processes. This book aims to guide you through all three, with clarity and realism.

For readers less familiar with the underlying cryptography, the Preface offers a concise primer. It explains foundational concepts such as symmetric and asymmetric encryption, key exchange, and digital certificates. Whether you're a technical leader brushing up on terminology or a business stakeholder seeking context, the Preface can help orient you before diving into the technical material.

Chapter 0 is an executive overview. It is written for CISOs, CIOs, business executives, and board members who need a high-level understanding of the quantum threat landscape and what to do about it. It outlines the stakes of Q-Day, defines key concepts like crypto-agility and algorithm migration, and introduces the Q-Ready Framework in plain language. It can also be used by CISOs as a standalone asset to educate their peers and brief the board. If you're a technical reader looking for help getting executive buy-in, Chapter 0 is where you start.

This book was written to help your team take action across the entire post-quantum lifecycle. Whether you're a CISO making strategic decisions, a security architect designing defenses, a program lead managing compliance, or a hands-on engineer deploying new tools, this book is your practical companion. It is built to turn quantum uncertainty into a structured path forward, step by step, decision by decision.

4.5 WHAT TO EXPECT NEXT

The first four chapters of this book have laid the foundation. We began by exploring why quantum computing presents a unique and urgent threat to traditional cryptographic systems. We explained what makes the risk different, why timelines matter, and how to measure exposure using the Mosca Model. We introduced the idea of Q-Day not as a distant possibility, but as a real inflection point that must be planned for now.

We also presented the Q-Ready Framework, a practical structure for responding to this challenge. This framework is built around five phases: Discovery, Planning, Implementation, Validation, and Maintenance. Each phase includes 3 steps, giving you 15 actionable points to guide your organization's transition from traditional encryption to quantum-resistant infrastructure.

The remainder of the book provides a detailed examination of each of these five phases. Every section contains three chapters, focused on the specific actions, tools, and strategies needed to carry out that phase successfully. The structure mirrors the way most real-world cybersecurity programs operate step by step, across teams, and always under pressure to balance innovation with risk.

In Section II, we begin with Discovery. These chapters guide you through identifying and documenting your cryptographic assets, assessing where quantum risk is highest, and prioritizing which systems should be addressed first. You will learn about tools like IBM Guardium, Sandbox AQ, and ISARA, and you will see how to construct a Cryptographic Bill of Materials. You will also be introduced to risk scoring methods and frameworks for evaluating the duration of privacy and the business impact.

Section III focuses on Planning. This phase is where strategy meets reality. You will learn how to design a migration plan, build test environments, and evaluate cryptographic toolkits. These chapters also provide techniques for gaining executive buy-in, briefing stakeholders, and defining success metrics. Because planning without alignment rarely succeeds, this section emphasizes both technical direction and organizational consensus.

In Section IV, we move into Implementation. Here, we walk through the process of replacing vulnerable algorithms, improving key generation and distribution, and integrating post-quantum encryption into systems like VPNs, TLS, firmware, and IoT devices. You will also explore emerging technologies such as Quantum Key Distribution and quantum random number generation. The practical challenges of upgrading long-lifecycle hardware and embedded systems are addressed head-on.

Section V covers Validation. In these chapters, we show you how to test your deployments, monitor for new cryptographic threats, and ensure that your implementation is audit-ready. We cover testing frameworks, simulation environments, and monitoring tools. We also include guidance on how to map your outcomes back to NIST, CISA, and other regulatory requirements, so you are prepared for both internal reviews and third-party audits.

Finally, Section VI focuses on Maintenance. This is where the work becomes ongoing. You will learn how to maintain crypto-agility, manage certificate lifecycles, and train your teams for a world where cryptographic standards are likely to continue evolving. This section also provides recommendations for building long-term organizational readiness, including training programs, tabletop exercises, and the designation of a quantum risk owner.

The book concludes with a chapter on moving from awareness to assurance. By that point, you will have the tools and frameworks to build a sustainable quantum readiness program. You will understand what readiness looks like, how to measure it, and how to defend it. What comes next is about action. The threat is real, the clock is ticking, and the first step is clarity. That is where we begin, with Discovery. Let's get to work.

Section II

Phase I

Discovery

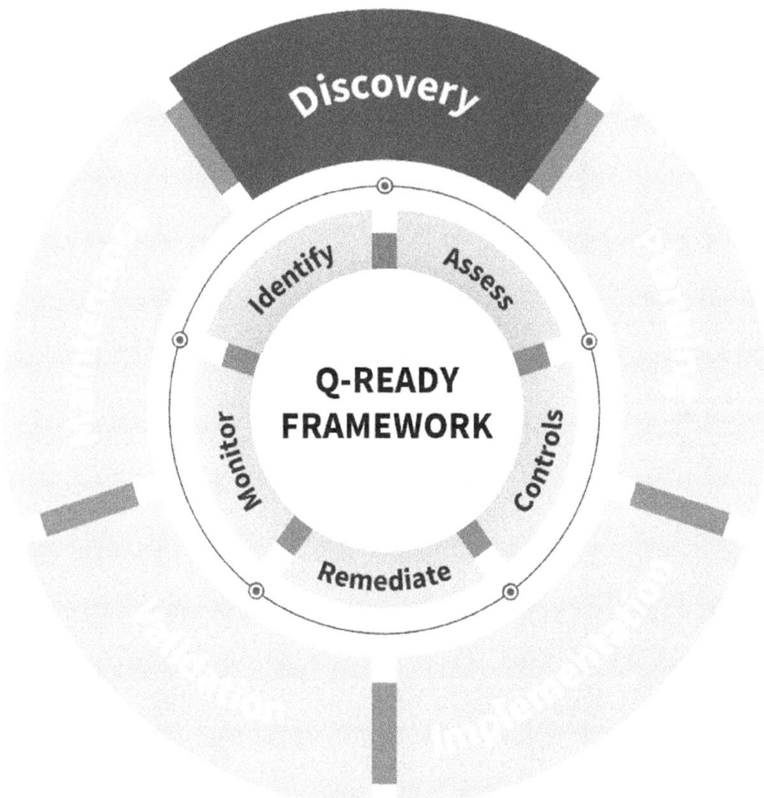

Figure SII.1 Discovery phase.

DOI: 10.1201/9781003685760-7

Chapter 5

Inventory your cryptographic assets

Before you can fix anything, you have to know where it lives. In the world of quantum readiness, that means understanding where cryptography is used, how it's configured, and what it protects. Cryptography is everywhere now, inside operating systems, woven through cloud platforms, embedded in APIs, baked into firmware, and hidden in hardware. Some of it is carefully maintained, while some of it is quietly forgotten, but all of it matters.

This chapter is about surfacing that complexity by mapping your environment and building the foundation for everything that follows. A successful quantum migration starts with discovery, and discovery starts with inventory.

5.1 THE FIRST STEP: KNOW WHAT YOU HAVE

Inventorying cryptographic assets may be the most difficult part of this transition. Unlike software updates or endpoint scans, cryptographic elements often lack centralized management. DevOps teams manage some, while others are embedded deep within legacy applications. Many organizations simply don't know how many certificates they have, let alone which algorithms those certificates use or how long they are valid.

You need to answer three questions:

- What crypto is used?
- Where is it used?
- Who or what is using it?

Begin with the protocols and systems most likely to contain vulnerable cryptographic components. These include TLS configurations on your web servers, VPN tunnels used for remote access, digital signatures that validate software, certificates that secure APIs, firmware with embedded encryption, IoT devices with hardcoded keys, and encrypted data-at-rest. Each of these may be using RSA, ECC, or other public key systems that will not

DOI: 10.1201/9781003685760-8

survive the quantum shift. Finding them is more than just a matter of inventory; it's strategic defense.

5.2 WHAT TO LOOK FOR

A good inventory goes beyond counting certificates. It includes every place where cryptographic functions appear.

That means scanning your infrastructure for:

- Transport Layer Security (TLS) settings in web applications and internal services.
- VPN connections relying on Diffie-Hellman or Elliptic Curve key exchange.
- Certificates used for authentication, code signing, and email encryption.
- Digital signatures on firmware, drivers, and packages, encrypted fields in databases, and backup archives.
- Cryptographic libraries embedded in IoT and operational technology.

Each item should be reviewed not only for the algorithm it uses but also for its purpose, lifespan, and level of exposure.

Start with the protocols and protections you know are in use. Begin with TLS and VPNs, the most widely deployed uses of cryptography in enterprise environments. Next, proceed to certificates, code signing mechanisms, firmware verification routines, data-at-rest encryption, and embedded encryption within IoT and OT devices.

Look for specific cryptographic artifacts, such as public and private key pairs, digital certificates, session keys, key exchange protocols, and the specific algorithms in use, including RSA, ECDSA, and AES. Trace how these elements are used to secure data-in-motion, data-at-rest, and identity validation. Examine API traffic, software build pipelines, and remote access tools. Inventory every piece of software and hardware that uses or depends on encryption.

Pay close attention to your endpoints. Determine which devices are used to access sensitive data, and how that data is protected at the endpoint. Identify what browsers, applications, and firmware versions are in use. In your network, trace how data moves, where it is encrypted, and which devices provide protection. This includes gateways, proxies, and edge devices. Don't overlook cloud infrastructure, especially when platform services abstract away encryption.

As you conduct this audit, note not only the presence of cryptographic tools but also the algorithms they rely on. Understanding whether a system uses RSA-2048 or AES-128 is essential to assessing quantum risk. When possible, document the length of the keys, the cipher modes used, and whether the system supports crypto-agility.

Additionally, consider whether these artifacts contain sensitive data and how long that data must be protected. Connecting encryption mechanisms to data privacy duration and classification makes the inventory much more valuable and actionable. Begin identifying which systems support regulated processes or business-critical workflows so that you can prioritize them during the quantum transition.

5.2.1 Tools to help

Several commercial tools have been built to support cryptographic inventory and discovery at scale. IBM Guardium specializes in data discovery, classifying sensitive information, and identifying the use of encryption across various environments. It can also flag weak configurations and identify compliance gaps, as well as generate Cryptographic Bill of Materials (CBOMs).

Sandbox AQ offers a powerful platform called AQtive Guard that combines artificial intelligence with quantum readiness analytics. It can scan your environment, identify cryptographic assets, assess their vulnerability, and support long-term crypto-agility. It goes beyond discovery by offering a structured Cryptographic Risk Assessment service. This service evaluates your current maturity, identifies security gaps, classifies data, and delivers actionable reports aligned to industry regulations. From there, Sandbox AQ helps develop and support a practical quantum transition plan. ISARA is another leading provider that helps organizations locate and replace vulnerable cryptographic protocols, especially in complex environments with embedded or legacy systems.

To keep the inventory current, integrate these tools into your asset management platforms or CI/CD pipelines. Automation ensures your inventory reflects changes as they happen. Set up alerting for unauthorized or unapproved cryptographic components so your team can respond before weaknesses are exploited.

5.2.2 Step-by-step: how to conduct a cryptographic inventory

Start by defining the scope. Determine which systems, environments, and networks you want to inventory first. Focus on high-value or high-risk areas. Then follow these general steps:

First, scan your network and systems using tools like AQtive Guard or Guardium to generate an initial list of where encryption is used. Second, validate those findings manually by working with system owners and reviewing configuration files, logs, and application settings. Third, document the specific algorithms in use, the key lengths, cipher modes, and protocol versions. Fourth, map each cryptographic element to the data or function it protects. Fifth, flag each artifact based on quantum vulnerability. RSA and ECC should be classified as high-risk. AES with 128-bit keys should be flagged for future upgrade. Finally, store this data in a centralized format that can be updated over time and reviewed by both security and compliance teams.

5.2.3 Building a Cryptographic Bill of Materials (CBOM)

To manage cryptographic assets at scale, you need a structure. That's where a Cryptographic Bill of Materials, or CBOM, comes in. A CBOM is a schema extension of the Software Bill of Materials (SBOM), built to describe cryptographic components and their dependencies.

A CBOM is particularly useful in development environments where cryptography is implemented within the software supply chain. It provides metadata about each cryptographic component, including the version, source, and dependencies. This makes it easier to track and manage vulnerabilities, plan replacements, and maintain crypto-agility.

In practical terms, a CBOM helps you document which algorithms, keys, protocols, and certificates are in use. It captures metadata such as expiration dates, key lengths, signing authorities, and usage context. This metadata enables you to assess not only whether something is vulnerable but also how difficult it will be to replace and what business processes depend on it.

When integrated with SBOMs, CBOMs provide greater visibility into software supply chains. They help identify inherited cryptographic risk from third-party packages, open-source libraries, and vendor-supplied tools. This integration enhances transparency, facilitates secure procurement, and aligns with broader software assurance initiatives.

Creating a CBOM is more than just a compliance checkbox. It is a working document that supports long-term management and security. As post-quantum standards evolve and vendor tools mature, the CBOM helps you track changes, identify obsolete components, and coordinate upgrades across teams. Use CBOMs during procurement reviews, third-party software assessments, or as part of your continuous integration and delivery pipelines. They are essential in regulated industries where proof of cryptographic controls is required, and they support automated compliance checks.

5.2.4 Step-by-step: how to create a CBOM

Start by integrating cryptographic scanning tools, like IBM Guardium, into your build pipeline. Use static analysis tools that can detect cryptographic function calls and identify libraries. Extract the relevant metadata for each cryptographic artifact. Document the algorithm name, version, key sizes, usage context, and whether it supports quantum-safe alternatives. Use a standardized format, such as the CBOM schema extension for CycloneDX, to structure this data. Store CBOMs in a version-controlled repository where they can be reviewed, updated, and audited for accuracy and consistency. Automate CBOM generation as part of your release process. This ensures that every new build has an associated cryptographic profile. Review CBOMs regularly as part of security assessments, vendor evaluations, and compliance reviews.

5.2.5 Triage and integration with SBOM tools

Once cryptographic artifacts have been identified through scanning and discovery, the next step is triage, where findings are categorized based on their risk level, relevance, and actionability. Effective triage transforms raw cryptographic data into prioritized intelligence, enabling teams to determine which issues require immediate remediation, which can be monitored, and which are safe to defer.

Start by categorizing each finding using three criteria: algorithm type, risk profile, and usage context. For example, findings involving RSA-2048 or ECC-based key exchange protocols should be flagged as high-risk due to their vulnerability to quantum decryption. AES-128 may be designated for monitoring, while AES-256 or SHA-3 components can be labeled as low-risk, pending further cryptanalytic research.

Next, align these categorized findings with your asset inventory and Software Bill of Materials (SBOM) systems. This integration allows you to link each cryptographic component to the software, system, or service it supports. For instance, if a vulnerable key exchange mechanism is tied to a third-party API or vendor library, your Software Bill of Materials (SBOM) should reflect that relationship. Likewise, if a certificate in your CBOM is used in both a cloud gateway and an internal microservice, those dependencies should be visible and traceable.

Many SBOM formats, such as CycloneDX and SPDX, support custom metadata fields or extensions for cryptographic attributes. This allows cryptographic inventories to be imported or enriched with additional risk data, such as key lengths, expiration dates, and quantum readiness status. Tying triaged findings into these formats improves traceability across the software supply chain and enables more dynamic risk modeling.

Triage also supports compliance tracking and remediation workflows. Once linked to an SBOM (Software Bill of Materials) or CMDB (Configuration Management Database), cryptographic findings can trigger tickets in vulnerability management systems, be included in audit checklists, or prompt review during patch cycles and third-party assessments.

To keep triage and inventory processes aligned:

- *Use tags or labels* (e.g., quantum-vulnerable, crypto-agile, legacy-only) in your SBOM entries.
- *Integrate scanning tools with CI/CD pipelines* so new cryptographic issues are triaged in real time as builds are created.
- *Establish service-level agreements (SLAs)* for cryptographic risk remediation based on severity, exposure, and business impact.
- *Correlate SBOM/CBOM entries* with incident response and risk management systems to ensure cryptographic failures can be quickly traced and mitigated.

By linking triaged cryptographic findings to Software Bill of Materials (SBOM) platforms and asset inventories, organizations gain not only visibility but also control. This enables coordinated upgrades, streamlined reporting, and faster response to evolving standards or emerging vulnerabilities, key enablers for sustaining crypto-agility in a post-quantum world.

5.3 BEYOND THE INVENTORY

A strong inventory is more than a list. It becomes the map you use to navigate your quantum transition. To make it actionable, you need to think beyond technical components. That means asking harder questions about the systems those components protect.

Start with your data. What are the highest-value datasets in your environment? Which ones are subject to privacy regulations or long-term confidentiality requirements? Some data only matters for a day. Other data, such as legal contracts, medical records, or source code, may need to remain trustworthy for decades. Those are your high-priority items. Look at your applications. How do they store and secure the data they handle? Who uses those systems, and what happens if trust is broken?

Examine your endpoints. Where is data stored? Which servers host sensitive information? What devices access it? Are any of them running old TLS configurations, outdated libraries, or unpatched firmware? Review your network paths. How does data move between endpoints? Is the traffic encrypted the entire way? Where does it hit the cloud? Are you relying on third-party integrations with unknown cryptographic practices? Classify each asset by readiness. Label artifacts that rely on vulnerable algorithms as quantum-vulnerable. Note where crypto-agility is supported and where post-quantum tools are already deployed. This pre-migration status will help prioritize transitions and support planning. We'll define and discuss crypto-agility in Section III, Chapter 8, when we cover planning.

Think about dynamic versus static inventory. A one-time scan is a snapshot, but cryptographic environments are constantly evolving. Keys are added or replaced, certificates expire, and code updates shift libraries. To stay current, implement continuous discovery, and integrate scanning tools into CI/CD pipelines and asset management systems. Enable logging and alerts for unauthorized or unapproved cryptographic changes.

Legacy systems and embedded devices present unique challenges. These often run on platforms that lack modern management interfaces. They may use hardcoded keys or outdated libraries. Manual audits or specialized firmware analysis tools may be required. Where automated tools fall short, coordination with OT and device manufacturers will be essential.

5.4 CONCLUSION

Developing your cryptographic inventory is not a one-time project. It is an ongoing process that must be built into the way you manage systems, evaluate risk, and maintain compliance. The more complete your inventory, the more confident you can be in your ability to identify quantum risk.

The work begins here, with inventory. It is tedious, detailed, and necessary. The better you understand what you have, the more effectively you can protect it. In the quantum era, knowing where cryptography resides is the first step in keeping trust alive.

When your inventory is complete, not only will you know what cryptographic assets you have, but you will understand what is at risk, where it is located, and what your options are for securing it. With the right tools and a clear process, you can gain a detailed understanding of where cryptography lives in your environment, what algorithms are in use, and where vulnerabilities exist. That understanding will form the foundation for everything that follows.

In the following chapter, we will begin assessing that inventory to determine where quantum threats pose the greatest risk. We will explore how to assign privacy duration, measure cryptographic exposure, and identify high-value targets that must be addressed first.

Chapter 6

Assess quantum vulnerabilities

Now that you have a clear view of the cryptographic assets in your environment, the next step is understanding which of them are at risk. Not all cryptographic elements are created equal, and not all are equally vulnerable to quantum computing. To make meaningful progress, you need to assess the current algorithms in use and measure their exposure to quantum threats. This chapter guides you through the process.

6.1 EVALUATING ALGORITHM RISK

The biggest quantum risk comes from public key encryption systems. RSA, DSA, and ECC are particularly vulnerable due to the way quantum algorithms, such as Shor's algorithm, break large-number factorization and discrete logarithm problems. A large enough quantum computer will render these algorithms useless for security purposes.

Begin by cataloging which systems rely on these vulnerable algorithms. These might include VPN key exchanges, TLS handshakes, digital signatures, and authentication mechanisms. Document not just the type of algorithm but the key size and usage. A system using RSA-2048 is at more immediate risk than one using AES-256, for example, because symmetric algorithms are weakened but not broken entirely by quantum techniques.

Use available tools to help generate a vulnerability snapshot. Sandbox AQ's AQtive Guard, for example, can analyze cryptographic assets and provide a detailed risk profile, complete with prioritization suggestions. IBM Guardium can generate real-time reports highlighting weak configurations and outdated algorithms. ISARA brings additional capabilities by mapping cryptographic components to business impact, helping prioritize what to fix first.

A cryptographic asset is considered vulnerable when it meets one or more of the following criteria. It utilizes a public key algorithm, such as RSA, DSA, or ECC, which are all vulnerable to being broken by quantum algorithms. It lacks crypto-agility, meaning the system cannot be updated or migrated without significant rework. The data it protects must remain secure beyond

DOI: 10.1201/9781003685760-9

the estimated timeline for quantum decryption, or it is exposed to environments where encrypted traffic can be captured, stored, and later decrypted.

6.2 MAPPING CRYPTO TO DATA AND EXPOSURE

Cryptographic controls only carry meaning in relation to the data they protect. They are not isolated technologies but deeply embedded layers of defense around systems, applications, and information flows. To evaluate quantum vulnerability with any degree of precision, organizations must connect their cryptographic assets to specific data classes, understand the context in which that data is used, and estimate how long its confidentiality and integrity must be preserved.

Begin by cataloging systems that handle sensitive, regulated, or high-value data. This includes personal information, financial records, intellectual property, source code, healthcare data, and classified government communications. For each of these systems, identify which cryptographic algorithms are in play. Are you relying on RSA for key exchange? ECC for digital signatures? AES for encryption at rest? Each algorithm carries different levels of susceptibility to quantum attack.

Equally important is understanding where cryptography sits in the broader data path. Consider a system that encrypts external web traffic but leaves internal service-to-service communication exposed. Or a backup archive that uses outdated encryption methods while production systems have been modernized. Exposure is not only about whether data is encrypted, but whether that encryption holds at every stage – during transmission, while stored, and when accessed or transformed. If an attacker can compromise a key during exchange, they may impersonate a server, intercept data, or alter commands. If a digital signature can be forged, malicious updates may be installed with full administrative trust.

Now layer in data longevity. Assign a privacy duration to each data class, estimating how long the information needs to remain confidential. An internal calendar invite might have no value after a week. A legal contract, a biometric identifier, or a national security document may need to stay protected for twenty years or longer. This duration is not an abstract number. It becomes a critical variable in your risk model. The longer the required confidentiality window, the greater the urgency to transition from quantum-vulnerable algorithms like RSA and ECC to quantum-resistant alternatives.

Some vulnerabilities emerge not from technical configurations, but from the mismatch between data value and cryptographic durability. For example, encrypted research data related to a new drug formula may be harvested today and decrypted ten years later, just as the patent reaches maturity. At that point, even if the original breach is never discovered, the financial and competitive consequences are irreversible. The same applies to state secrets, whistleblower disclosures, or long-term confidential negotiations. The threat is not only immediate decryption, but long-term compromise through stored ciphertext.

Healthcare systems face a uniquely high level of exposure to quantum-related risks. Patient records often contain immutable data such as birth dates, Social Security numbers, diagnoses, genomic profiles, and diagnostic image information that cannot be revoked or reissued once compromised. These records routinely move between hospitals, insurers, and research institutions through a patchwork of legacy systems and embedded medical devices that were never designed with post-quantum resilience in mind. Many electronic health record (EHR) platforms and imaging systems still rely on outdated cryptographic modules or hardcoded libraries that are difficult to replace. Some systems continue to use VPN tunnels based on aging key exchange protocols. If this sensitive data is intercepted today, quantum decryption capabilities in the future could expose it, leading to severe privacy violations, reputational harm, and regulatory consequences. Compounding the challenge, frameworks like HIPAA, GDPR, and HITECH impose strict requirements around the confidentiality and longevity of healthcare data. For providers, adopting post-quantum cryptography involves more than just technical upgrades; it requires careful coordination with vendors, device manufacturers, and compliance teams. The risks are significant, and effective remediation demands a methodical, precision-focused approach.

Similar risks exist in sectors that handle intellectual property, proprietary models, or legal evidence. Think of an architecture firm's designs, a manufacturing blueprint, or source code for a new software product. Even if the underlying encryption appears strong today, it may not withstand future attacks. And once the data is exposed, the harm cannot be undone.

Mapping cryptography to data exposure is not just an inventory task. It is a way to uncover blind spots, prioritize remediation, and make informed trade-offs. It helps differentiate between systems that can wait and those that must be addressed now. And when paired with accurate cryptographic scanning and classification tools, it becomes a cornerstone of any serious quantum readiness strategy.

Ultimately, cryptography is only as strong as the assumptions you make about the data it protects. By understanding those assumptions – and the consequences if they fail – you gain a far more realistic picture of what's truly at stake.

6.3 UNDERSTAND THE SYSTEM LANDSCAPE

Vulnerability is about more than algorithms; it's about context. That means examining where cryptographic assets reside.

First, understand your data and applications. Categorize data by sensitivity, regulatory constraints, and privacy duration. Understand how applications use cryptography, including whether they rely on hardcoded keys or external certificate authorities. Identify who can access that data and from where.

Next, assess your endpoints. Identify which devices store or process encrypted data and what protections are in place. Determine which servers issue and serve certificates, how they are maintained, and whether firmware supports crypto-agile updates.

Then, examine your network. Trace how data moves, where it is encrypted, and which protocols are used. Consider cloud workloads and SaaS integrations. Many services use encryption that is abstracted from your direct control. Collaborate with vendors and cloud providers to determine the cryptographic protections in place.

6.3.1 Third-party dependencies and supply chain considerations

Evaluating quantum risk extends beyond your internal systems. Once you have identified internal vulnerabilities, the next step is to assess third-party software, hardware, and services through the lens of quantum exposure. You may already be familiar with the vendors and platforms you rely on. The question now is what cryptographic algorithms they use and how exposed those systems are to compromise.

Begin by collecting CBOMs and SBOMs from your vendors. These documents can help you evaluate what algorithms are in use, whether the systems support crypto-agility, and if they have a defined path to post-quantum standards. Evaluate key sizes, cipher suites, and certificate validity durations. Consider the vendor's ability to respond quickly to cryptographic vulnerabilities.

Classify each third-party system as quantum-vulnerable, crypto-agile, or post-quantum ready. Use this information to determine whether to mitigate, monitor, or replace. Ensure these third-party assessments are incorporated into your overall quantum risk profile.

If your supplier cannot provide cryptographic transparency or fails to meet your readiness standards, escalate the risk and review contractual obligations. Treat high-risk dependencies with the same scrutiny as internal systems. Where possible, include quantum readiness requirements in future procurement language and renewal agreements.

6.4 THREAT PATTERNS TO WATCH FOR

Beyond the technical inventory, you should recognize patterns that increase quantum exposure. Systems that rely on RSA and ECC for long-term key storage or archival data are particularly vulnerable. Similarly, systems with minimal crypto agility or those that use outdated TLS versions are also vulnerable.

Attack methods like Harvest Now, Decrypt Later (HNDL) make this even more urgent. In this scenario, attackers capture encrypted data today, intending to decrypt it once quantum capabilities are available. This is especially concerning for protocols like DNSSEC, which currently use RSA-based digital signatures to validate domain records. Since DNSSEC relies on publishing cryptographic material (such as public keys and signatures) in publicly accessible DNS records, it presents a tempting target. An adversary could archive DNSSEC-signed records and later apply Shor's Algorithm to extract private keys and retroactively forge or manipulate DNS responses. This would undermine domain integrity and enable broad spoofing or redirection attacks, with impacts ranging from service disruption to credential theft and malware distribution.

Other sources of quantum-sensitive data include certificate transparency logs and cached network traffic. These publicly logged or widely captured artifacts, if encrypted with pre-quantum algorithms, become low-hanging fruit in a post-quantum world.

Certificate scraping *and* man-in-the-middle (MITM) attacks also benefit from weak or misconfigured encryption. Certificates that aren't rotated regularly or that rely on RSA/ECC are especially vulnerable. Attackers who collect large volumes of certificates or intercept traffic using compromised or forged certificates could eventually decrypt or impersonate trusted parties when quantum capabilities mature.

Weak key generation processes and poor entropy sources also contribute to vulnerability. If keys are generated using low-entropy or predictable methods, they may be easier to brute-force, especially under Grover's search algorithm. Systems that fail to validate cryptographic parameters or allow weak cipher suites to persist increase the overall attack surface.

Threat modeling should also include insider threats, vendor-based risks, and supply chain exposure. Some attackers may already have access to cryptographic materials through compromised third parties or poorly segmented environments.

Integrating your quantum vulnerability assessment into established threat modeling practices strengthens your understanding of risk. Align your cryptographic risk profiles with frameworks like STRIDE, DREAD, or MITRE ATT&CK. This can help you identify which threat actors are most likely to target quantum-vulnerable systems, how those systems might be exploited, and what tactics may be used to compromise them.

6.5 STEP-BY-STEP: HOW TO PERFORM A VULNERABILITY ASSESSMENT

Start by reviewing your cryptographic inventory and segmenting assets by algorithm. For each algorithm, document the key length, protocol, and purpose. Next, assess the business context of each asset. Identify what data it protects and how long that data needs to stay confidential. Consider whether the asset is exposed to the public internet or lives behind internal protections. Then, evaluate whether each asset supports crypto-agility. If the system cannot be updated without major rework, it should be considered higher risk. Label each asset using a readiness status. Quantum-vulnerable means it uses RSA, ECC, or similar. Crypto-agile means it can be updated without a redesign. Post-quantum ready means it is already using quantum-safe protocols.

6.6 BUILDING A RISK PROFILE

To take action, translate your observations into a working risk profile. Consider likelihood, impact, and exploitability.

Likelihood is based on a timeline. How far out is quantum decryption for the algorithms in question? As we discussed in Section I, Q-Day may arrive by 2035, but you must weigh that against how long your data needs to remain confidential.

Impact is about business harm. What happens if encryption fails? Will customer data be exposed? Will system trust be compromised? Would you be out of compliance with legal standards?

Exploitability focuses on whether attackers can access encrypted traffic today. If so, you are at risk even before quantum computing becomes practical.

From these factors, begin assigning a readiness status to each asset. Label them as quantum-vulnerable, crypto-agile, or post-quantum ready. Use this to create migration tiers and focus your efforts where they will have the highest payoff.

6.6.1 Risk scoring examples and quantification

To simplify risk communication, consider using a scoring matrix that translates qualitative factors into an actionable risk tier. A basic rubric might classify:

- *Likelihood* as high, medium, or low based on proximity to Q-Day and length of privacy duration.
- *Impact* as catastrophic, moderate, or minimal depending on business consequences.
- *Exploitability* as external, internal, or archived based on the accessibility of the asset.

Combine these to assign a resulting risk tier such as critical, high, medium, or low.

For example, a customer-facing API using RSA-2048 that supports authentication for financial transactions would likely be of high likelihood, catastrophic impact, and externally exploitable. This would result in a critical risk tier.

Risk quantification frameworks such as FAIR can also be adapted. These allow you to estimate the frequency of quantum-relevant exposure and the monetary loss associated with breach or decryption. Although predicting quantum timelines is difficult, you can use scenarios to express potential financial exposure and model return on investment for migration activities.

6.6.2 Crypto Agility Risk Assessment Framework (CARAF)

The Crypto Agility Risk Assessment Framework (CARAF) is a structured model developed by the National Cybersecurity Center of Excellence (NCCoE) as part of the NIST Special Publication 1800-38 series, which focuses on migrating to post-quantum cryptography. It is designed to help organizations assess cryptographic exposure and prioritize remediation based not only on risk but also on adaptability, also known as crypto-agility. CARAF appears in Volume B of NIST SP 1800-38, which focuses on cryptographic discovery, system architecture, and migration planning.

While traditional risk assessments often center on static vulnerabilities, CARAF introduces agility as a critical dimension. This makes it particularly valuable in quantum readiness initiatives, where timelines are uncertain, but consequences are potentially severe. By combining threat modeling with adaptability analysis, CARAF helps decision-makers move from awareness to action.

CARAF is especially useful in situations where organizations need to move beyond simple asset classification and instead tie cryptographic vulnerabilities directly to broader business strategy. It provides a way to contextualize technical risk in terms that business and executive leaders can understand and act upon. It is also valuable when aligning cryptographic planning with enterprise risk management and roadmapping processes. Rather than treating cryptographic upgrades as isolated IT tasks, CARAF integrates them into organization-wide planning efforts, ensuring that quantum readiness becomes part of long-term transformation initiatives.

Another important use case is when you need to justify budget or resource allocation to executive stakeholders. CARAF enables teams to present cryptographic migration as a structured, phased risk reduction initiative, complete with prioritization, timing, and measurable milestones. This framing can help secure funding and leadership support.

Finally, CARAF is helpful for bridging the gap between technical discovery efforts, such as cryptographic inventory scans, and a high-level understanding of the organization's evolving risk posture. It turns raw data into actionable intelligence and connects frontline analysis with executive decision-making.

6.6.2.1 The five steps of CARAF

1. *Threat identification*
   Identify which cryptographic protocols, algorithms, and assets are vulnerable to quantum decryption. This includes documenting encryption at rest and in transit, understanding the use of public keys, and identifying externally facing interfaces and dependencies.
2. *Impact mapping*
   Map the consequences of cryptographic compromise to business operations. Consider regulatory risk, customer trust, reputational harm, operational disruption, and legal exposure. This step brings risk context into business language.
3. *Agility evaluation*
   Assess each system's ability to support algorithm replacement. This includes evaluating code modularity, use of standards-based libraries, certificate management practices, and third-party dependencies. Systems with hard-coded algorithms or non-standard cryptography are flagged as low-agility.
4. *Remediation prioritization*
   Prioritize systems based on their quantum risk (likelihood, impact, exploitability) and their crypto-agility score. This step guides the development of remediation tiers or migration waves, enabling phased upgrades based on urgency and feasibility.
5. *Roadmap development*
   Translate priorities into a migration roadmap. Define target states, timelines, ownership, and resource requirements. Align these efforts with budget cycles, compliance mandates, and broader IT transformation programs.

6.6.3 Comparing quantum risk assessment models

As organizations consider how to assess risk and prioritize migration to post-quantum cryptography, several risk models and guidance frameworks have emerged. Each offers a unique perspective and emphasis; some prioritize mathematical exposure, while others focus on agility or organizational readiness. This section introduces and compares four leading models: Mosca's Inequality, the Crypto Agility Risk Assessment Framework (CARAF), the Cryptographic Agility Implementation (CAI) Matrix, and the DHS/CISA Quantum Readiness Roadmap.

6.6.3.1 *Mosca's Inequality: cryptographic shelf life at a glance*

As discussed in Chapter 3, Mosca's Model, sometimes referred to as Mosca's Inequality, is a conceptual equation proposed by Dr. Michele Mosca to estimate when quantum cryptography becomes an urgent concern. It posits that:

$$X + Y > Z$$

Where:

- X = Time it takes to replace cryptography
- Y = Desired duration of confidentiality
- Z = Estimated arrival of a cryptanalytically relevant quantum computer (CRQC)

If the time to migrate and the time your data needs to remain secure exceeds the projected arrival of quantum decryption, then quantum risk is already relevant. Mosca's model is especially effective for framing urgency with executives, offering a high-level conceptual anchor for understanding long-term data confidentiality exposure.

Use case: Use Mosca's model to communicate urgency and establish thresholds for when migration should begin. It is most effective when applied early in the strategic planning process.

6.6.3.2 *CARAF: Crypto Agility Risk Assessment Framework*

The *CARAF* model, introduced by NIST's NCCoE in SP 1800-38B, adds depth and structure to quantum risk modeling by incorporating both technical vulnerability and cryptographic agility. It emphasizes five steps:

1. *Threat identification*
2. *Impact mapping*
3. *Agility evaluation*
4. *Remediation prioritization*
5. *Roadmap development*

CARAF is designed to be used after inventory and discovery have taken place and is intended to create a prioritized, tiered roadmap based on both quantum vulnerability and an organization's ability to respond. Agility becomes a measurable factor in decision-making alongside traditional risk dimensions.

Use Case: Use CARAF for programmatic risk reduction and structured decision-making. Ideal for organizations conducting technical readiness assessments and roadmap planning.

6.6.3.3 CAI Matrix: cryptographic agility implementation

The *CAI Matrix* is a complementary maturity model featured in NIST SP 1800-38B. It focuses on evaluating cryptographic agility across six dimensions: awareness, documentation, automation, responsiveness, interdependency, and sustainment. Each dimension is scored across a five-tier maturity scale, from Reactive to Strategic.

The CAI model does not replace risk scoring but enhances it by highlighting how well an organization can adapt to cryptographic change. It helps teams recognize where rigidity exists in their architecture or processes and where investment is needed to support agile cryptographic transitions.

Use case: Use CAI to measure agility maturity and to track improvement over time. It's particularly useful for internal benchmarking and preparing business cases for investments related to agility.

The CAI matrix is discussed in more depth in Chapter 17, which focuses on maintaining crypto-agility.

6.6.3.4 DHS/CISA Quantum Readiness Roadmap

The *DHS/CISA guidance*, developed in partnership with NIST and NSA, offers a policy-driven roadmap for public and private sector organizations. It outlines five key strategic actions:

1. Establish a Quantum-Readiness Roadmap
2. Prepare a cryptographic inventory
3. Assess supply chain readiness
4. Engage with vendors
5. Begin testing quantum-resistant algorithms

Rather than a formal risk model, this guidance provides a readiness checklist and is designed to align with national security directives and compliance expectations. It's oriented toward CIOs, CISOs, and government-aligned agencies preparing for executive mandates, such as NSM-10 and OMB M-23-02.

Use case: Use DHS/CISA guidance when aligning with federal mandates or when developing policy-level programs that require executive visibility and cross-agency coordination.

6.6.3.5 Comparison summary

Choosing the right risk model or readiness framework depends on where your organization is in the quantum migration journey and what outcomes you're trying to achieve. Some models are better suited for framing executive awareness, while others help guide technical prioritization, internal capability building, or alignment with government policy. Understanding when

Table 6.1 Model comparison

Model	*Focus*	*Strengths*	*Best for*
Mosca	Time-based urgency	Simple, conceptual, executive-friendly	Early awareness and urgency framing
CARAF	Risk and agility	Actionable, roadmap-driven	Prioritization, remediation planning
CAI Matrix	Agility maturity	Self-assessment, benchmarking	Internal capability improvement
DHS/CISA	Strategic readiness	Policy alignment, vendor coordination	Government, regulated enterprise programs

and why to use each model ensures that your strategy remains both effective and appropriately scoped for your audience and goals. See Table 6.1 for a model comparison.

Start with Mosca to establish a sense of urgency and to help frame executive conversations. Its simplicity and time-based perspective make it an effective way to communicate the impending risk of quantum decryption to nontechnical stakeholders.

Use CARAF when your organization has completed cryptographic discovery and asset inventory. CARAF allows you to develop a migration roadmap that prioritizes systems based on both quantum vulnerability and their ability to adapt, tying remediation efforts directly to risk and agility.

Apply the CAI Matrix when your goal is to understand and improve your organization's cryptographic responsiveness. It provides a structured approach to benchmarking agility maturity, identifying internal bottlenecks, and tracking progress over time across multiple operational dimensions.

Follow DHS/CISA guidance when your migration strategy must align with federal programs, policy timelines, or regulatory expectations. This guidance is especially useful when engaging vendors, coordinating across agencies, or demonstrating compliance with directives such as NSM-10 or OMB M-23-02.

Each model offers a distinct perspective on the problem of quantum readiness. Used together, they offer a layered approach that combines conceptual urgency, technical prioritization, agility assessment, and policy compliance, ensuring your migration is not only timely but also strategic and sustainable.

6.7 CONCLUSION

Assessing quantum vulnerabilities requires more than checking for outdated algorithms. It means understanding the broader context of how cryptography is used in your environment, how long the data it protects must remain secure, and how exposed those systems are to modern threat models. You must assess the business impact of a cryptographic failure, evaluate the exploitability of your systems, and categorize assets by their readiness. It also requires looking outward, beyond your own environment, to assess third-party cryptography, supplier trust chains, and software dependencies.

By combining these technical, operational, and business insights into a unified risk profile, you can begin to prioritize where change is most urgent. Assigning readiness labels and quantifying exposure provides a clear way to communicate quantum risk and take steps to mitigate it before those vulnerabilities become real in quantum computing.

In the next chapter, we will take this work one step further. We will look at how to prioritize your systems and assets based on risk, business value, and operational feasibility. This will enable you to create a migration timeline that is informed, structured, and achievable. You have seen what is vulnerable. Now it's time to decide what to fix first.

Chapter 7

Prioritize critical systems

By this point, you have a full view of your cryptographic environment and a clear understanding of the vulnerabilities that matter most. The next step is deciding where to begin. Not every system needs to be upgraded immediately. The goal is to prioritize your efforts based on risk, exposure, and business impact. This chapter provides a framework to do exactly that.

7.1 WHAT MATTERS MOST

Critical systems are not just those labeled as mission-critical in a traditional sense. In the context of quantum readiness, the most important systems are often those that process or store data with a long privacy duration. A customer record with a social security number or a healthcare transaction might not be sensitive today, but could still be exploitable ten years from now. That time horizon is what gives certain systems a higher priority for quantum remediation.

Start by evaluating data transfers over the internet, such as TLS traffic, that contain information with long privacy durations. Focus on encrypted sessions that may involve sensitive communications, intellectual property, or personally identifiable information intended to remain confidential for years. Public Key Infrastructure (PKI), digital certificates, and cryptographic keys used in these sessions should be closely examined. If compromised, they could allow attackers to retroactively decrypt historical data, impersonate services, or undermine authentication processes. VPNs, secure email gateways, and other encrypted communications systems handling high-value or long-retention data should also be prioritized.

7.2 RISK, SENSITIVITY, AND EXPOSURE

Knowing which cryptographic algorithms are in use is only part of the equation. Effective prioritization starts with understanding the potential impact each system's failure or compromise would have on the organization.

DOI: 10.1201/9781003685760-10

Which means you need to evaluate each system through the three key lenses of business impact, data sensitivity, and exposure to external threats.

Start with business impact, and ask what the consequences would be if a given system's cryptographic protections were broken. Would service availability be disrupted? Would it trigger financial penalties or regulatory fines? Would customers lose trust in your ability to protect their information? For example, a system that signs software updates for a widely deployed medical device has a significantly higher business impact than an internal logging server. In one case, compromised signatures could endanger patient safety; in another, the consequence might be minimal.

Conduct a business impact analysis (BIA) session during the early stages of your quantum migration planning. These reviews should be done in partnership with application owners, compliance teams, and business stakeholders. Use existing risk registers, disaster recovery plans, or business continuity frameworks to help quantify impact where possible.

Next, assess data sensitivity. This includes both the nature of the data and how long it must remain protected. Transient data, like temporary caches or ephemeral session keys, may not need long-term protection. However, long-lived data, such as legal documents, health records, or customer identity information, often must remain secure for years or even decades. The longer the privacy duration, the more urgent it becomes to replace vulnerable cryptographic protections.

For example, encrypted human resources records containing social security numbers and background checks may need to be secure for a decade or more. If the key for those records is stored using asymmetric encryption, they could be decrypted even if the bulk encryption for the file storage is symmetric.

Perform data sensitivity reviews at the data classification level. Start with systems tagged as handling "restricted", "regulated", or "confidential" data. Evaluate retention policies, privacy requirements, and the contractual or regulatory obligations associated with each data set. Then, engage legal, compliance, and data governance teams to help assign appropriate privacy durations and protection tiers.

Then, examine exposure. Some systems are buried deep within the organization's internal network, behind multiple layers of access control. Others sit directly on the internet, where they are exposed to a wide range of threat actors. Systems that interface with third parties, rely on externally accessible APIs, or serve customer-facing services have a larger threat surface and higher exposure.

Take, for instance, a VPN concentrator that uses traditional key exchange methods and is accessible from the public internet. If that system relies on Diffie-Hellman or Elliptic Curve cryptography, it is a likely candidate for a Harvest Now, Decrypt Later attack. Encrypted sessions can be captured and stored today, and potentially decrypted when a sufficiently powerful quantum computer becomes available. Compare that to a backup server protected by the same algorithm but physically segmented from the network. While still vulnerable, its lower exposure shifts its priority for remediation.

Incorporate exposure analysis during vulnerability assessments, penetration tests, and threat modeling exercises. Cross-reference asset exposure with your vulnerability management program to identify which systems are most accessible to adversaries. Be sure to include third-party interfaces and supply chain integrations in this review.

As you complete these evaluations, revisit the readiness labels introduced in Chapter 6. Assets marked as quantum-vulnerable and lacking crypto-agility should be moved to the top of the priority list. These are systems that will be both difficult to fix and dangerous to leave as-is. Crypto-agile systems may offer more flexibility and can be scheduled for upgrades later in the timeline, but they still require attention. Post-Quantum Ready systems can be monitored for changes or regressions, but do not require immediate remediation.

When done well, this analysis does more than create a ranked list. It provides the foundation for a risk-informed strategy that aligns with your organization's values, regulations, and business objectives. By anchoring this strategy in clear examples, formal processes, and cross-functional participation, you make it easier to communicate priorities and justify resource decisions as your quantum readiness program progresses.

Here lies a key challenge: the actual risk is hard to determine because we don't know who will reach Q-Day first, or what they will do when they get there. If IBM or Google achieves quantum supremacy, it's unlikely they'll turn those multi-million-dollar systems toward decrypting your old TLS handshakes. But if a nation-state like China gets there first, we may never hear about it. They might not announce their success and rather quietly leverage it for intelligence gathering and persistent access, especially in high-value sectors like government, finance, defense, and critical infrastructure.

There's also likely some wiggle room in the Mosca model, which estimates how long you have to act. Q-Day may not arrive all at once; there will be a lead time when quantum capabilities are still rare and expensive, accessible only to a small group of elite actors. Your three-year-old VPN conversations may not interest them. But your VPN concentrator still uses RSA for authentication? That's a live target. If left unfixed, it could offer direct network access to exactly the kind of system someone with quantum capability might be curious enough to explore.

It's important to keep that actual risk in mind when prioritizing your remediations. Not every vulnerability needs to be addressed immediately, and not every system carries the same level of exposure or consequence. There will likely be risks your business is willing to accept, especially during the early stages of quantum readiness. That's part of the exercise, determining, through structured analysis, which risks can be tolerated and which must be remediated based on their potential impact on your organization. The goal isn't to eliminate all risk, but to make informed decisions that align with your threat landscape, operational realities, and long-term resilience strategy.

7.3 BUILDING A PRIORITIZATION MODEL

Use a risk-based model to rank systems. This might take the form of a matrix with dimensions like likelihood, impact, and exploitability. Assign scores to each asset based on these factors. For example, a customer-facing application using RSA for authentication might be scored as high in likelihood, high in impact, and externally exploitable. That puts it in the critical tier.

Consider adapting a template that assigns each dimension a simple scale. Likelihood might be rated high, medium, or low based on the proximity to Q-Day and the lifespan of the protected data. The impact may range from minimal to catastrophic, depending on the consequences of a breach. Exploitability could be defined as internal, external, or archived, depending on the asset's exposure to threat actors.

Combine these scores to determine the overall risk tier: critical, high, medium, or low. This framework provides a method for objectively comparing systems and helps justify decisions about where to begin.

Dependency mapping should be incorporated into this model. Low-priority systems may act as critical dependencies for high-priority assets, especially those related to authentication, identity services, or data movement. Trust chains such as certificate authorities, single sign-on systems, and directory services should be evaluated for their downstream influence. If these components are compromised or not updated in time, they can undermine the security of otherwise remediated systems.

Tooling can assist with this level of analysis. Vendors like Sandbox AQ, IBM, and ISARA provide platforms with embedded prioritization models that take into account interdependencies, readiness states, and threat exposure. These tools can also be integrated into your existing risk platforms to provide live updates to readiness scores over time.

7.3.1 Quantifying crypto risk for prioritization

A numerical rubric can help formalize this process. Likelihood can be scored from 1 to 5, with 1 representing a low chance of compromise before transition, and 5 representing a high chance due to long-term data exposure or poor crypto-agility. Impact might follow a similar scale, ranging from 1 (minimal disruption) to 5 (catastrophic data loss or regulatory failure). Exploitability can also be scored from 1 to 5 based on whether the asset is internal only, partially exposed, or publicly accessible.

Add these three scores to determine a total risk score between 3 and 15. For example, a high-value public API might score a 5 for likelihood, 5 for impact, and 4 for exploitability. That gives it a total risk score of 14 and places it in the critical remediation tier. An internal-only legacy system protecting low-sensitivity data might score 1s across the board, landing in the low-priority range.

For organizations seeking a more detailed approach, the FAIR (Factor Analysis of Information Risk) framework can provide a model for quantifying quantum exposure in financial terms. FAIR breaks down risk into frequency and magnitude of loss, offering a way to calculate the expected value of a potential quantum-related breach. While FAIR was not designed for quantum specifically, it can be adapted to evaluate long-term data exposure, projected migration costs, and the probability of post-quantum decryption scenarios.

This fusion of scoring and quantification allows for both strategic prioritization and executive-level reporting. The better your ability to express risk in clear, comparative terms, the easier it becomes to secure funding and assign responsibility.

7.3.2 Visual tools and communication

Communicating priority tiers effectively is just as important as calculating them. Use heatmaps, dashboards, or tiered scorecards to share prioritization outcomes with business units. These tools are especially useful when working with non-technical stakeholders, such as finance or legal teams, who may need to approve funding or policy changes.

Tools that support visual modeling can also highlight system dependencies, showing where delays in one system could affect the readiness of others. Consider layering prioritization outcomes with operational maps or service architectures to make risk patterns more visible.

7.4 ASSIGNING RESOURCES AND TIMELINES

Once you have your risk tiers, you can begin assigning migration priorities and timelines. Critical systems should have dedicated remediation plans and funded transition paths in place. Medium-priority systems can be phased in over time. Low-priority systems should still be documented and monitored, especially if their risk profile changes.

When building your migration roadmap, consider internal capacity, vendor support, and dependencies between systems. A system may appear low-risk on its own, but it could play a key role in supporting a higher-risk function. These dependencies must be mapped and understood to avoid creating new vulnerabilities during the migration.

Budget and resource allocation are also part of this process. Engage stakeholders early to ensure that critical efforts are properly funded and staffed. This may include procurement of new tools, training for teams, and updates to compliance documentation. We will discuss both planning and stakeholder engagement in the next section.

Compliance mandates may also shape priorities. Industries such as healthcare, finance, and defense may already be subject to executive orders, international regulations, or specific cryptographic standards. In these cases, your prioritization model should incorporate external timelines and reporting requirements to ensure alignment with relevant external stakeholders. Maintain traceability between prioritization decisions and compliance mandates to simplify audit preparation and demonstrate alignment with regulatory expectations.

7.4.1 Exception handling and justification framework

Even with a well-scored prioritization model and a clear migration roadmap, not every high-risk asset can or should be remediated immediately. Some systems may be too deeply embedded, have no available post-quantum replacement, or be tied to vendor contracts that delay your ability to act. Others may serve functions so critical that reconfiguration requires long testing cycles or specialized coordination. In these cases, an exception handling and justification framework becomes essential.

An exception framework provides a structured method for acknowledging these constraints without letting them fall off the radar. It formalizes the rationale behind delayed remediation, ensures compensating controls are applied where possible, and guarantees regular follow-up. This kind of documentation also plays an important role in demonstrating due diligence to regulators, auditors, and executive stakeholders.

Start by establishing exception request and approval procedures. These should define who can request an exception, under what conditions, and what documentation must be submitted to support the request. Typically, an exception request should include:

- A description of the asset and its cryptographic risk score
- The business function it supports and why remediation is not currently feasible
- The duration of the requested exception
- The date of the next review
- Any compensating controls in place, such as restricted access, enhanced monitoring, or physical isolation
- A roadmap or milestone plan, if applicable

For example, a payment processing gateway that uses RSA for certificate validation might be too tightly integrated with multiple banking partners to be upgraded mid-cycle. In this case, the organization might approve a six-month exception while it coordinates a phased rollout across dependent systems. During that time, it may increase audit frequency, reduce key lifetime, and monitor traffic more aggressively to reduce risk.

It is important to separate legitimate exceptions from organizational inertia. Exceptions should never be used to indefinitely avoid action. Build a tracking mechanism, such as a dashboard or dedicated register, that logs all approved exceptions, their expiration dates, and their associated business owners. Review this register during quarterly security governance meetings or change management cycles. Include an escalation path for expired or non-renewed exceptions. If a system remains unremediated past its approved timeline, flag it for executive attention. Reassess its impact, and if no path to remediation is in sight, consider broader risk acceptance discussions with legal and compliance teams.

Where applicable, align your exception handling with industry frameworks like NIST RMF, ISO 27001 corrective actions, or CIS control deviation registers. This alignment provides consistency and ensures your exception framework is both operationally and auditor-friendly.

Finally, make sure exception justifications tie back into your larger prioritization model. For example, a high-risk asset with no available fix might remain on the critical list but be labeled as deferred, accompanied by relevant notes. This allows reporting tools to reflect its status accurately while preventing accidental omission from planning discussions.

7.5 STEP-BY-STEP: HOW TO PRIORITIZE QUANTUM CRYPTOGRAPHIC ASSET VULNERABILITIES AND REMEDIATIONS

Step 1 is to classify assets by risk category using your cryptographic inventory. Separate them based on the algorithms in use, their privacy duration requirements, and system exposure.

Step 2 is to assign each asset a readiness label. Determine whether it is quantum-vulnerable, crypto-agile, or post-quantum ready.

Step 3 is to evaluate business impact. Review how critical each asset is to operations, compliance, customer trust, and service availability.

Step 4 is to assess exploitability. Determine if the asset is accessible externally, internally, or if it is part of archived infrastructure. This will shape your prioritization logic.

Step 5 is to calculate risk scores using your chosen model. Sum the scores for likelihood, impact, and exploitability to arrive at a prioritized list of remediation targets.

Step 6 is to define remediation actions. Identify whether each system will require replacement, upgrades, reconfiguration, or monitoring. This will inform your timeline and resource planning.

Step 7 is to group assets into migration waves. Group high-risk assets for immediate remediation. Plan medium-priority systems for mid-term transition. Place low-risk assets on a monitoring track with defined future review cycles.

Step 8 is to build your roadmap. Create a migration schedule that is aligned with your budget, capacity, and vendor timelines.

Step 9 is to secure cross-functional buy-in. Share the risk assessment results with stakeholders to validate assumptions and assign accountability.

Step 10 is to review and update regularly. Risk profiles evolve over time; reassess your prioritization at least annually or whenever there is a major cryptographic event or system change.

7.6 CONCLUSION

Prioritizing your cryptographic systems for post-quantum remediation is not about checking off a list of tasks. It is about building a roadmap rooted in risk, business impact, and technical feasibility. The systems that need attention first are often not the loudest or most visible. They are the ones that protect long-lived data, sustain trust relationships, and support critical authentication and communications. These assets, if compromised, would expose your organization to lasting damage, even if the actual attack comes years from now.

This chapter has laid out a framework for making those prioritization decisions in a structured, defensible way. You've seen how to assess risk through the combined lenses of impact, sensitivity, and exposure, and how to apply readiness labels and risk scores to quantify your findings. You've explored the role of business context, system interconnectivity, and external compliance pressures in shaping what should come first. You now have a model to not only identify high-priority assets but also communicate their urgency to stakeholders who control resources, policies, and timelines.

Exception handling is just as critical. No organization can fix everything at once, and not every high-risk system can be remediated on schedule. By creating a clear process to document and justify those delays, you keep control of the narrative and maintain visibility over the full scope of your quantum transition.

What matters most is that prioritization is not a one-time exercise. The threat landscape will change, vendor capabilities will improve, and your own architecture will evolve. That's why it is essential to revisit your prioritization model regularly. Make it part of your quarterly or biannual security review cycles so that your roadmap reflects today's risk, not yesterday's assumptions.

With your critical systems identified and your roadmap taking shape, you are now ready to shift from strategy to execution. In the next chapter, we move into the planning phase, where you will begin outlining your migration, testing, and stakeholder alignment efforts. The foundation you've built here will give structure and momentum to that work, making the road ahead clearer and more achievable.

Section III

Phase 2

Planning

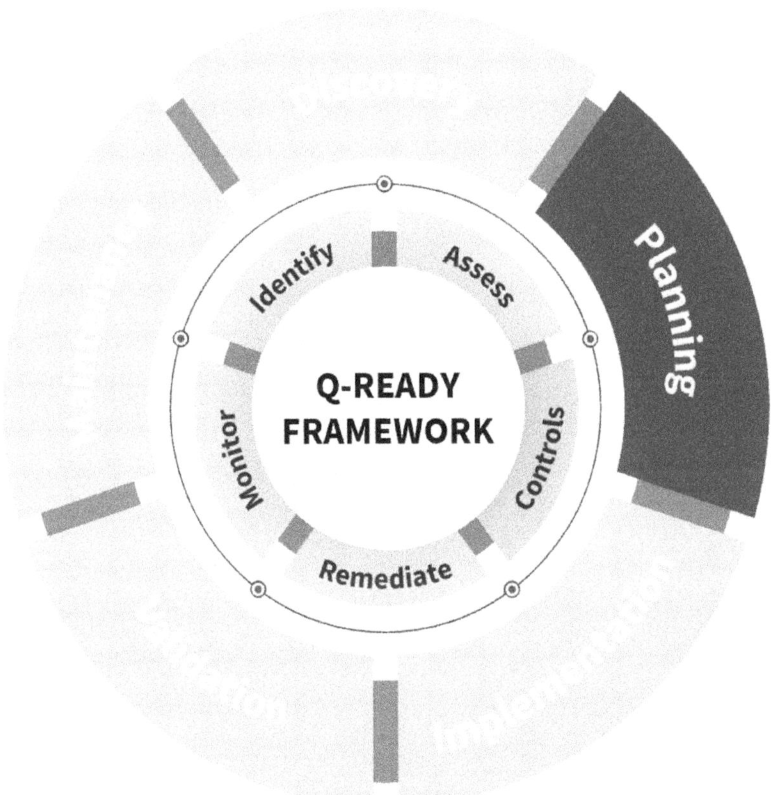

Figure SIII.1 Planning Phase

DOI: 10.1201/9781003685760-11

Chapter 8

Develop a migration and testing plan

With your cryptographic assets inventoried, your risks assessed, and your priorities defined, the next step is transformation. This chapter focuses on turning strategy into action through structured migration planning, targeted testing, and the policies that support secure execution.

> Pro Tip: Before building a complex plan to upgrade algorithms or re-architect services, take a moment to consider a simpler mitigation: take confidential data offline. If certain high-risk records cannot be transitioned to post-quantum protections in time, temporarily removing them from exposure may be your best defense against Harvest Now, Decrypt Later attacks. Once offline, encrypted data can't be intercepted, stored, or cracked later.

8.1 CREATING A POST-QUANTUM CRYPTOGRAPHY POLICY

Establishing a formal post-quantum cryptography (PQC) policy is one of the most effective ways to set expectations, build organizational alignment, and create repeatable standards across teams. A PQC policy brings structure to what is often an abstract or highly technical problem. It connects the cryptographic transition to business goals, compliance mandates, and operational planning.

Start by defining the purpose and scope of the policy. Make clear that the organization is proactively adopting post-quantum cryptographic standards to maintain data confidentiality, integrity, and availability in light of emerging threats. Describe which systems the policy applies to. This may include customer-facing applications, internal systems, third-party integrations, and long-term data archives.

A well-crafted policy should include several core elements. First, it should specify cryptographic readiness classifications, such as "quantum-vulnerable", "crypto-agile", or "post-quantum ready". These labels create a shared

DOI: 10.1201/9781003685760-12

vocabulary that teams can use during audits, architecture reviews, and roadmap discussions.

Next, outline minimum requirements. For example, the policy might state that all new systems must support crypto-agility by default, or that all certificates with expiration dates beyond 2030 must be issued using hybrid or post-quantum algorithms. It should also define approved algorithms for various functions, aligned with NIST's current recommendations. Include guidance for key sizes, certificate durations, and accepted libraries or toolchains.

Don't overlook governance and enforcement. The policy should designate ownership for cryptographic standards, often within a security architecture or enterprise risk team. It should establish review timelines, such as annual policy updates or post-incident reassessments, to ensure ongoing effectiveness. Exception handling procedures should also be included, along with clear instructions for requesting waivers and assigning compensating controls.

For example, a strong PQC policy might contain a clause like:

> *Beginning in FY26, all new externally facing services must use TLS configurations that support at least one NIST-approved post-quantum key exchange algorithm. Hybrid deployments may be used for transitional compatibility, but legacy-only configurations must be remediated within 12 months of launch.*

To craft your policy, draw from other enterprise documents such as your encryption standard, procurement checklists, risk registers, and key lifecycle management procedures. Align the PQC policy with your broader information security policy, ensuring that all relevant teams, including legal, compliance, and architecture, contribute. The goal is to make quantum readiness a living part of the organization's security baseline, not just a project with an expiration date.

Here is an example PQC Policy Template

> *Post-Quantum Cryptography (PQC) Policy*
> *Policy ID*: SEC-CRYPTO-PQC-001
> *Effective Date*: [Insert Date]
> *Next Review Date*: [Insert Date]
> *Owner*: [Security Architecture / Enterprise Risk Team]

8.1.1 Policy statement

This policy establishes the organization's commitment to proactively transitioning from quantum-vulnerable cryptographic systems to quantum-resistant alternatives. It reflects our responsibility to protect sensitive data, maintain regulatory compliance, and preserve trust in the face of emerging quantum computing threats. This policy is an extension of our broader information security objectives and is intended to ensure long-term resilience across all cryptographic systems.

8.1.2 Purpose

This policy sets requirements and expectations for identifying, mitigating, and transitioning from traditional public-key cryptographic algorithms (e.g., RSA, ECC) to post-quantum cryptographic (PQC) alternatives, in alignment with NIST guidance and emerging global standards. It provides a structured approach to cryptographic modernization that supports data confidentiality, integrity, and availability.

8.1.3 Scope

This policy applies to all systems, applications, services, and infrastructure that:

- Store, transmit, or process data with confidentiality or integrity requirements beyond three years,
- Rely on public-key cryptography for encryption, signing, or authentication,
- Interface with third-party platforms through cryptographic mechanisms,
- Manage or store long-lived data archives, including backups and digital records,
- Fall under regulatory or contractual obligations requiring encryption.

Excluded from this policy are ephemeral test environments without production data and systems with operational life cycles under six months, unless otherwise specified.

8.1.4 Definitions and readiness classifications

The following classifications are used to evaluate cryptographic readiness:

- *Quantum-vulnerable*: Uses RSA, DSA, DH, or ECC without crypto-agility or PQC support.
- *Crypto-agile*: Designed with modular cryptographic components capable of adopting PQC without major redesign.
- *Post-quantum ready*: Implements NIST-approved PQC algorithms or hybrid models.

These labels will be applied during architecture reviews, asset inventories, and risk assessments.

8.1.5 Roles and responsibilities

- *CISO/Security architecture team*: Maintain and enforce this policy; define standards; approve exceptions.
- *Application and infrastructure owners*: Implement crypto-agility and execute remediation plans.
- *Procurement and vendor risk teams*: Ensure third-party cryptographic compliance.
- *Compliance/legal*: Advise on regulatory impacts and contractual obligations.

8.1.6 Minimum requirements

8.1.6.1 New deployments

- Starting FY26, all externally facing services must support at least one NIST-approved PQC key exchange algorithm.
- All new systems must be crypto-agile and avoid hardcoded cryptographic primitives.
- Certificates with expiration dates beyond 1 January 2030 must use hybrid or PQC-approved algorithms.

8.1.6.2 Legacy systems

- All quantum-vulnerable systems must be inventoried and prioritized for remediation based on risk.
- TLS configurations using only RSA or ECDHE must be upgraded to hybrid or PQC-supported options by [Insert Deadline].

8.1.6.3 Certificate lifecycle management

- In alignment with CA/Browser Forum mandates, all TLS certificates must be rotated every 47 days by 2029.
- The organization will phase in this change via certificate lifecycle automation:
  - 200-day maximum by 2026
  - 100-day maximum by 2027
  - 47-day maximum by 2029
- All certificate issuance and renewal must be automated using approved tooling.

8.1.6.4 Approved algorithms and libraries

- PQC algorithms must align with NIST selections (e.g., ML-KEM, ML-DSA).
- Approved libraries include OpenSSL v3+, liboqs, and other security architecture-approved platforms.
- Key sizes, certificate lifetimes, and algorithms must follow NIST and enterprise crypto standards.

8.1.7 Risk-based prioritization

Systems must be prioritized based on:

- *Data sensitivity* (e.g., personal, financial, regulated data)
- *Business impact* (e.g., customer trust, operational disruption)
- *Exposure* (e.g., internet-facing, third-party access)

Prioritization will align with enterprise risk registers and business continuity frameworks.

8.1.8 Training and awareness

All developers, security engineers, architects, and system owners must complete annual training covering:

- Post-quantum cryptography principles
- Crypto-agility implementation
- Policy compliance requirements

8.1.9 Monitoring and metrics

The following metrics will be tracked and reported quarterly:

- % of cryptographic assets inventoried and classified
- % of systems transitioned to PQC or hybrid crypto
- % of certificates managed by automated tooling
- % of developers trained on crypto-agility

8.1.10 Legal and regulatory alignment

This policy supports compliance with:

- NIST CSF & NIST SP 800 series (208, 56C, 57, 175B)
- FIPS 140-3
- ISO/IEC 27001 Annex A.10.1

- GDPR, HIPAA, and relevant regional encryption mandates

8.1.11 Technology lifecycle integration

- PQC requirements must be embedded in procurement checklists, project kickoff reviews, and secure SDLC.
- PQC posture must be assessed during architecture reviews and change management.

8.1.12 End-of-life and sunset requirements

- RSA, DH, and ECC-based algorithms must be fully deprecated by 31 December 2028 unless formally exempted.
- All exemptions must include compensating controls and must be revalidated annually.

8.1.13 Exceptions and waivers

- All exception requests must include a business justification, duration, and compensating controls.
- Waivers must be approved by the CISO and documented in the risk register.

8.1.14 Change management and version control

Policy changes must be approved by the Security Governance Committee and documented in the revision history.

Revision history

Version	*Date*	*Description*	*Approved By*
1.0	[Insert]	Initial policy creation	[Name / Title]

Approval
[Name, Title, Date]
[Name, Title, Date]

8.2 BUILD A MIGRATION PLAN

Every organization will approach quantum remediation at its own pace. The most effective plans are phased, risk-informed, and aligned to business goals. Begin with high-priority assets as defined in your risk profile. These will often include VPN key exchanges, PKI systems, externally facing APIs, and long-lived sensitive data sets. Use the readiness labels from earlier chapters to guide where to start. Assets marked quantum-vulnerable and lacking crypto-agility should take precedence.

Define what success looks like. A clear migration plan should set targets such as the percentage of systems to be transitioned each quarter, how crypto-agility will be implemented, and which protocols or algorithms will be prioritized. Consider hybrid solutions for transitional states. You may need to adopt hybrid key schemes, where classical and post-quantum algorithms are combined, to maintain compatibility while enhancing protection. Vendors like Sandbox AQ and IBM offer tools that streamline this process. Their platforms help align migration timelines with system risk scores, vendor readiness, and technical dependencies.

As organizations transition to post-quantum cryptography, legacy decryption capabilities may still be needed for specific use cases. Certain regulatory, legal, or forensic scenarios might require access to data encrypted with older algorithms. This makes it important to build key escrow mechanisms into your migration plans. Ensure that historical keys are stored securely and are accessible under strict controls. Retaining the ability to decrypt archived data with legacy keys is not a contradiction to quantum preparedness; it is a bridge that allows continuity, compliance, and evidence preservation while transitioning to new standards. Migration should not happen in isolation. Align your cryptographic transition with broader business continuity and disaster recovery strategies. Run tabletop exercises and business impact analyses to ensure your crypto migration does not disrupt critical services.

8.3 DEFINE CRYPTO-AGILITY

Crypto-agility is not a buzzword; it is a core survival trait. The ability to rapidly replace algorithms, rotate keys, and adapt to new standards is now a baseline requirement. Crypto-agility refers to the ability of a system, platform, or application to rapidly and securely change its cryptographic algorithms when needed. At its core, it means having the flexibility to adapt to new cryptographic standards without having to rebuild entire systems. This is particularly important in a post-quantum world, where algorithms may need to be updated rapidly in response to new vulnerabilities.

NIST IR 8105 defines crypto-agility as "the recognition that cryptographic infrastructures must evolve quickly in response to vulnerabilities". IBM expands the definition by stating that "crypto-agility allows systems, platforms, and applications to adapt their cryptographic mechanisms in response to changing threats or technologies". Crypto-agility is also called out in PCI-DSS 4.0 under control 12.3.3, which requires entities to be capable of replacing cryptographic protocols as threats evolve.

In simpler terms, crypto-agility is the ability to swap out old locks for new ones, without having to replace every door in the building. If one encryption method becomes unsafe, a crypto-agile system can adopt a safer alternative with minimal disruption.

To support long-term readiness, build agility into your policies now. Architect systems to support modular cryptographic implementations. Update procurement checklists to favor vendors who provide agility by design, and include agility controls in your risk registers, security reviews, and key lifecycle management.

Crypto-agility is more than a best practice; it is the foundation that will determine whether your post-quantum transition is manageable or painful. The more agile your environment, the more options you will have as standards evolve and vulnerabilities surface.

8.4 KEY COMPONENTS OF A MIGRATION STRATEGY

A successful migration strategy must be more than a set of upgrade tasks. It must be a coherent, phased roadmap rooted in real risk data, business priorities, and operational capacity. Below are the core elements that every organization should build into their post-quantum cryptographic migration strategy:

Understand your security options

Start by assessing your current protocols. Do you need to migrate to newer protocols such as those recommended by NIST? Are there specific key exchange methods, signature schemes, or encryption techniques that are no longer viable? Are hybrid key models necessary to bridge classical and post-quantum compatibility?

Identify PQC-targeted assets

Using the inventory built in earlier phases, list systems that depend on public key cryptography. Pay particular attention to those using RSA, DSA, or ECC. Tag each with their quantum vulnerability, expected transition effort, and level of business impact.

Match technology to priority levels

High-priority systems may need immediate re-platforming or hybrid deployments. Medium-priority systems can be planned for transition in the next budget cycle. Low-priority or internal-use systems may simply require monitoring and readiness documentation.

Select your post-quantum algorithms

Base your selection on NIST's standards and guidelines. Not all PQC algorithms are equally suited to every use case. Consider performance, interoperability, and key size. Lattice-based encryption schemes, for instance, may offer high security but come with large payloads that can negatively impact performance.

Plan for hybrid key implementations

Some systems will require hybrid approaches that use both classical and quantum-safe algorithms to ensure backward compatibility. This allows you to maintain service availability and security during the transition period.

Address crypto-agility requirements

Make crypto-agility a design principle. This includes selecting libraries and frameworks that support algorithm replacement and ensuring that update mechanisms are robust enough to roll out cryptographic changes at scale.

Update key lifecycle policies

Revise key lifecycle policies to reflect quantum risk. Ensure that you not only rotate keys regularly but also use key lengths and formats that anticipate PQC requirements. For long-lived data, special attention should be paid to archival protection strategies.

Ensure compliance alignment

Confirm that your migration strategy aligns with relevant compliance frameworks. This includes PCI-DSS, HIPAA, FedRAMP, ISO/IEC 27001, and others. Trace each decision back to its corresponding requirement whenever possible to facilitate audit preparation.

Evaluate advanced cryptographic tools

Determine if your systems require specialized capabilities such as quantum random number generators (QRNGs) or quantum key distribution (QKD). These technologies can provide an additional layer of assurance in certain high-risk or compliance-sensitive environments. However, these are advanced controls, and most corporate enterprises will not need to leverage QRNGs or QKD. In most cases, organizations will be better served by focusing on implementing standard post-quantum cryptographic algorithms and achieving crypto-agility before considering more specialized quantum-enhanced solutions.

Define your certificate and authentication transition plans

Set dates for moving to post-quantum certificates. Prioritize systems exposed to the public or involved in identity verification. Establish timelines and milestones to track this progress across vendors and partners.

Migration is not just about replacing cryptography; it is about redesigning trust at scale. Your architecture must support these changes without introducing new vulnerabilities or disruptions. The technical concepts mentioned above, such as quantum random number generators (QRNGs) and quantum key distribution (QKD), will be covered in Section IV – Implementation, starting in Chapter 11.

8.4.1 Step-by-step: how to build a migration plan

1. *Conduct a readiness review*: Identify current systems that rely on classical cryptographic protocols and assess their associated risk levels.
2. *Prioritize systems*: Use risk scores to sort systems into immediate, mid-term, or deferred migration groups.
3. *Select appropriate algorithms*: Choose suitable post-quantum algorithms based on NIST guidance and performance profiles.
4. *Engage vendors*: Collaborate with providers to verify their PQC roadmap and crypto-agility support.
5. *Design Hybrid Rollouts*: Where needed, plan for hybrid deployments that include both classical and quantum-safe algorithms.
6. *Build your timeline*: Set migration milestones, from pilot rollouts to production changes, mapped to your internal resources and budget.
7. *Establish feedback loops*: Track key performance indicators (KPIs) such as the percentage of PQC adoption, crypto-agility coverage, and unremediated vulnerabilities.
8. *Develop your test lab*: Ensure that every stage of your plan is validated in a controlled environment before rollout.

This structured approach turns a long-term strategic problem into a series of manageable steps. Testing, flexibility, and communication will ensure your migration succeeds with minimal disruption.

8.5 QUANTUM READINESS MATURITY MODEL

Preparing for the post-quantum era is not a one-time checklist but an evolving process that unfolds across multiple disciplines, systems, and decision layers. As organizations move into Phase 2 of the Q-Ready Framework,

Planning, they need a structured way to assess their current posture, define future goals, and prioritize improvements. That structure is provided by a maturity model.

A maturity model serves two critical purposes. First, it helps during the planning phase by giving organizations a framework to baseline where they are today and identify realistic, actionable steps to improve. Without that clarity, planning often becomes a wish list or a disconnected set of technical projects. Second, it becomes even more important in Phase 4 Validation. It enables repeatable measurement, performance tracking, and a means of demonstrating progress to stakeholders, auditors, and boards. It helps connect technical activities to business outcomes.

The Quantum Readiness Maturity Model included in this book aligns directly to the Q-Ready Framework. It breaks down each phase into key capability domains, then defines a progression of maturity levels from ad hoc to optimized. This is not theory for theory's sake. The model was designed to reflect real-world challenges and practical realities faced by CISOs, security architects, product leaders, and engineers. It exists in this book to turn the concept of "quantum readiness" into something measurable, communicable, and manageable.

Readiness is often treated as a yes-or-no question. But in practice, most organizations are ahead in some areas, lagging in others, and unclear about how to measure improvement. This model helps answer that. It provides a shared vocabulary to facilitate internal alignment, cross-functional coordination, and consistent evaluation. Most importantly, it offers a concrete way to link planning activities with future-state goals and ongoing operational validation.

What follows is a detailed breakdown of the model's structure, its domains, and its five maturity levels. We explain how to assess your posture, how to score each domain, and how to use the results to drive prioritization and reporting. This model is not a separate tool; it is a built-in instrument for navigating both the planning and validation phases of your quantum migration.

Each Q-Ready phase contains three capability domains. These domains are the core areas where action is required. For example, in the Discovery phase, the organization must develop a detailed cryptographic inventory, assess risk, and integrate with software and supply chain visibility efforts. Each domain is evaluated using a five-level maturity scale:

1. *Initial*
   Practices are informal or ad hoc. There is no consistent process in place. Success depends heavily on individual effort and institutional knowledge.
2. *Managed*
   Basic procedures exist and are repeatable, though they may not be standardized. The work is largely reactive, often triggered by specific issues or mandates.

3. *Defined*
   Formal processes have been established and documented. Activities are proactive, and ownership is clear. Training, governance, and measurement practices are emerging.
4. *Quantitatively managed*
   Performance is measured consistently. Metrics are used to inform decision-making and to optimize execution. There is a feedback loop that guides improvements.
5. *Optimizing*
   Capabilities are fully integrated into the organization's strategic planning. Processes are continuously reviewed, refined, and aligned to evolving threats and standards.

Let's walk through each domain and explore what these levels look like in practice.

8.5.1 Discovery phase

Cryptographic inventory
At the initial level, cryptographic assets are unknown or tracked manually. By the time an organization reaches Level 3, it maintains a detailed Cryptographic Bill of Materials (CBOM) integrated with software development practices. Level 5 includes automated inventory updates across environments and tight alignment with Software Bill of Materials (SBOM) and DevSecOps pipelines.

Risk assessment
Early-stage organizations may rely on outdated or generic threat models. At higher levels, risk assessments are customized for quantum impact, conducted regularly, and include data sensitivity mapping and third-party exposure. At Level 4 and above, scoring models (like CARAF or a bespoke framework) quantify exposure to PQC-relevant threats.

SBOM/CBOM integration
This domain examines how well cryptographic visibility is linked with software and system inventory. Initial efforts may be disconnected from the development lifecycle. Mature organizations treat CBOMs as part of building pipelines, ensuring that crypto-related components are visible from commit to deployment.

8.5.2 Planning phase

PQC policy
At lower levels, post-quantum considerations may be buried in broader IT or security policies, if mentioned at all. A defined policy, complete with

roles, responsibilities, and lifecycle triggers, signals Level 3. At the highest levels, the policy drives investment and reporting, and is reviewed annually against evolving standards.

Crypto-agility strategy
Crypto-agility moves from a buzzword to a practice. At Level 1, agility is nonexistent. Level 3 marks the introduction of design patterns and interface abstraction. At Levels 4 and 5, organizations simulate deprecation scenarios and have mechanisms to swap cryptographic primitives without significant reengineering.

Migration roadmap
Initial levels involve vague timelines and unassigned tasks. Level 3 includes a published, resourced roadmap aligned to enterprise architecture. At Level 5, this roadmap is integrated with vendor risk management, procurement, and product development lifecycles.

8.5.3 Implementation phase

TLS/VPN upgrade
Organizations begin by cataloging endpoints and libraries. Middle maturity levels include pilot deployments using hybrid cryptographic modes, such as implementing PQC candidates alongside classical algorithms in TLS 1.3. At the highest level, systems perform automated certificate provisioning and compliance scanning, with metrics tracking latency, error rates, and successful negotiation rates.

Modern certificates
This domain evaluates the enterprise's ability to issue, manage, and validate certificates that include both classical and post-quantum public key material. Early stages may involve lab testing only. Higher levels include policy-backed deployment, chain-of-trust mapping, and operational integration with enterprise PKI and third-party CAs.

Code signing and APIs
Organizations start with legacy code signing mechanisms and manual certificate management. Maturity improves with cryptographic abstraction layers, automated signature enforcement in build pipelines, and PQC-algorithm support. At higher levels, security testing and API integrations validate the integrity of signed artifacts across supply chains.

IoT and OT hardware
Long-lifecycle systems, especially industrial control systems (ICS), embedded devices, and IoT endpoints, pose distinct challenges in a quantum migration. Early-stage organizations may not even know what cryptography is

embedded in their hardware. Middle maturity involves firmware analysis, supplier questionnaires, and proof-of-concept upgrades using lightweight PQC. At Levels 4 and 5, organizations work closely with vendors to adopt PQC-aware hardware, manage root-of-trust cryptography, and embed lifecycle monitoring into product and manufacturing design. Integration with hardware security modules (HSMs), secure elements, and field-upgradable firmware is essential for full readiness.

8.5.4 Validation phase

Interoperability testing
Initial tests are informal and undocumented. By Level 3, regression and interoperability testing are formalized in test plans. Level 5 introduces test automation pipelines, metrics reporting, and active collaboration with vendors and standards bodies.

Security testing
Beyond functional testing, mature organizations simulate post-quantum threat vectors. Level 4 includes fuzzing, crypto abuse simulation, and PQC-specific vulnerability hunting. Level 5 integrates these into DevSecOps workflows.

Audit readiness
Early stages involve scattered documentation. A defined audit trail appears at Level 3. Level 5 includes continuous control monitoring, formal evidence packaging, and internal audit playbooks specific to PQC.

8.5.5 Maintenance phase

Key and certificate lifecycle
Manual renewal and inconsistent key handling mark the early stages. Higher levels introduce automated rotation, short-lived certificates, and full integration with HSMs and vault systems. Level 5 organizations practice continuous validation and entropy monitoring.

Standards monitoring
Level 1 may rely on outdated guidance. At Level 3, teams subscribe to NIST, ETSI, and ISO updates. Level 5 organizations actively participate in working groups, publish adaptations, and influence vendor compliance.

Crypto-agility governance
This domain reflects institutional maturity. Level 1 has no central oversight. Level 3 includes a steering committee with KPIs and board visibility. Level 5 embeds agility as a strategic capability with formal review cycles and scenario planning.

Start by assembling a cross-functional team that includes stakeholders from security, engineering, legal, compliance, and enterprise architecture. Review each domain together and score your current level from 1 to 5. Use evidence, not just instinct. Reference documentation, architectural patterns, vendor contracts, and operational workflows. Be honest. It is better to recognize gaps than to assume readiness. Once each domain is scored, document the specific criteria that must be met to move up a level. This turns the model into a roadmap for capability development. Use a simple worksheet or dashboard with one row per domain. Record your current maturity level, a brief justification, and the actions required to reach the next level. For example, please see Table 8.1.

Once scored, map the results to a radar chart. A radar chart allows you to visualize organizational readiness at a glance. Each axis represents one domain. Plot the maturity level (1 through 5) on each axis and connect the dots. The resulting shape gives you an intuitive sense of strengths and weaknesses. A lopsided shape highlights an imbalance. A tight, small shape shows low readiness. A broad, balanced chart with values clustered at 4 or 5 reflects strong enterprise maturity (Table 8.2).

Use these charts in leadership briefings and board updates. They are powerful tools for communicating progress and justifying investment. More importantly, they remind stakeholders that readiness is a process, and that quantum preparedness is both a technical and strategic imperative.

8.6 USING TECHNICAL READINESS LEVELS (TRLs) TO PRIORITIZE MIGRATION

Planning a post-quantum migration is not just about identifying what needs to change. It's also about understanding *when* it's realistic to act. Some solutions are enterprise-ready today. Others are still maturing in labs or locked behind vendor roadmaps. Knowing the difference – and planning accordingly – is essential for building a credible and effective roadmap.

This is where Technical Readiness Levels (TRLs) come into play. Originally developed by NASA and widely adopted in defense, aerospace,

Table 8.1 Maturity model

Domain	*Current Level*	*Justification*	*Next Steps*
Crypto-Agility Strategy	2	Interfaces exist but lack abstraction	Design crypto-abstraction layer for modularity
TLS/VPN Upgrade	3	Pilot completed for TLS 1.3 w/ hybrid certs	Expand deployment and monitor latency under load
Standards Monitoring	1	No formal tracking process	Subscribe to NIST PQC mailing list and RSS feeds

Table 8.2 Maturity radar

TRL	*PQC Readiness Description*
1	**Conceptual research**: Basic scientific principles are observed. PQC algorithm is experimental or academic. No practical implementation exists.
2	**Applied research**:Algorithm is being modeled or simulated. Some early code may exist, but no real-world deployment.
3	**Proof-of-concept**: Prototype created in a controlled lab setting. Performance and interoperability are not yet optimized.
4	**Bench-tested solution**:The solution is working in isolated systems. May be tested against known classical protocols. Interoperability is limited.
5	**Field-tested prototype**:Technology tested in a non-production environment (e.g., sandbox, demo environment). Feedback informs redesign.
6	**Enterprise pilot**: Deployed in a limited production setting (e.g., PQC-enabled VPN in one business unit). Integrated with some operational systems.
7	**Initial operational capability**: Deployed more broadly. Maintained with policy and monitoring, though issues may still emerge.
8	**Full operational deployment**: Stable, integrated, and supported across business-critical systems. Included in standard engineering practices.
9	**Optimized and strategic**: Fully embedded in enterprise security architecture. Aligned with business goals and lifecycle processes. Continuously improved.

and critical infrastructure, TRLs provide a standardized way to assess the maturity of a specific technology or solution. Rather than simply asking, "Can we implement this?" TRLs help teams answer, "How close is this to being operational in *our* environment?"

In the context of post-quantum cryptography, TRLs offer a practical way to evaluate the tools, protocols, and controls being considered. Is that PQC library just a research proof-of-concept? Has that hardware vendor completed production certification? Is the algorithm approved by NIST or still under evaluation? TRLs help teams askand answer these kinds of questions with more structure and less guesswork.

Here is a simplified adaptation of the TRL scale specifically for quantum migration initiatives:

When evaluating any technology or control as part of your quantum readiness strategy always assign it a TRL, whether it's a PQC-capable library, an upgraded TLS stack, or a new code-signing process. This helps teams visualize where each item stands in terms of maturity, vendor support, integration complexity, and deployment feasibility.

Let's look at a few examples:

- *ML-KEM support in OpenSSL 3.2*
  TRL 6: Available in release, widely tested, but not yet mainstream in enterprise environments.

- *Quantum-safe VPN tunnel using hybrid certificates (RFC 8784)*
  TRL 7: Supported by some vendors and deployable in production with the right configuration.
- *QKD key exchange for enterprise communication*
  TRL 2–3: Still mostly theoretical or piloted in highly specialized research environments.
- *Firmware signing using Dilithium in embedded devices*
  TRL 4–5: Some early-stage integrations exist, but full supply chain adoption is limited.
- *Hybrid certificate support in Microsoft Windows Server*
  TRL 5–6: Available in Insider builds and supported via registry-level configuration, but not fully documented for production-grade use. Suitable for pilot testing in isolated environments, particularly with Windows-integrated PKI.
- *PQC-ready HSMs from leading vendors*
  TRL 5: Some vendors now offer support for PQC algorithms (e.g., Dilithium or ML-KEM) in test firmware or through SDK extensions. These are mostly restricted to evaluation licenses or partner programs and are not yet included in general availability releases.
- *TLS libraries with PQC cipher suites in major browsers*
  TRL 3–4: While Chrome and Firefox have experimented with PQC hybrid ciphers, these are not enabled by default and are intended for developer testing. Production readiness varies significantly across platforms.
- *API security using PQC signatures in serverless environments*
  TRL 4: Prototype implementations exist, especially in Python or Go SDKs. However, performance, key size constraints, and cloud service provider support make it unsuitable for large-scale adoption today.

These examples show the wide variance in readiness across technologies. Some controls are nearly plug-and-play, while others remain several years from practical enterprise use. The example TRLs provided reflect the state of the ecosystem as of Q4 2025/Q1 2026 and are fairly accurate within that window, but they will naturally evolve as standards finalize, vendors mature their offerings, and broader adoption drives integration. Incorporating TRLs into your planning process helps distinguish between promising ideas and viable tools, both now and as the landscape continues to shift.

This process helps prevent one of the most common mistakes in security planning: building timelines based on assumptions instead of maturity. A technology that scores TRL 3 should not be on next quarter's deployment roadmap. Conversely, tools already at TRL 7 or 8 deserve urgent planning attention.

The maturity model in the previous section helps organizations assess their *own internal capability* to plan, implement, and sustain post-quantum security practices. The TRL framework complements this by evaluating the *external maturity* of specific technologies or controls.

Think of it this way:

- The *Q-ready maturity model* tells you *how prepared your organization is* to take action.
- The *TRL scale* tells you *how ready the solution is* for your organization to adopt.

Both are necessary. For example, you might score high on crypto-agility readiness, perhaps Level 4 on the maturity model, but discover that the PQC libraries required for implementation are only at TRL 5. That disconnect often explains delays, shifting deadlines, or the inability to scale a pilot into production. Understanding both organizational and technological readiness allows for more accurate planning and expectation management.

When used together, the maturity model and TRL framework help prioritize pilot efforts on controls that are both internally mature and externally deployable. They allow teams to communicate roadmap expectations more clearly to stakeholders and vendors. Most importantly, they guide the sequencing of upgrades in a way that reflects real-world feasibility, not just aspirational planning.

In practice, TRLs are especially useful during key phases of the Q-Ready Framework. During Phase 2 Planning, they help assess which technologies are mature enough to be included in near-term projects and which should be postponed or isolated for further testing. In Phase 4 Validation, they help teams reassess the maturity of previously selected tools and determine whether pilots are ready for full deployment or still require refinement. TRLs also play an important role in procurement and vendor management. They can offer a shared vocabulary when working with suppliers. Instead of relying on vague timelines or marketing claims, teams can ask direct, grounded questions such as, "What's the TRL of your PQC integration for this product or protocol?" This grounds the conversation in a framework that ties directly back to operational risk and implementation strategy.

8.7 DEVELOP A TESTING PLAN

Planning is necessary, but testing is decisive. Theoretical planning cannot capture the complexity of interoperability, performance trade-offs, or real-world constraints.

Start by defining the goals of your testing effort. These might include verifying algorithm compatibility, measuring system latency, or identifying broken trust chains in third-party integrations. Create test cases based on actual system dependencies. Include certificate authorities, identity providers, backup services, and partner APIs. Aim for completeness, not convenience. Define metrics for each test. These should include success rates, error tolerances, fallback behavior, and end-to-end quantum resistance. Also, measure how easily your team can swap out algorithms, rotate keys, and reconfigure services, a practical measure of crypto-agility. The act of testing will often reveal roadblocks that no risk model predicted. That is not a failure. It is an insight.

8.7.1 Build a proof-of-concept lab

To validate your plan and policies, you need a dedicated lab environment. This lab should simulate critical components of your production environment and include real data flows where appropriate.

Your proof-of-concept lab should allow you to:

- Test the full lifecycle of PQC deployment, including key generation, distribution, and rotation.
- Compare performance and latency between classical and PQC algorithms. Larger key sizes and digital signature lengths may affect application responsiveness and file sizes.
- Identify incompatible libraries, APIs, or devices that cannot handle PQC cryptography.
- Validate crypto-agility by forcing algorithm swaps in simulated failure scenarios.
- Test end-to-end encryption scenarios, including between external partners and vendors.

Include platforms like OpenSSL, BoringSSL, liboqs, and Qiskit in your environment. These tools allow for experimentation with post-quantum algorithms and help simulate deployment paths without placing production systems at risk.

To ensure robustness and resilience in post-quantum cryptographic systems, testing should go beyond functional correctness. Integrate fuzz testing and fault injection to simulate unpredictable input conditions and uncover implementation flaws in cryptographic modules. These methods help catch edge cases that typical unit tests might miss.

Incorporate CI/CD pipeline integration into your testing process. Add automated tests for PQC algorithm compliance and interoperability within your continuous integration environments. Every code commit or system build should trigger validations that confirm cryptographic compatibility, key negotiation success, and fallback behavior.

Cross-platform compatibility also demands attention. Ensure your testing environment includes modern browsers, mobile platforms, legacy clients, and IoT endpoints. These systems may exhibit inconsistent support for emerging protocols or require additional configuration to maintain compatibility with PQC deployments. Interoperability failures at these touchpoints could delay deployment or weaken security guarantees.

Ensure your lab includes partners and suppliers. Some of your dependencies may not be ready for PQC, and this will impact your migration timeline. Better to learn that in the lab than during deployment.

8.7.2 How to develop a testing plan

A well-structured testing plan is essential to ensure that your migration to post-quantum cryptography (PQC) proceeds smoothly, without unintended side effects or security regressions. Testing validates assumptions, uncovers compatibility issues, and helps refine your overall migration roadmap. The following steps outline a practical approach for developing your testing strategy.

Step 1: Define the objectives of testing

Start by clarifying what you are trying to validate. Are you testing for interoperability, performance, algorithm compatibility, or regulatory compliance? Ensure each objective is directly tied to your migration goals. Typical objectives include verifying the integration of post-quantum algorithms, ensuring crypto-agility functionality, or assessing the behavior of hybrid key systems.

Step 2: Identify scope and assets to test

Select systems, applications, and components based on your prioritization model. Focus initially on high-risk or high-impact assets, such as PKI systems, authentication frameworks, VPNs, and systems that protect long-lived sensitive data. Include both internal and third-party systems where possible.

Step 3: Select testing environments

Set up isolated, controlled environments for proof-of-concept (PoC) testing. These environments should closely mirror production configurations, including relevant software stacks, hardware dependencies, and external interfaces. Avoid testing directly in production environments unless the changes have been fully validated and risk assessed.

Step 4: Choose the right tools and libraries

Use trusted cryptographic libraries that support PQC and hybrid implementations. Common options include:

- *OpenSSL* and *BoringSSL* with PQC extensions
- *liboqs* (Open Quantum Safe library) for integrating NIST candidate algorithms
- *Qiskit* for simulating quantum behavior or modeling quantum-safe key management schemes

Ensure the tools are properly configured and their versioning is documented.

Step 5: Define success criteria and metrics

Establish what a successful test looks like. Include criteria such as:

- Successful handshake using post-quantum key exchange
- Round-trip encryption and decryption without data loss
- Maintenance of latency or performance within defined thresholds
- Compatibility with adjacent systems or APIs

Define metrics such as:

- Time to complete a post-quantum handshake
- Encrypted payload size
- CPU/memory impact of new algorithms

Step 6: Run unit tests and integration tests

Begin with isolated testing of cryptographic libraries and components. Then proceed to full integration testing across applications, APIs, and network flows. Test fallback logic and failover scenarios. Ensure that systems gracefully handle unsupported algorithms or negotiation failures.

Step 7: Test hybrid and crypto-agile configurations

If you are using hybrid key exchanges, ensure they function as intended, especially in multi-party environments. Verify that crypto-agile configurations allow seamless switching between algorithms without service interruption. Test dynamic key rotation and algorithm update procedures to ensure optimal performance.

Step 8: Involve vendors and external partners

Your systems do not exist in a vacuum. Coordinate testing with cloud service providers, software vendors, and trusted third parties whose cryptographic posture can impact your environment. Test interoperability across the full communication chain.

Step 9: Log, monitor, and document results

Capture detailed logs from each test run. Include configuration files, test inputs, outputs, error messages, and observed behavior. Store this documentation in a version-controlled repository. Use dashboards or scorecards to visualize progress and pinpoint failures.

Step 10: Use results to inform your migration plan

Incorporate lessons from testing into your broader migration roadmap. If a particular algorithm causes performance bottlenecks or compatibility issues, you may need to defer its adoption or seek vendor alternatives. Testing should feed directly into prioritization, procurement, and risk mitigation discussions.

8.8 CONCLUSION

The goal of this chapter is not just to outline the work ahead, but to give you a clear starting point. Developing a post-quantum migration and testing plan is where strategic intent becomes operational reality. It is the step where risk assessments, inventory reviews, and prioritization models translate into decisions about timelines, protocols, and resource allocation.

A well-structured plan reveals both strengths and gaps. It exposes areas where systems are brittle, where vendor dependencies require attention, and where business continuity intersects with cryptographic changes. It also forces organizations to confront practical questions. Which protocols are we standardizing on? How will we test hybrid configurations? What counts as good enough in terms of crypto-agility? These are not theoretical debates. They are planning decisions that carry technical, financial, and organizational consequences.

Testing will sharpen that clarity. Every lab simulation, every failed handshake, and every successful integration strengthens your team's understanding of what post-quantum readiness really means. The earlier these lessons surface, the easier it becomes to prevent disruption and to correct course before issues reach production. Your proof-of-concept environments, vendor coordination, and interoperability exercises are not side projects, and they are safety nets.

As you move into execution, remember that this is not just a cryptographic upgrade. It is a shift in how trust is managed, how resilience is measured, and how your organization prepares for the future. Migration is never finished in a single phase. However, every system you upgrade now, every policy you publish, and every test you run closes the window of exposure that quantum threats are counting on.

In the next chapter, we will explore how to coordinate across departments and scale your remediation efforts. Planning sets the direction, execution moves the organization, but only collaboration turns individual fixes into systemic resilience.

Chapter 9

Engage stakeholders and secure buy-in

Post-quantum cryptography is not only a security problem; it's a coordination challenge, a communication exercise, and, at times, a political process. Success depends on aligning teams that often speak different languages: technical, legal, operational, and financial. That alignment begins with deliberate engagement and ends with lasting support.

Quantum migration represents a shift in how an organization approaches long-term security, risk, and resilience. While the engineers and cryptographers will write the code and run the tests, the success of a post-quantum transition depends just as much on organizational alignment. Getting buy-in across technical and executive teams is what transforms a roadmap into a reality.

9.1 START WITH ALIGNMENT, NOT AWARENESS

Most leaders are familiar with quantum computing. Fewer understand its impact. Even fewer are aware of what it means for their organization's cryptography. Your first task is not to alarm or overload, but to align. Explain how post-quantum cryptography fits into broader business risk. Link it to familiar concepts, such as data privacy, zero-trust security, ransomware readiness, or regulatory compliance. Use stories and analogies when helpful. For example, "Quantum migration is like replacing the locks on a building before thieves learn how to pick them".

Workshops and strategic sessions are effective tools for achieving goals. Gather IT leaders, risk managers, and security architects in the same room. Walk through your cryptographic inventory, share the prioritization model, and explore real-world use cases. Use data from vendors like IBM Guardium or ISARA to show what other organizations are doing. Bring the scenarios to life, like what happens if your VPN tunnels are harvested now and decrypted in 2033? How would you explain that to regulators, or customers, or your own board?

DOI: 10.1201/9781003685760-13

9.1.1 Speak the board's language

Communicating with senior leadership requires translation. Technical risk must be framed in terms of business impact. Use the language of cost, liability, trust, and continuity, not bits and keys. Boards don't need to know how Kyber works; they need to understand what would happen if a quantum-enabled adversary were to access customer data.

Start by explaining the "Harvest Now, Decrypt Later" threat. Help the board understand that data stolen today may be decrypted tomorrow. Focus on the lifetime of the data and the likelihood of exposure over time.

Present post-quantum cryptography as a form of long-term business resilience. Draw analogies to previous shifts, like Y2K or the move to the cloud. Stress that this is not just a theoretical concern. Some governments and nation-state actors are already believed to be harvesting encrypted data in anticipation of future quantum breakthroughs.

Frame quantum risk in terms of fiduciary duty. Highlight how encrypted data in transit today may still be valuable ten years from now. Use terms like "compliance readiness", "third-party assurance", and "strategic continuity". Quantify risk wherever possible, drawing from FAIR models or cost-of-breach calculators. When sharing your plan, do not just ask for funding; instead, demonstrate how the investment directly ties to risk reduction, reputation protection, and operational continuity.

Utilize visuals, such as heatmaps, maturity models, and migration timelines, to effectively communicate risk and readiness. A scorecard showing how many systems are classified as "quantum-vulnerable" makes it tangible. A timeline that aligns quantum readiness with broader transformation programs makes it strategic.

A good board briefing includes three parts: a simple explanation of the risk, a clear description of what's already being done, and a request for support that aligns with long-term business goals. This is where a well-articulated migration and testing plan becomes your best tool. It signals that your team is not reacting but leading.

If you're looking for a way to start that conversation, the Introduction of this book can help. It's designed as a business-focused, executive-level summary of the risks, challenges, and opportunities of post-quantum cryptography. It can be used to frame discussions with leadership or serve as a briefing tool for boards of directors.

9.2 BUSINESS AND FINANCIAL PLANNING FOR PQC

No cryptographic transition succeeds without financial support. Post-quantum cryptography introduces new tooling, new vendor relationships, and new complexity. Planning for these costs early and communicating their value clearly can be the difference between a stalled initiative and a strategic win. CISOs who regularly apply ROI, TCO, and cost avoidance analyses are well-positioned to make this case. For post-quantum cryptography, a robust investment model can clarify how proactive migration minimizes future losses, limits breach exposure, and extends the value of existing infrastructure.

Begin with a basic cost estimation model. Break down your systems into categories such as endpoints, applications, network infrastructure, and cryptographic services. Estimate the average cost to assess, test, and migrate each category. This might include labor hours for engineers, licensing fees for crypto-agile libraries, upgrades to incompatible devices, and training for teams. Use your cryptographic inventory as a starting point and assign rough dollar values to each risk tier. For example, you might estimate that migrating a critical API service costs five times more than updating an internal dashboard.

Some organizations use cost-per-asset models. These apply a standard estimate for classes of systems, such as \$10,000 to migrate a VPN cluster, \$1,000 for a low-risk internal service, or \$50,000 for a hybrid cloud application requiring third-party coordination and key management updates. While these are only approximations, they help budgeting teams prepare ahead of procurement and resourcing cycles.

However, financial planning for PQC should not stop at cost. The return on investment for crypto-agility is equally important. A PQC ROI model should compare the all-in cost of migration, tools, labor, vendor enablement, test infrastructure, and audit scope against the estimated financial impact of a quantum-enabled compromise. For instance, if an organization invests \$4 million over three years to modernize its cryptographic infrastructure, it may be avoiding a \$50 million loss scenario, factoring in breach response, litigation, downtime, customer churn, and reputational erosion. This frames the investment as risk reduction with a potential ROI of over 1000 percent, based on a 10–15 percent probability of breach within a decade. That said, I wouldn't present a 1000%+ ROI to a board of directors, because this is a cost avoidance scenario – you're not actually getting money back. A more credible framing might be a "dollars of risk reduced per dollar invested" calculation. In this example, dividing the \$50 million in avoided risk by the \$4 million investment yields \$12.50 of risk reduction for every dollar invested.

TCO modeling extends this logic, capturing both capital and operational expenses across the program lifecycle. Upfront line items may include asset discovery, steering committee resourcing, and vendor assessments. Migration costs cover integration and testing. Ongoing obligations range from key lifecycle management and crypto-agility testing to internal awareness campaigns. Compared to traditional refresh cycles or post-breach costs, a well-scoped PQC transition often presents a lower long-term cost basis.

That said, calculating Total Cost of Ownership (TCO) for PQC initiatives presents real challenges. Unlike traditional infrastructure investments with well-defined boundaries, PQC touches nearly every aspect of an organization's IT and risk landscape. Costs may be fragmented across teams, security, architecture, compliance, vendor management, and not easily centralized. Indirect costs, like system downtime during migrations, delays from vendor lag, or the time spent revalidating crypto-dependent integrations, are difficult to forecast and often underestimated. Moreover, many existing systems lack accurate cryptographic inventories, making scope definition a moving target. CISOs should treat early TCO estimates as directional rather than definitive and expect adjustments as discovery and testing unfold. A phased budgeting model, with checkpoints at major milestones like asset discovery completion or pilot deployments, can help manage uncertainty and avoid overcommitting based on incomplete data.

To conduct a meaningful TCO analysis for PQC, start by breaking the effort into distinct cost domains. Even if not every cost can be precisely calculated at the outset, building a structured framework will surface hidden dependencies and improve accuracy over time.

1. *Establish the scope and boundaries*
   Begin with a list of systems, applications, vendors, and cryptographic processes that may be affected. If you don't yet have a full cryptographic inventory, treat this as a dependency and budget placeholder. Be explicit about what's in scope now versus what may be added later.
2. *Organize costs into lifecycle phases*
   Use a phased approach that mirrors the typical PQC program structure. For each phase, identify potential costs and whether they are fixed, variable, one-time, or recurring:
   - *Discovery phase*:
     - Cryptographic asset inventory tools (e.g., AppViewX, Keyfactor)
     - Internal staff time or contractor support
     - Gap analysis reports and compliance assessments
   - *Planning phase*:
     - Time for steering committee and architecture review
     - Vendor readiness assessments
     - Legal reviews for contractual crypto-agility clauses
   - *Implementation phase*:
     - Engineering and development hours for integration
     - Test environments and sandboxing for PQC libraries
     - Purchase or customization of toolkits (e.g., liboqs, BoringSSL, PQShield SDKs)
   - *Validation phase*:
     - Penetration testing and algorithm verification
     - Compliance audits
     - User acceptance testing (UAT)

- *Sustainment phase*:
    - Staff training refreshers
    - Certificate lifecycle and key rotation management
    - Monitoring of standards evolution and vendor SLAs

3. *Estimate labor costs by role*
   List the roles involved: security engineers, application developers, legal counsel, vendor managers, and estimate time commitments in FTEs or hours. Multiply by loaded salary rates. For example:
   - Security Architect: 0.3 FTE for 12 months = $60,000
   - DevOps Engineer: 100 hours for integration and testing = $10,000
4. *Account for indirect and opportunity costs*
   Estimate productivity loss during migration windows, delays from incompatible vendor systems, or reputational exposure due to missed timelines. While harder to quantify, a 5–10% buffer on project totals for unforeseen issues is a reasonable starting point.
5. *Revisit and refine*
   TCO should not be treated as a fixed number. Build in checkpoints for review after major milestones like pilot completions or vendor selections. Treat each revision as an opportunity to increase fidelity and reduce risk.

Example output (for a mid-sized organization over 5 years):

- *Discovery phase*: Approximately $350,000
  This includes tooling for cryptographic asset inventory, plus staff effort to perform discovery, analysis, and initial scoping.
- *Planning phase*: Approximately $500,000
  Covers time allocated to the steering committee, architecture reviews, vendor assessments, and legal review of contracts and crypto-agility clauses.
- *Implementation phase*: Approximately $2,400,000
  Reflects the bulk of the migration cost, including integration of PQC toolkits, development and testing, infrastructure upgrades, and vendor coordination.
- *Validation phase*: Approximately $600,000
  Includes compliance audits, penetration testing, user acceptance testing, and remediation work necessary for rollout approval.
- *Sustainment phase*: Approximately $850,000
  Captures ongoing cryptographic key management, monitoring of vendor readiness, refresher training, and long-term support for crypto-agility.

Total 5-year estimated TCO: *Approximately $4.7 million*, which includes a built-in contingency buffer to account for unanticipated costs.

Scenario modeling is particularly effective when aligning with finance. Rather than advocating for a single course of action, CISOs can present tiered pathways:

The minimal compliance route targets only the highest-risk systems, minimizing near-term spend while leaving significant exposure. A balanced mitigation plan aligns with key systems and vendor dependencies, offering moderate protection and budget predictability. Full quantum readiness provides enterprise-wide crypto-agility, robust third-party oversight, and continuous monitoring, with a price point to match.

Here's how those trade-offs might be modeled (Table 9.1):

This approach supports executive-level decision-making by tying investment levels to specific operational outcomes.

A well-prepared budget proposal should include FTE allocations by workstream, vendor audit costs, toolkit acquisition, and any external support for assessment or program governance. Including a worksheet or investment summary in board or budget planning packets can streamline discussions.

Executive messaging might sound like: "Our cryptographic infrastructure has a known shelf life. A planned $4 to $5 million investment not only ensures continuity and compliance, it materially reduces exposure to emerging risks that could cost ten times that amount in the event of failure".

To secure budget and executive buy-in, tie PQC initiatives to real business risk. Map cryptographic exposure to data breach costs, reputational damage, or regulatory fines. Use FAIR-based models or similar frameworks to assign dollar values to the risks mitigated by PQC investments. Emphasize that this is not theoretical; encrypted data is already being harvested today, and the cost of inaction will show up not now, but when a quantum-capable adversary makes use of it.

Finally, align PQC efforts with broader initiatives already underway. If the organization is modernizing identity services, expanding zero trust architectures, or rewriting APIs, use those moments to insert PQC upgrades. This piggybacks on existing momentum and reduces marginal cost. It also makes the case that PQC is not just a security concern but a strategic enabler. In this way, business and financial planning become more

Table 9.1 Scenario modeling

Scenario	*Estimated Cost*	*Residual Risk Level*	*Staff Involved*	*Business Impact*
Minimal Compliance	$1.2M	High	Core security	Meets regulatory baseline, high breach risk
Balanced Mitigation	$3.8M	Medium	Multi-team	Moderate protection, aligned with key priorities
Full Quantum Readiness	$7.5M	Low	Org-wide	Comprehensive coverage and resilience

than funding an upgrade. It becomes a shared exercise in managing long-term trust and building a resilient digital foundation for the years ahead.

9.3 CREATE A POST-QUANTUM STEERING COMMITTEE

No major technology shift succeeds without someone at the wheel. Post-quantum cryptography goes well beyond being just a cryptographic upgrade; it is a foundational change that affects nearly every aspect of modern IT architecture. Without dedicated oversight, the effort can become fragmented, reactive, or simply stall. A Post-Quantum Steering Committee provides the structure and accountability needed to coordinate planning, align stakeholders, and drive measurable progress.

To build a committee with real impact, start by assembling representatives from the business functions most directly affected by cryptographic change. This usually includes security and infrastructure teams, enterprise architecture, application development, risk and compliance, procurement, legal, and data governance. In larger organizations, you may also want to include delegates from internal audit, vendor management, or specific business units handling regulated workloads.

Be intentional with role assignments. For example, security engineering may own the technical evaluation of candidate algorithms, while enterprise architects assess crypto-agility readiness across platforms. Procurement can review vendor agreements for contract clauses that address crypto-agility or post-quantum readiness. Legal may be tasked with reviewing data retention policies and breach notification obligations related to Harvest Now, Decrypt Later risks. Assigning specific responsibilities helps avoid the trap of committee members attending passively without taking ownership.

Once your team is assembled, establish a formal charter to guide its operations. This document should include:

- Mission Statement: Why the committee exists and how it aligns with organizational goals (e.g., "To coordinate and oversee the organization's transition to post-quantum cryptography in a manner that protects data, ensures compliance, and maintains service continuity").
- Scope of Work: The boundaries of what the committee will address, such as cryptographic policy development, algorithm selection, migration planning, vendor coordination, and compliance mapping.
- Roles and Responsibilities: A breakdown of who owns what, both by function (e.g., compliance lead reviews regulatory alignment) and by deliverable (e.g., architecture lead authors the crypto-agility requirements spec).

- Decision-Making Process: How proposals are evaluated and approved. Some committees use a voting model; others rely on consensus or executive arbitration for unresolved issues.
- Reporting and Escalation Pathways: Who the committee reports to, how frequently it shares updates, and how budget requests or blockers are escalated.

A sample list of deliverables from a PQC steering committee might include:

- A formal PQC migration roadmap with phases and milestones
- A post-quantum certificate and key management strategy
- Vendor readiness reports and scorecards
- Updated procurement and architecture standards with crypto-agility requirements
- Communications templates for internal awareness and executive briefings
- Quarterly status reports and board-level summaries

As for cadence, the committee should meet at least monthly during the initial planning and assessment phases. During active migration windows, biweekly or even weekly check-ins may be necessary to address interdependencies and maintain alignment among workstreams. Meeting agendas should be tight and action-oriented, with clearly tracked follow-ups. Shared dashboards and a central repository for test results, risk scores, migration plans, and remediation status are key to maintaining visibility and accountability.

Here is a simple framework for creating and running a Post-Quantum Steering Committee:

Step 1: Identify and invite members
Focus on individuals with the authority to make decisions or influence workstreams. Ensure cross-functional representation.

Step 2: Draft a charter
Define the purpose, scope, decision-making structure, and accountability model. Secure buy-in from executive sponsors.

Step 3: Assign deliverables
Assign each member a clear responsibility that aligns with their area of expertise. Create timelines for deliverables.

Step 4: Schedule recurring meetings
Set a standing cadence with pre-read materials and consistent reporting. Use structured agendas that allow for time to address issue escalation.

Step 5: Create a reporting mechanism
Use a shared dashboard, progress tracker, or repository for all steering committee artifacts. This improves continuity and transparency.

Step 6: Review and iterate
Hold quarterly retrospectives to refine the committee's focus, address obstacles, and realign priorities.

By giving the Post-Quantum Steering Committee a mandate, a structure, and a rhythm, you create a governance engine that can translate strategic intent into operational momentum. Without it, even the most thorough plans risk stagnation. With it, your organization has a forum where security, operations, and business leaders can collaborate toward a secure and agile post-quantum future.

9.3.1 Example program charter

Post-Quantum Cryptography Program Charter
Program Name: Quantum Resilience Initiative (QRI)
Sponsor: Chief Information Security Officer (CISO)
Steering Committee Chair: [Insert Name]
Charter Date: [Insert Date]
Review Date: [Insert Date Annually or Semiannually]

9.3.1.1 Mission and vision

Mission
To ensure cryptographic resilience in the face of quantum computing by identifying, upgrading, and future-proofing vulnerable systems across the enterprise.

Vision
To establish a world-class center of excellence for post-quantum cryptography, enabling secure, compliant, and uninterrupted operations in the quantum era.

9.3.1.2 Purpose

The Quantum Resilience Initiative (QRI) prepares the organization for quantum-induced cryptographic risk by migrating critical assets to NIST-approved post-quantum algorithms. This program will implement the five-phase Q-Ready Framework from *Quantum Ready*, ensuring alignment with standards from NIST, CISA, IEEE, and other regulatory bodies. The initiative will strengthen enterprise security, reduce long-term costs, and build trust with customers, partners, and regulators.

9.3.1.3 Scope

QRI addresses cryptographic risk across all global business units, including:

- Cryptographic inventory and asset mapping
- Quantum vulnerability assessments and risk scoring
- PQC migration planning and pilot testing
- TLS, VPN, and API protocol remediation
- Certificate and key lifecycle modernization
- Crypto-agility architecture and policy updates
- Vendor PQC readiness and integration
- Compliance, audit, and reporting alignment

9.3.1.4 Objectives and Key Results (OKRs)

- *Security*: Ensure confidentiality of long-lived data and resilience of critical systems
- *Continuity*: Avoid disruption by remediating cryptography before Q-Day
- *Compliance*: Align with FIPS 203–206 and other emerging standards
- *Cost control*: Lower remediation costs through early crypto-agility
- *Trust*: Demonstrate readiness to customers, partners, and regulators

Key results

- 100% cryptographic asset inventory and risk classification
- 75%+ of critical systems migrated to PQC or hybrid configurations
- 100% vendor crypto roadmaps collected and reviewed
- PQC education delivered to key stakeholder groups
- Q-Day exposure window reduced by [Target %]

9.3.1.5 Governance

PQC steering committee
Cross-functional leadership from Security, IT, Risk, Legal, Compliance, Procurement, and Architecture provides strategic oversight, funding guidance, and milestone approval.

Roles and responsibilities

- *Compliance lead:* Reviews regulatory guidance and ensures audit readiness.
- *Architecture lead:* Authors crypto-agility framework and system design requirements.
- *Vendor management lead:* Evaluates and reports on vendor cryptographic readiness.

- *Program manager:* Manages timeline, resources, and cross-functional collaboration.
- *Communications lead:* Develops internal messaging and executive briefings.

Crypto Center of Excellence (CoE)
A dedicated technical working group that evaluates algorithms, builds test environments, defines crypto-agile standards, and guides implementation across business units.

Working groups
Formed to address domain-specific needs such as PKI modernization, third-party integrations, DevSecOps crypto hygiene, and TLS/VPN remediation.

9.3.1.6 Decision-making process

Committee decisions will be made by consensus during regularly scheduled PQC Steering Committee meetings. For urgent matters or if consensus is not reached, the Steering Committee Chair may escalate the issue to the CISO or designated executive sponsor for final arbitration. Emergency decisions may be conducted via asynchronous vote with majority approval documented in writing.

9.3.1.7 Phased roadmap (aligned to Q-Ready Framework)

- *Phase 1 – Discover*
  Build CBOM, identify vulnerable algorithms, and map to data sensitivity levels.
- *Phase 2 – Plan*
  Set KPIs, define migration paths, secure funding, and prepare test labs.
- *Phase 3 – Implement*
  Migrate algorithms, deploy hybrid certs, update key management workflows.
- *Phase 4 – Validate*
  Conduct interoperability testing, simulate crypto-failure scenarios, and prepare audit documentation.
- *Phase 5 – Maintain*
  Monitor evolving standards, rotate keys, update policies, and maintain crypto-agility.

9.3.1.8 Metrics and reporting

- % cryptographic assets inventoried and assessed
- % of critical systems migrated to PQC or hybrid mode

- % of third-party vendor crypto-readiness assessed
- Workforce PQC awareness training completion rate
- Compliance readiness scores and audit findings
- Estimated Q-Day exposure window reduction

Monthly reports and quarterly steering committee updates will track status and escalate risks.

9.3.1.9 Key deliverables

- Enterprise PQC policy and CBOM
- Post-Quantum certificate and key management strategy
- Migration plan with technical readiness levels (TRLs)
- PQC test lab reports and interoperability results
- Crypto-agnostic architecture templates
- Vendor readiness reports and scorecards
- Updated procurement and architecture standards
- Internal communications templates for awareness campaigns and executive briefings
- Quarterly steering committee status reports
- Board-level PQC readiness summaries

9.3.1.10 Risks and assumptions

Risks

- Incomplete visibility into legacy or embedded crypto
- Lack of cooperation from vendors or supply chain partners
- Talent shortages in cryptographic engineering and architecture
- Evolving regulatory timelines or uncertainty in standards

Assumptions

- NIST standardization stabilizes within 12–18 months
- Migration may take 3–7 years across the enterprise
- PQC compliance will become mandatory in future audits and RFPs

9.3.1.11 Funding and resources

Budget and staffing will be aligned with IT capital and operational risk programs. Key investments include:

- Cryptographic scanning and SBOM tooling
- PQC test and validation environments
- External vendor assessments and consulting
- Crypto-agility architecture refactoring
- PQC education and internal communications

9.3.1.12 Review and updates

This charter will be reviewed semiannually by the PQC Steering Committee. Updates will reflect regulatory changes, NIST releases, operational findings, and shifts in enterprise risk posture.

9.4 STAND UP A CRYPTO CENTER OF EXCELLENCE

A Crypto Center of Excellence (CCoE) serves as the internal hub for cryptographic strategy, standards, and execution. It is a dedicated, technically focused body responsible for driving cryptographic maturity, architectural consistency, and quantum readiness across the enterprise. While the Post-Quantum Steering Committee provides strategic oversight, setting direction, funding, and risk tolerance, the CCoE is where the work happens. It translates vision into implementation, serving as both a think tank for innovation and a support desk for teams upgrading legacy cryptography.

The distinction between these two entities is essential. The Post-Quantum Steering Committee is composed of executive and senior leaders from Security, Risk, IT, Legal, Compliance, and Enterprise Architecture. Its responsibilities include governance, milestone approvals, cross-functional coordination, and aligning PQC initiatives with regulatory expectations and enterprise risk posture. In contrast, the CCoE is staffed by practitioners, including cryptographers, security architects, protocol engineers, DevSecOps leaders, and application security specialists, who define cryptographic standards, evaluate tools and protocols, and build reference implementations to support post-quantum adoption.

The CCoE becomes the nerve center for PQC experimentation and policy development. Among its responsibilities is the creation and maintenance of cryptographic policy documents, including lists of approved and deprecated algorithms, key length requirements, hybrid certificate guidelines, and crypto-agility strategies. It vets and benchmarks quantum-safe libraries such as liboqs, PQCrypto-SIDH, QSC, and PQC-enabled forks of OpenSSL or BoringSSL. These evaluations extend to key management solutions and crypto-linting tools that can be embedded into CI/CD pipelines.

Equally important is the development of reference architectures and reusable code. These assets provide implementation guidance for securing TLS, VPN, PKI, and APIs with post-quantum algorithms, enabling teams to integrate quantum-safe cryptography without having to completely rewrite existing systems. The CCoE maintains interoperability testing environments that mirror internal infrastructure, allowing it to simulate PQC upgrades and hybrid deployments under realistic operational conditions.

To support delivery teams, the CCoE publishes how-to guides, integration templates, developer SDKs, and maintains shared documentation portals or internal wikis. These resources serve as a knowledge base for application teams grappling with cryptographic changes, capturing lessons learned, known issues, regulatory updates, and recommended practices. The CCoE also plays a key role in reviewing vendor cryptographic readiness, evaluating third-party products and services for post-quantum alignment, and mapping results to internal risk frameworks.

Operationalizing a CCoE doesn't require a massive upfront investment. In fact, the best approach is to start small. A working group of three to five engineers, including security architects, application security experts, and cryptographic analysts, with enough bandwidth to evaluate tools like liboqs or Qiskit, can seed the initiative. Early wins, such as testing PQC in a TLS handshake or creating a hybrid certificate proof-of-concept, help demonstrate value and build momentum. Documentation should be a priority from the start: a shared repository or wiki should capture everything from test results to architecture patterns.

Initial deliverables within the first six months may include a Cryptographic Standards Playbook, evaluation reports on quantum-safe libraries, a test lab environment simulating TLS/PQC integration, a reference implementation of hybrid TLS 1.3, and a vendor cryptographic discovery checklist. A community of practice, such as a dedicated Slack or Teams channel, can help disseminate knowledge and foster engagement.

The composition of the CCoE should grow with demand. A core team might include one to two security architects with crypto-agility experience, one to two platform or application security engineers, and a cryptographer or protocol analyst. Rotating support from DevOps, PKI, IAM, and network teams enhances cross-functional reach. As the program matures, the CCoE should integrate contributors from internal audit, vendor risk management, and compliance to ensure full lifecycle coverage.

The evolution of a CCoE can be measured through four maturity stages. In the "Start" phase, the team functions as an ad hoc working group focused on initial evaluations, standards drafts, and limited testing. In the "Build" phase, it establishes a formal charter, delivers enterprise-wide policies, and begins producing reusable architecture assets. The "Scale" phase embeds CCoE activities into SDLC workflows, procurement processes, and audit programs, providing tooling like CI/CD crypto linters and standardized vendor reviews. Finally, in the "Sustain" phase, the CCoE becomes a continuous innovation engine, rotating algorithms, managing deprecation cycles, influencing standards bodies, and supporting long-term cryptographic resilience.

To launch a CCoE, executive sponsorship is critical. With formal backing from the CISO or CTO and alignment with the PQC Steering Committee, the CCoE can operate with clear authority and scope. Once initiated, the CCoE should begin outreach across the organization through tech talks, office hours, internal demos, and hands-on workshops. This visibility not only encourages adoption but also helps uncover cryptographic blind spots across systems and vendors.

Ultimately, the CCoE is not just a technical function; it is a cultural shift. It builds shared accountability for cryptographic resilience, fosters collaboration between architecture and delivery teams, and ensures that the enterprise is prepared not just for post-quantum threats, but for the next wave of cryptographic innovation.

9.5 DESIGNATE A CHAMPION: THE PQC CZAR

Every transformational effort needs a leader who will push it forward when attention drifts or priorities shift. Post-quantum cryptography is no exception. The role of a PQC Czar, whether formalized with a title or not, is to ensure that someone is consistently thinking about the long arc of cryptographic readiness.

In some organizations, this person may be a senior enterprise architect, a cryptographic engineer, or even a director within infrastructure or application security. In others, it may be the CISO, the CTO, or someone from the risk function. What matters is not where they sit on the org chart, but whether they have the authority, credibility, and time to coordinate the initiative across teams. They must be able to make decisions, rally stakeholders, and escalate blockers without being sidelined by day-to-day firefighting. Whether this person reports to the CIO, CISO, or CTO is less important than whether they can marshal the support of all three. They need executive backing, cross-departmental visibility, and enough latitude to shape timelines and influence budgets. Without this level of empowerment, the cryptographic migration program will remain a paper exercise.

The PQC Czar's responsibilities are wide-ranging. They set the direction for the migration roadmap, chair the steering committee, and meet with vendors to evaluate their cryptographic roadmaps. They coordinate with compliance to ensure new crypto standards align with regulatory expectations, and when there is confusion, delay, or resistance, they are expected to bring clarity and urgency.

Just as importantly, the PQC Czar serves as the translator between worlds. They explain crypto-agility to business leaders in terms of operational flexibility; they help developers understand why algorithm choices matter years down the line, and they connect legal and compliance teams to the technical realities of key management and algorithm replacement. Their job is not to do everything but to connect the dots and keep the momentum alive.

Even if your organization is not ready to create a formal title, appoint someone to serve in this capacity. Treat it as a defined role with assigned time, not a side project. Document their responsibilities, ensure they have executive sponsorship, and make it clear that they speak for the program.

Having a clear point of leadership, someone who wakes up thinking about PQC every day, is the difference between good intentions and real progress.

9.6 FACILITATE CROSS-FUNCTIONAL TASK FORCES

PQC readiness cannot live solely in security or infrastructure. Legal, procurement, compliance, engineering, and product development all have a stake in cryptographic transitions. That is why it is essential to formalize a cross-functional post-quantum task force as part of the Crypto Center of Excellence.

This group should include representatives from across the organization. Its job is to coordinate efforts, share updates, remove blockers, and ensure that quantum-related decisions are not made in silos. The center should meet regularly, track progress against key performance indicators (KPIs), and manage exceptions or escalations.

Responsibilities may include reviewing vendor contracts for crypto-agility clauses, updating development standards to reflect new key lengths, or tracking certificate transition deadlines. It should also provide feedback loops to leadership, giving executives real-time visibility into quantum preparedness.

Each task force should have a sponsor, a deadline, and a clear objective. These focused efforts create small wins and build confidence. They also reinforce that PQC readiness is not owned by any one team. Everyone, from product to legal to finance, has a role to play.

Large organizations often suffer from initiative fatigue. Dozens of projects compete for attention, and unless PQC is positioned as a shared risk, it may never rise to the top. Establishing cross-functional task forces is one way to cut through this inertia. Task forces are short-term, high-impact teams that focus on a specific deliverable or objective. For PQC, this might include a task force to convert legacy PKI systems to hybrid certificates or another to assess the readiness of third-party vendors. Workshops, strategy sprints, and executive readouts can be useful touchpoints to sustain alignment. These moments allow teams to share progress, raise blockers, and recalibrate in real time.

9.7 MAKE QUANTUM READINESS PART OF THE CULTURE

Getting support once is not enough. Sustained alignment and adoption require that quantum resilience become embedded in the organization's broader security culture. This transformation goes beyond updating algorithms. It calls for a mindset shift across the enterprise. This involves training development teams on crypto-agile design practices, educating infrastructure teams on protocol transitions, and ensuring that PQC milestones are accurately reflected in product roadmaps and release schedules. It also means reviewing and updating incident response and business continuity plans to account for cryptographic failure scenarios, including how to respond if a post-quantum algorithm is broken or a hybrid configuration is exploited.

Quantum readiness does not live in a single department. Cryptography underpins authentication, data privacy, system integrity, and regulatory compliance. As such, PQC planning touches nearly every part of the business, from customer-facing apps and cloud platforms to procurement, legal, compliance, and even marketing teams working with privacy-sensitive analytics platforms. Success requires coordinated support across these domains. Bring departments and business units together at an early stage. Make space for their input, clarify their responsibilities, and help them understand how their work is affected. The more ownership people feel, the more resilient and distributed your post-quantum effort becomes.

Change of this scale rarely succeeds through technical planning alone. Strong change management practices are essential. That includes creating clear communication plans, aligning changes with department-level KPIs, and building feedback loops into your rollout. Behavioral change takes time. Resistance is often rooted in uncertainty or disruption fatigue, especially when the transformation involves deep technical complexity. Make it easier for teams to participate by giving them what they need: practical guidance, test environments, job-specific training, and clear escalation paths for concerns.

Every strategic transition needs visible champions. Identify individuals throughout the organization who can help carry the message and guide their teams through the changes. These might be engineering managers, compliance officers, product owners, or architects who have both the credibility and the trust of their peers. Support them with tools, resources, and recognition. Provide them with updates they can share, training materials tailored to their roles, and a forum where they can ask questions and share insights.

Finally, remember that buy-in is not just about agreement; it is about ownership. It is one thing for teams to know the plan; it is another for them to see themselves in it and shape it with their input. That is how a cryptographic upgrade becomes something more meaningful: a shared mission to protect the business long-term, and a proof point that security and innovation can move forward together.

9.8 ORGANIZATIONAL CHANGE MANAGEMENT FOR POST-QUANTUM CRYPTOGRAPHY

To succeed, the PQC migration must be managed as an enterprise-wide change initiative, not just an IT project. Organizational Change Management (OCM) is the bridge between technical readiness and operational adoption. Successful OCM ensures that stakeholders understand why change is happening, what is being changed, and how it impacts their work. It builds support across teams, fosters accountability, and reduces resistance. Without this alignment, even the most technically sound migration plan risks stalling in execution due to miscommunication, budgetary friction, or lack of buy-in from key roles.

A critical first step is to create a compelling, non-technical narrative that explains the "why" behind PQC migration. Avoid reducing it to a compliance checkbox or technical upgrade. Instead, link the effort to broader business drivers such as regulatory readiness, long-term data protection, brand trust, and resilience against emerging threats. This narrative should be tailored to each stakeholder group, including executives, legal, compliance, and operations. For executives, frame PQC as a strategic investment that safeguards digital assets, preserves shareholder value, and ensures business continuity in a future where legacy cryptography may fail. For example: "Quantum-resilient infrastructure will become table stakes for investor confidence and competitive differentiation". For legal teams, emphasize the contractual and liability implications of failing to adopt quantum-safe measures – particularly around long-lived data or IP protection clauses. A suitable message might be: "Our contracts assume strong encryption; if that encryption becomes obsolete, so does our legal assurance". For compliance stakeholders, highlight the alignment with evolving regulatory frameworks such as NIST, GDPR, and ISO/IEC standards. You might say: "PQC migration prepares us for upcoming mandates and keeps us ahead of audit and certification expectations". For operations, stress how crypto-agility and quantum readiness reduce the risk of outages, interoperability failures, or future emergency patches. A relevant message could be: "Adopting crypto-agile systems now avoids a rushed, high-risk response later, when legacy cryptography becomes a vulnerability under pressure".

For all groups, a unifying statement might be: "Quantum computing threatens the encryption we rely on for customer data, contracts, and supply chain transactions. Transitioning to post-quantum cryptography isn't just a technology refresh, it's a strategic defense of our digital foundation".

Next, identify the internal stakeholders and change champions who will drive this effort. These may include product managers, developers, infrastructure engineers, PKI owners, legal advisors, and vendor risk leads. Within each group, appoint individuals who can advocate for the migration, raise concerns early, and serve as communication conduits. Empowering these champions helps build credibility and momentum from within.

OCM also requires a well-structured communication plan. Establish a cadence for updates, internal blogs, Q&A sessions, training events, and policy rollouts. Use clear, visual tools to illustrate cryptographic risk and the organization's current state of readiness. It's also important to develop a shared vocabulary, using terms like "crypto-agile", "quantum-vulnerable", and "hybrid secure", to give teams across disciplines a common frame of reference.

Change must be embedded into existing governance processes to gain real traction. Post-quantum milestones should be integrated into enterprise architecture reviews, change control processes, and procurement workflows. This ensures that PQC adoption is not treated as a side project but becomes part of the organization's strategic planning and investment cycle.

Equipping teams with the right training is another essential step. Go beyond surface-level awareness sessions. Developers, for instance, need hands-on training in crypto-agile design patterns and supported libraries. Procurement staff must learn how to assess vendor roadmaps for PQC support. Legal teams should understand contract implications and upcoming regulatory expectations. Deliver this training through multiple formats, including wikis, microlearning modules, and project-specific documentation. Training is a key part of Phase 5, Step 3, Organizational Readiness, and is covered further in Chapter 19.

Recognizing progress and rewarding participation accelerates adoption. Celebrate the first team to implement a PQC-enabled system or to automate short-lived certificate issuance. These early wins reinforce the program's momentum and demonstrate leadership commitment. Recognition programs help foster a sense of ownership and pride across teams.

Of course, some resistance is inevitable. It may stem from technical debt, competing priorities, or fear of introducing instability. Address this head-on by engaging skeptics early and listening to their concerns. Tailored mitigation strategies, such as phased rollouts or additional support for legacy systems, can help ease transitions. Empathy and transparency are essential in maintaining trust throughout the process.

To ensure the program stays on track, establish clear feedback loops and track key performance indicators. Metrics might include the percentage of teams trained on PQC, the percentage of systems with assigned migration plans, or the number of stakeholder groups with designated change champions. After major milestones, hold retrospectives to evaluate what worked, what didn't, and how the strategy should evolve.

A useful example comes from a global manufacturing firm that launched its PQC program with a town hall co-led by the CIO, CISO, and Chief Legal Officer. They positioned PQC as essential to protecting intellectual property, complying with upcoming European mandates, and minimizing supply chain risk. Each department nominated a PQC point of contact, who received tailored onboarding and a quarterly roadmap.

In summary, PQC migration is not just a cryptographic challenge; it is an organizational one. Change management ensures that policies become practice, strategies become action, and teams understand their role in securing the future. Without structured OCM, even the best-laid technical plans risk stalling. With it, organizations gain the alignment, energy, and adaptability needed to future-proof their security posture.

9.9 CONCLUSION

Getting to quantum readiness is more than just updating code or swapping out algorithms. It is about getting people aligned. The real challenge lies in navigating organizational complexity across silos, disciplines, and hierarchies. A cryptographic transformation of this scale demands that security professionals become educators, translators, and coalition builders.

Throughout this chapter, we explored how to lay the foundation for that work. We examined how to brief executive leaders in language that effectively connects cryptographic risk to business impact. We laid out the structure for a Post-Quantum Steering Committee and the role of a dedicated program champion. We discussed the formation of cross-functional task forces and Crypto Centers of Excellence, and how they serve as engines for momentum and coordination. We emphasized the role of culture, noting that lasting buy-in is not about a one-time agreement, but rather ongoing participation and shared accountability.

What makes PQC unique is its reach. It affects everything from procurement and vendor contracts to application architecture and data retention policies. No one person or team can manage that alone. Getting stakeholder engagement right means setting up systems that outlast the kickoff meeting. It means turning initial support into institutional commitment.

In the next chapter, we will continue the planning phase by defining success metrics and setting risk tolerance. These elements are essential for measuring progress, securing funding, and managing uncertainty as your post-quantum program evolves. With the right indicators in place, you will be better equipped to track impact and steer your organization with confidence.

Chapter 10

Success metrics and risk tolerance

Success in post-quantum cryptography requires you to measure whether your organization is making steady, meaningful progress. Without clear metrics, programs drift without a defined risk tolerance, and decision-making stalls. This chapter lays out how to define both.

Every transformation effort needs a compass. In a PQC initiative, that compass is your success metrics. These indicators turn abstract strategies into concrete signals, helping teams answer questions like: Are we moving fast enough? Where are we behind? What is working, and what is not?

Along with defining metrics, organizations must determine their risk tolerance. This starts with understanding which systems hold long-term sensitive data, which are internet-facing, and which lack crypto-agility. These factors determine the acceptable level of residual risk during the migration timeline. Some teams may decide that a non-critical internal system using RSA can be deprioritized for the time being. Others may classify any internet-facing workload without hybrid encryption as unacceptable. These are judgment calls, but they need to be made explicitly, not ad hoc.

Your risk tolerance also defines when escalation is required. For instance, if the number of quantum-vulnerable systems increases over a quarter due to newly discovered dependencies, does that trigger a program review? If a critical vendor is unable to provide PQC support in time, do you pause rollout or isolate them with compensating controls? Codifying thresholds allows risk management to move from opinion-based to process-driven.

Audit readiness is another critical driver. Whether you are subject to PCI, HIPAA, FedRAMP, or internal risk reviews, demonstrating cryptographic control maturity will soon become a table-stakes requirement. That means dashboards, document repositories, and executive briefings must be kept current and accurate. It also means that your metrics need to map back to real policies and controls, not just track activity for its own sake. The rest of this chapter explores how to set the right metrics and tie them to outcomes that truly matter. We begin with a detailed look at tracking mechanisms.

DOI: 10.1201/9781003685760-14

10.1 DEFINING WHAT SUCCESS LOOKS LIKE

Post-quantum cryptography initiatives are complex, long-term transformations that span disciplines, technologies, and timeframes. Without a clear definition of success, these efforts risk becoming endless pilots or disconnected upgrades. Defining success is not about guessing what "good" looks like, but deliberately deciding what outcomes matter most and how you will measure progress toward them.

Start by capturing your current state. This includes identifying the cryptographic protocols in use, the percentage of systems classified as quantum-vulnerable, the presence or absence of crypto-agility, and any known interoperability or vendor readiness issues. Use your cryptographic inventory and prioritization data to create a baseline. This is your starting point.

Whenever possible, risk quantification is your best starting point. The ability to define risk exposure in financial terms, whether as potential losses, regulatory fines, or operational disruptions, provides a more grounded and defensible picture of what success actually looks like. If you can estimate the amount of risk you're buying down, or align cryptographic remediation with specific client requirements, regulatory obligations, or system criticality, you can begin to establish meaningful Key Risk Indicators (KRIs). These strategic measures go beyond technical outcomes to reflect organizational risk posture. In this section, however, we are primarily focused on developing Key Performance Indicators (KPIs) to track tactical progress. More info on how to perform risk quantification and how to develop meaningful KRIs can be found in my book *The CISO 3.0 – A Guide to Next-Generation Security Leadership*, available from CRC Press.

Next, define your desired future state. Think of this as a detailed description of what your organization will look like once it achieves quantum readiness. This may include full migration of externally facing services to post-quantum algorithms, complete implementation of crypto-agility across all new applications, or documented vendor compliance for third-party integrations. These goals should reflect both technical outcomes and business objectives. Ask what level of quantum resistance will give your organization confidence that it can maintain continuity, trust, and compliance in the years ahead. The more specific your future state, the easier it becomes to prioritize actions and measure progress.

From there, define what success looks like. Use both qualitative and quantitative criteria. Qualitatively, success may mean your board has signed off on a roadmap and your application teams understand how to apply hybrid keying. Quantitatively, success might be achieving 75 percent crypto-agility across production systems or reducing the number of quantum-vulnerable APIs by half within 18 months. These success statements should be tailored to your industry, size, and risk profile.

Develop success metrics that are durable and actionable. These should not be one-time statistics, but rather indicators that you can track continuously. Common examples include the number of quantum-vulnerable systems remaining, the number of systems tested with post-quantum cryptography (PQC) algorithms, or the number of vendors under contract who have declared crypto-agility roadmaps. Ensure that your success metrics align with your governance calendar. Use them to inform steering committee meetings, board briefings, and budget discussions.

For example, success may be defined as migrating 95 percent of high-risk systems to PQC within three years. It may include reaching a state where all long-lived data is protected by hybrid or post-quantum encryption. It may even mean completing vendor coordination, system upgrades, and crypto-agility testing within four years. Documenting this definition aligns teams and allows stakeholders to evaluate progress objectively. With a working definition of success in place, determine how it will be measured. Choose KPIs that correspond to your goals, such as the number of post-quantum certificates in use, the reduction in quantum-exposed data, or the number of systems capable of algorithm replacement. These KPIs should be displayed on dashboards, reviewed in governance meetings, and support reporting up to the board or executive sponsors.

The timing for capturing your current and future states should align with the major phases of your migration lifecycle. Ideally, conduct a current-state assessment immediately after completing your cryptographic inventory and use it as the foundation for stakeholder engagement. Set your future state vision just before or in parallel with migration planning, so your goals shape the prioritization. Documenting this journey is critical. Use charts, readiness scorecards, and architectural overviews to show what progress looks like. Share this material broadly. The more people understand what success means and how it will be measured, the more likely they are to contribute to it.

10.1.1 Define success for testing

Proof-of-concept testing is often where quantum readiness efforts gain or lose credibility. Yet too often, testing is informal and unbounded. To make testing meaningful, it must be deliberate, focused, and tied to clear outcomes.

Mature IT organizations should already have established testing processes for new deployments, whether through DevOps pipelines, release management playbooks, or formal QA environments. If such processes exist, they should be leveraged and adapted to address quantum-specific concerns. This not only ensures consistency and operational alignment but also accelerates time-to-validation by integrating quantum testing into existing governance and tooling frameworks.

Begin by defining the success criteria for each test cycle. These criteria should be based on what you are trying to learn or validate. For example, success for a hybrid key exchange test might mean completing a TLS handshake using Kyber in combination with RSA across three browser environments. For a certificate validation test, it may mean successfully issuing, deploying, and rotating a post-quantum certificate through an existing identity provider.

Establish your testing scope, set pass/fail criteria, and specific performance thresholds before you begin. Identify the systems, applications, or libraries that will be tested and explain why. Include a rationale, like "these services support critical customer transactions and rely on RSA-2048", or "this component sits between internal services and handles encrypted API traffic". Document both functional and performance goals. Are you testing for successful handshakes? Acceptable latency under load? Graceful fallback behavior? Use test plans with defined start and end points, and avoid allowing pilot environments to drift into a permanent state of limbo. Don't let testing become an exploratory exercise with no end. For example, a successful proof of concept might demonstrate that a PQC-enabled VPN can establish stable tunnels using hybrid key exchanges across modern and legacy endpoints, with no more than 10 percent performance degradation and full interoperability with current logging and monitoring tools.

Define what constitutes a pass, what triggers additional investigation, and what stops a test from proceeding to production. Track test completion and results using defined metrics. These might include time-to-handshake, encryption overhead, or test coverage across your critical service map. Store logs, outputs, and results in a central repository with version control. This enables traceability for audits and simplifies debugging when issues arise. You should also set organizational criteria for ending testing and moving forward. For instance, you might decide that 95 percent of services must pass PQC integration tests with zero-impact rollbacks before migration begins, or that all critical paths through your application stack must be crypto-agile in staging before a new release can go live. Once those outcomes are achieved, the pilot can be declared complete, the results documented, and the lessons folded into the broader deployment plan.

The goal is to uncover brittle areas in your environment, highlight gaps in documentation, and expose vendor dependencies that could slow your progress. Defining success clearly helps avoid endless cycles of "almost working" and instead gives you actionable proof that your migration is real, measurable, and repeatable. When teams know what success looks like, they are more likely to build toward it, test for it, and deliver it.

10.2 TRACK PROGRESS WITH METRICS AND KPIS

PQC Migration is a cross-functional, time-bound effort that requires planning discipline, stakeholder alignment, and measurable progress. As with any transformation initiative, success depends on knowing where you are, where you're going, and how you will know when you've arrived.

To support this visibility, organizations should define and implement a clear set of metrics and key performance indicators (KPIs) that align with their quantum migration strategy. These indicators should not only track deployment outcomes but also monitor the progress of planning, testing, remediation, and risk reduction activities.

Metrics should be developed early in the program, ideally during the planning phase, and refined throughout the lifecycle of the migration effort. Start with baseline measurements immediately following the initial cryptographic inventory. As prioritization models are built and test plans are implemented, extend your metrics to cover planning progress, testing coverage, and stakeholder engagement. Regularly scheduled governance meetings or quarterly security reviews offer natural checkpoints to introduce or update KPIs. Dashboards and reports should be accessible to technical leads, compliance officers, and executives alike. Effective metrics are specific, measurable, and actionable. They should reflect real change, not just activity. Use a combination of lagging indicators (e.g., systems remediated) and leading indicators (e.g., tests completed or plans approved) to maintain balance. Group metrics into categories aligned with your program milestones, here are some examles.

10.2.1 Planning and policy metrics

- Percentage of systems with assigned quantum readiness labels
- Number of applications with formal remediation plans in place
- Coverage of exception handling framework (e.g., how many assets have open exceptions)
- Percentage of critical systems with defined migration timelines

10.2.2 Testing and validation metrics

- Number of test cases executed for PQC algorithms
- Percentage of systems tested for crypto-agility
- Number of successful end-to-end PQC tests (e.g., encrypted transmission, certificate validation)
- Test coverage of hybrid configurations across critical services
- Number of interoperability issues identified and resolved

10.2.3 Deployment and remediation metrics

- Percentage of quantum-vulnerable systems migrated
- Number of PQC-ready applications in production
- Percentage of applications supporting dynamic algorithm switching
- Number of legacy cryptographic libraries removed or replaced

- Reduction in average time to update or swap crypto configurations (a measure of improved agility)

10.2.4 Risk and exposure metrics

- Total number of known quantum-vulnerable systems
- Change in aggregate risk score across prioritized systems
- Estimated volume of data still exposed to long-term decryption risk
- Number of systems exposed to Harvest Now, Decrypt Later scenarios

10.2.5 Examples in practice

If your migration roadmap includes transitioning VPN tunnels to quantum-safe key exchanges, track the number of VPN concentrators upgraded to RFC 8784 or RFC 9370-compliant implementations. If your test plan includes evaluating PQC in mobile applications, log the number of apps that successfully validate post-quantum certificates or complete a hybrid key handshake.

For organizations using tools from vendors like Sandbox AQ, IBM, or ISARA, these platforms often include built-in dashboards that automatically track readiness states, crypto-agility scores, and algorithm usage trends. Integrating these dashboards into your enterprise risk platform allows for unified reporting across both classical and quantum risk dimensions.

Build dashboards that speak to the needs of each audience. Your technical teams will want detailed timelines and system-level tracking, while executives and board members are better served by high-level scorecards, trendlines, and heatmaps that highlight business impact, risk reduction, and overall strategic progress.

For example, a color-coded heatmap showing the quantum vulnerability status of business-critical services can drive urgency and accountability in leadership discussions. A dashboard that flags systems without assigned owners, overdue testing phases, or open exceptions can help program managers unblock stalled efforts before they impact timelines.

KPIs shouldn't exist in a vacuum. They need to be connected to real decision-making, whether that's funding discussions, planning meetings, or performance reviews. Use them to flag roadblocks, guide resource allocation, and make sure teams stay on the hook for hitting key milestones. When done right, metrics don't just measure progress; they help drive it.

10.3 INCORPORATING KEY RISK INDICATORS (KRIs)

While Key Performance Indicators (KPIs) help you track activity and execution,such as the number of systems migrated or tests completed. Key Risk Indicators (KRIs) help you monitor your exposure to potential failure.

In short, KPIs measure what you're doing, while KRIs measure what might go wrong.

KRIs are proactive. They offer early warning signs that your program may be drifting into unacceptable risk territory. Where KPIs assess delivery progress, KRIs assess the program's risk posture and its alignment with business, legal, and security thresholds.

Both are necessary for a successful PQC initiative. KPIs ensure projects move forward, but without KRIs, you may move in the wrong direction, miss risk blind spots, or become overly focused on activity without understanding residual exposure.

Understanding your audience is essential when designing and using these indicators. KPIs are primarily designed for program managers, technical leads, and engineers. These stakeholders use KPIs to guide day-to-day activities, track project velocity, and support tactical decision-making. KRIs, on the other hand, are aimed at CISOs, CIOs, risk officers, internal audit teams, compliance leaders, and the board. These audiences need to understand how much risk remains in the system, whether exposure is decreasing fast enough, and if any established risk thresholds are being breached. By using both KPIs and KRIs, you create a complete picture: KPIs show whether the work is getting done, and KRIs reveal whether the right risks are being reduced.

Post-quantum cryptography is a risk-driven transformation. The need to migrate isn't motivated by efficiency or short-term ROI—it's driven by exposure to future decryption threats, reliance on vulnerable vendors, and the need to comply with regulatory expectations. As such, the ability to measure and communicate risk reduction is just as important as tracking technical progress. KRIs provide visibility into the pace of risk reduction, areas where exposure is not falling fast enough, when residual risk exceeds agreed-upon thresholds, and the likelihood of failure due to missed dependencies or stalled vendors. They allow organizations to identify when tolerable risk becomes intolerable and act accordingly. These insights help CISOs and executives prioritize resources, escalate decisions, and make timely corrections before security or compliance is compromised.

To develop effective PQC-related KRIs, you must begin with your defined risk tolerances. Review the boundaries your organization has set for acceptable risk. For example, "no customer-facing system should lack crypto-agility after Q3". These thresholds become the starting point for KRI development. Next, identify high-impact failure scenarios. These may include a missed migration milestone for a critical system, a vendor failing to meet crypto-agile contract requirements, or a spike in exposed long-term data. From there, define observable indicators that reflect these scenarios. Look for signs of negative trends, stagnation, or regression. For instance, you might track the number of newly discovered quantum-vulnerable systems as a leading signal of exposure. You can find KRI development examples in Table 10.1.

Table 10.1 KRI examples

KRI	*Description*	*Threshold Example*
% of business-critical systems lacking crypto-agility	Measures residual exposure in high-priority services	Trigger if >10% after Year 2
Number of high-risk vendors without a PQC roadmap	Tracks third-party risk related to cryptographic dependency	Trigger if 2 or more Tier 1 vendors remain noncompliant
Change in quantum-vulnerable data volume	Measures the amount of sensitive data still exposed to long-term decryption risk	Trigger if reduction trend stalls for more than 2 quarters
% of cryptographic exceptions past remediation date	Identifies where compensating controls have become indefinite	Trigger if >15% of exceptions go overdue
Average time to escalate and resolve cryptographic findings	Assesses how fast the organization addresses known risks	Trigger if average resolution time exceeds 90 days
% of migration milestones delayed beyond tolerance window	Tracks schedule reliability against critical migration targets	Trigger if more than 25% of tasks are 30+ days behind

Each KRI must have an assigned owner and a documented escalation path. This ensures accountability and responsiveness. It doesn't matter if your KRIs are based on FAIR, NIST RMF, COSO, or ISO 27005, integrating them into your broader enterprise risk management framework strengthens your governance and alignment.

10.3.1 Examples of KRIs for PQC

You may also track changes in the volume of quantum-vulnerable data over time. If the amount of sensitive, long-lived data exposed to outdated algorithms fails to decline quarter over quarter, it suggests that risk is stagnating rather than falling. Similarly, you can measure the percentage of cryptographic exceptions that remain unresolved past their remediation deadlines. If more than 15 percent of exceptions are overdue, it may reflect governance breakdowns or resourcing issues. Another KRI could focus on operational responsiveness, such as the average time required to escalate and resolve cryptographic findings. If this time regularly exceeds ninety days, it points to systemic friction in the decision-making process.

You might also assess deployment risk by tracking the percentage of migration milestones delayed beyond their acceptable time window. For instance, if more than 25 percent of key activities are thirty or more days behind schedule, it may indicate under-resourcing, technical bottlenecks, or stakeholder disengagement.

By integrating KRIs with your existing KPI tracking, steering committee processes, and executive dashboards, you give leadership the ability to make informed decisions about prioritization, resource reallocation, and vendor strategy. KRIs keep the program grounded, not just in what is being done, but in how well the organization is being protected as those activities unfold. As your post-quantum roadmap moves from planning to execution, these indicators will help guide which systems are ready to advance, which need reassessment, and where risk exposure must be addressed before momentum can resume.

10.4 ESTABLISHING RISK TOLERANCE FOR PQC

Every security program must draw a line between acceptable and unacceptable risk. In post-quantum cryptography, that line can be difficult to place. The timeline of the threat is uncertain, the attack vectors are abstract, and the technologies are still evolving. The good news is that defining risk tolerance doesn't require perfect data; it only requires you to set boundaries that reflect your business priorities, compliance obligations, and operational realities.

To begin, identify the categories of risk that your PQC program will need to manage. These typically include long-term data exposure, a lack of crypto-agility, vendor readiness issues, and deployment delays. For each of these categories, establish what levels of risk are acceptable during different phases of the migration. For example, you might accept that 30 percent of internal systems remain quantum-vulnerable in year one, but expect that number to drop below 10 percent by year two. Alternatively, you may decide that any customer-facing system without crypto-agility is considered a red flag, regardless of the timeline.

Use existing frameworks like FAIR or your enterprise risk management model to quantify these tolerances. If FAIR is already used to estimate cyber risk in financial terms, incorporate PQC scenarios into those calculations. How much would it cost to remediate a breach involving long-lived encrypted records? What would be the impact of a vendor failing to meet crypto-agile contract requirements? Converting abstract risk into financial terms makes it easier to communicate and justify thresholds.

Once your tolerances are defined, document them in a risk register or program charter. Make them visible to stakeholders. These boundaries should not just live in the minds of technical leads. They should be written down, reviewed periodically, and tied to escalation procedures. If an upgrade milestone is missed or a critical vendor is noncompliant, the documented tolerance helps determine whether to pause, escalate, or continue with compensating controls.

Design your metrics to reflect these tolerances. For example, if you decide that no more than five percent of your high-priority systems should lack crypto-agility by Q3, create a KPI that tracks this percentage on a weekly basis. If you decide that any system storing data with a retention period over ten years must migrate to PQC by 2026, track the number of systems that meet that threshold each quarter.

Deployment risk should also be monitored. Track metrics such as delay variance in rollout schedules, the number of failed PQC integrations, or the percentage of deployments requiring rollback. These help ensure that program velocity is not coming at the cost of quality.

By turning your risk tolerances into measurable, visible indicators, you create guardrails that keep your program aligned with business intent. You also enable faster decision-making when things do not go as planned. Rather than debating whether a delay is serious, teams can compare it to the agreed threshold and respond accordingly. Ultimately, risk tolerance is what allows a migration roadmap to stay flexible without becoming directionless. It is what helps translate uncertainty into action.

10.4.1 PQC risk tolerance assessment questionnaire

To guide your organization in establishing formal risk boundaries for post-quantum cryptography, use the following questions to facilitate executive and cross-functional dialogue. These prompts are designed to assess your organization's tolerance for cryptographic exposure, vendor dependency, remediation pace, and operational risk during the PQC migration lifecycle.

Data sensitivity and long-term risk

1. What categories of data do we consider sensitive for more than 5, 10, or 20 years?
2. Are we willing to tolerate any quantum-vulnerable encryption for long-lived data assets? If so, for how long?
3. What retention period triggers a requirement for hybrid or PQC encryption by default?

Crypto-agility and internal readiness

1. What percentage of our systems must support dynamic algorithm replacement (crypto-agility) by the end of each fiscal year?
2. How much residual quantum-vulnerable infrastructure are we willing to accept in:
   - Internal systems?
   - Internet-facing systems?
   - Third-party hosted systems?

3. Are there any business units or use cases that we consider exempt from PQC requirements? If so, why?

Vendor dependency and supply chain exposure

1. What percentage of our critical vendors must have a documented PQC roadmap by the end of the year?
2. How long are we willing to rely on third parties that do not support hybrid or post-quantum cryptography?
3. What triggers escalation or replacement of a vendor that cannot meet PQC expectations?

Deployment and integration risk

1. What level of migration delay (in days or percent deviation) is considered acceptable for:
   - High-priority systems?
   - Medium-priority systems?
2. How many failed PQC integrations or rollbacks are tolerable per quarter?
3. What is the maximum acceptable window for running outdated cryptographic libraries in production before escalation?

Compliance and strategic alignment

1. Which regulatory, audit, or contractual requirements impose mandatory PQC milestones? How closely must we align to them?
2. Are we willing to accept residual risk if full PQC migration would delay other business objectives? If so, under what conditions?
3. Who has final authority to approve risk acceptance or compensating controls when thresholds are exceeded?

Financial risk

1. What is the maximum annual budget our organization is willing to allocate toward PQC migration efforts, including tooling, vendor support, and staff resources?
2. What level of unexpected cost overrun (as a percentage of the original PQC program budget) would require executive-level review or formal reauthorization?
3. How much financial exposure (e.g., through fines, breach-related costs, or reputational damage) from quantum-vulnerable cryptography would our leadership consider acceptable over the next 3 to 5 years?

4. Are we willing to delay or reallocate funding from other cybersecurity initiatives to accelerate PQC readiness if the threat timeline shortens or regulatory requirements tighten unexpectedly?

Responses to this questionnaire should be discussed in risk committee meetings, reviewed alongside your enterprise risk register, and formally documented as part of the PQC program charter or risk governance model. By defining and socializing these boundaries early, you equip your organization to respond with discipline when quantum-related risks materialize. You also ensure your migration roadmap reflects not just technology goals, but strategic intent.

10.5 METRIC EVOLUTION

As your PQC program matures, so too must your success metrics. What is meaningful in early phases may no longer provide actionable insight during later stages. Metrics must evolve in parallel with your program lifecycle, transitioning from discovery and planning to implementation and long-term sustenance.

In the Discovery Phase, the focus is on understanding the current state. Relevant metrics include the percentage of cryptographic assets inventoried, the percentage of systems labeled by risk category (e.g., internet-facing, long-lived data, legacy protocols), and the number of critical systems dependent on quantum-vulnerable algorithms. These KPIs give visibility into scope and provide a foundation for prioritization.

In the Planning Phase, metrics should shift toward preparedness. Track the percentage of systems with remediation plans, the number of applications mapped to migration timelines, the breadth of crypto-agility assessments, and test coverage rates across prioritized systems. KRIs in this phase might highlight planning delays, exceptions without timelines, or gaps in vendor disclosures.

In the Implementation Phase, execution takes center stage. Metrics include the percentage of systems migrated to PQC or hybrid configurations, the number of successful end-to-end PQC handshakes, and the rate of vendor upgrades completed. KRIs may track the number of rollout failures, schedule variance beyond agreed tolerances, or the emergence of previously undiscovered quantum-vulnerable services.

In the Sustainment Phase, attention turns to maintaining posture. Metrics should reflect adherence to ongoing crypto hygiene, such as the percentage of systems with crypto-agility features enabled, the frequency and success rate of certificate rotations, and the number of systems participating in continuous algorithm scanning. KRIs might include increases in overdue crypto upgrades, missed certificate expiration dates, or regression in vendor compliance.

Adjusting your metrics as the program progresses ensures that success remains visible and relevant. For example, in discovery, success may be defined as achieving 100 percent cryptographic asset visibility. In sustainment, success may be defined as ensuring all newly deployed systems support crypto-agility by default. Similarly, a KRI focused on third-party roadmap disclosure in the planning phase might evolve into one tracking SLA adherence in the sustainment phase.

These evolving indicators help executives and program managers anticipate what success looks like at each step. They also enable better forecasting, resource allocation, and accountability. Metrics should not be static; they should mirror the maturity and focus of your program over time.

10.6 CONCLUSION

Defining success and setting risk tolerance are the anchors of any well-run transformation. Without them, programs chase activity instead of outcomes. With them, teams can track progress, make tradeoffs with clarity, and course-correct with confidence. This chapter provided the tools to do both.

Success is not a static target. It evolves in tandem with your strategy, tools, and risk landscape. Unless it is defined, both at the enterprise level and within your proof-of-concept labs, it remains impossible to measure or replicate. Whether your goal is migrating a percentage of systems, reducing quantum exposure, or achieving crypto-agility across the board, success must be visible, documented, and understood across teams.

The same applies to risk tolerance. Post-quantum cryptography carries uncertainty. That is unavoidable, but uncertainty does not mean indecision. When you clarify your appetite for delay, for exposure, or dependency on legacy vendors, you gain the ability to act with discipline rather than react out of urgency.

By combining clearly defined metrics with an explicit tolerance for residual risk, your PQC initiative becomes more than a list of tasks. It becomes a measurable, managed program, one that can withstand change, meet compliance demands, and earn stakeholder trust.

In the next chapter, we move from planning to execution. Section IV begins with a detailed look at how to replace vulnerable algorithms across your environment. You will explore practical strategies for implementing post-quantum replacements for RSA, Diffie-Hellman, ECC, and SHA-1, as well as how to integrate hybrid certificates and dual-stack cryptography into existing systems. From TLS and VPN tunnels to code signing and public APIs, the chapter will walk through real-world applications and standards, such as RFC 8784, RFC 9242, and RFC 937, that enable quantum-resistant configurations. This is where your roadmap becomes real, and migration begins in earnest.

Section IV

Phase 3

Implementation

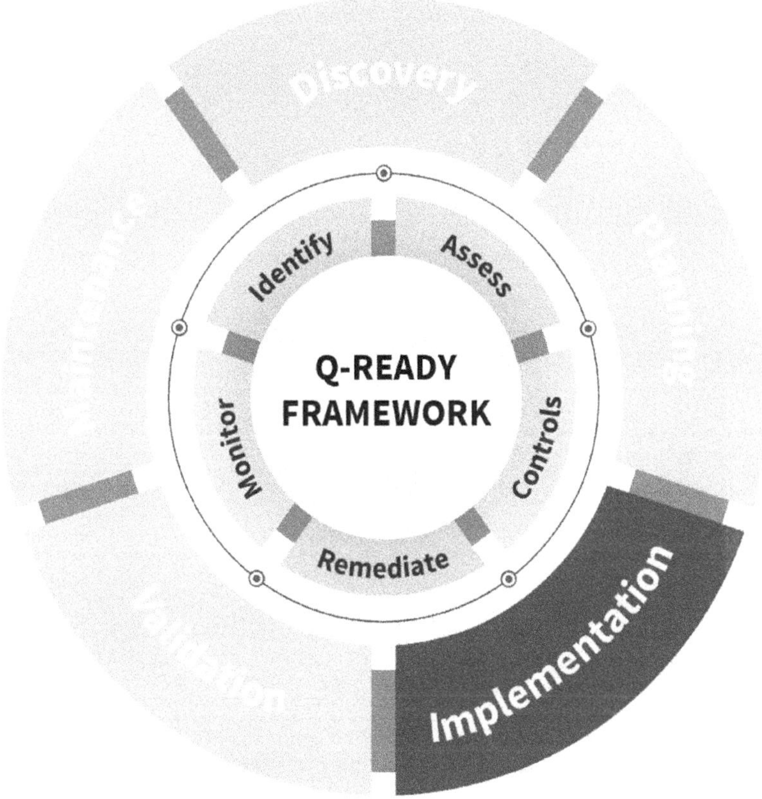

Figure SIV.1 Implementation phase.

DOI: 10.1201/9781003685760-15

Chapter 11

Replacing vulnerable algorithms

Cryptographic algorithms like RSA, Diffie-Hellman, ECC, and SHA-1, which have long formed the foundation of digital security, are now at risk from quantum-enabled adversaries. This chapter focuses on replacing vulnerable algorithms with quantum-safe alternatives across critical systems, including TLS, VPNs, code signing, and APIs. It also addresses the transition path through hybrid certificates and dual stacks, providing practical guidance on how and when to implement them.

11.1 FROM CLASSICAL TO QUANTUM-SAFE: WHAT NEEDS REPLACING

RSA, Diffie-Hellman, and elliptic curve cryptography all rely on mathematical problems that quantum computers are expected to solve with ease. Using Shor's Algorithm, a sufficiently powerful quantum machine could factor large integers and compute discrete logarithms, breaking the security guarantees these algorithms provide.

The same applies to SHA-1, which has been deprecated for years due to its known weaknesses, yet it still appears in legacy systems. While Grover's Algorithm only offers a quadratic speedup against hash functions, it still means the effective bit strength of even SHA-128 is probably too low for a post-quantum world.

The replacements are now established. NIST's selection of Kyber for key exchange and Dilithium and Falcon for digital signatures lays the groundwork for future-proofed implementations. However, rolling out these algorithms at scale involves far more than updating a single library.

11.1.1 Understanding NIST-standardized post-quantum cryptography

Post-quantum cryptography (PQC), also referred to as quantum-resistant cryptography (QRC), encompasses cryptographic algorithms that are believed to be secure against both classical and quantum adversaries. These

DOI: 10.1201/9781003685760-16

new methods have been developed to counter the unique threats posed by quantum computers, particularly the threat of Shor's Algorithm to break traditional public-key systems, such as RSA, Diffie-Hellman, and elliptic-curve cryptography.

In 2022, the National Institute of Standards and Technology (NIST) began the process of selecting and standardizing a new generation of quantum-resistant cryptographic algorithms. After years of global collaboration and extensive testing, NIST released its initial set of recommendations. In late 2024, NIST finalized and announced the Module-Lattice-Based Digital Signature Standard, marking a significant milestone in the evolution of cryptography.

Most of the selected algorithms are built on lattice-based cryptography, a field that has garnered attention for its potential to remain secure even in the presence of quantum computing. In the context of cryptography, a lattice refers to a grid-like structure of points in multidimensional space, formed by all linear combinations of a basis of vectors with integer coefficients. To imagine a lattice, think of a three-dimensional city grid, but extended into many more dimensions. Each point is like an intersection where multiple streets meet, and the challenge lies in figuring out the shortest path between distant points or identifying which intersection you started from, given only your destination. These problems become extraordinarily difficult as the number of dimensions increases. The security of lattice-based schemes hinges on the assumed hardness of these mathematical puzzles, which have been studied for decades without efficient solutions, even on quantum machines. Unlike RSA or elliptic-curve methods, lattice-based algorithms appear to resist known quantum attacks. They also tend to support a wide range of cryptographic functions, including encryption, signatures, and key exchange, which makes them especially versatile.

11.1.2 Leading post-quantum algorithms

CRYSTALS-Kyber

Kyber is a key encapsulation mechanism (KEM) that supports encryption and is used for establishing secure keys in a quantum-safe manner. It is efficient and well-suited for high-performance environments. Kyber is expected to be widely deployed in secure TLS configurations and VPN protocols where quantum-safe key exchange is essential.

CRYSTALS-Dilithium

Dilithium is a lattice-based digital signature algorithm known for its speed and relatively small signature sizes. It is particularly effective in server and embedded contexts, where both performance and memory efficiency are important.

Falcon
Falcon is another digital signature algorithm, selected for its compact key and signature sizes. While more challenging to implement securely, Falcon offers strong performance benefits in constrained environments where size is critical.

SPHINCS+
Unlike Kyber and Dilithium, SPHINCS+ is a hash-based signature scheme. It offers strong theoretical security guarantees but comes with larger signatures and slower performance. Its inclusion in the NIST suite provides a non-lattice-based option, useful as a fallback if lattice assumptions are ever challenged.

Classic McEliece
Classic McEliece is a code-based encryption scheme that has resisted cryptanalysis for decades. Its large public keys limit its practicality for certain applications, but it remains an important hedge in the overall portfolio due to its fundamentally different structure.

NTRU
An alternative lattice-based KEM, NTRU, is also part of the NIST portfolio. It offers similar security properties to Kyber with a distinct mathematical foundation. NTRU is often favored for its resilience and historical pedigree.

These algorithms are not just theoretical constructs. They have undergone extensive rounds of academic review and real-world testing. However, the cryptographic community acknowledges that it may take five to ten years of operational deployment, attempted exploitation, and continued refinement before confidence in the long-term resilience of these algorithms is fully established. Which is why crypto-agility is so important.

Organizations should monitor the ongoing work from the IETF and industry standards bodies as they finalize support for post-quantum integration in protocols like TLS, X.509 certificates, and PKCS#11. At the same time, deployment should begin now through hybrid configurations and dual stacks, even as the ecosystem around these algorithms continues to mature. By embracing the NIST PQC standards today, organizations can position themselves to meet the security demands of tomorrow on their own terms, rather than in reaction to a breach.

11.2 TRANSPORT PROTOCOL SECURITY

Transport protocols such as TLS and VPNs are central to the security posture of modern organizations. They protect the integrity and confidentiality of data in motion, whether that data is moving across a public website, within internal APIs, or through encrypted tunnels like IPsec and OpenVPN. However, these protections are only as strong as the cryptographic foundations upon which they are built. Traditional protocols rely on asymmetric algorithms, such as RSA and ECDH, for key exchange and authentication, methods that are vulnerable to quantum attacks. Once quantum computers mature, the handshake mechanisms that secure today's encrypted traffic could be retroactively broken.

Organizations must begin upgrading their transport protocols to include quantum-resistant capabilities. This means moving away from outdated TLS versions, adopting hybrid key exchange algorithms, and preparing for the eventual support of post-quantum digital signatures. TLS and VPN upgrades should be coordinated across endpoint infrastructure, application delivery networks, and certificate management processes to ensure seamless integration. These updates must align with vendor readiness and pending standards from IETF and NIST.

11.2.1 TLS security

Transport Layer Security (TLS) is the protocol responsible for encrypting a vast portion of internet traffic. It secures browser connections, API requests, mobile apps, and internal communication across cloud services and enterprise environments. As such, TLS is one of the most critical components to modernize for post-quantum readiness.

The first requirement for post-quantum TLS is the adoption of TLS 1.3. This version streamlines the handshake process, removes vulnerable algorithms, and supports the integration of hybrid key exchange mechanisms. TLS 1.2 and earlier versions lack the extensibility and structural efficiency required to support PQC methods. Any organization still using TLS 1.2 should prioritize this migration as a foundational prerequisite.

Post-quantum TLS upgrades center on replacing vulnerable key exchange algorithms with hybrid approaches that combine classical and quantum-safe algorithms. Kyber, NIST's selected key encapsulation mechanism, is now supported in OpenSSL and BoringSSL through contributions from the Open Quantum Safe project. These libraries allow organizations to prototype and deploy hybrid TLS configurations today, even as the IETF finalizes formal integration standards. Vendors like ISARA provide enterprise-grade tools for managing these transitions.

Equally important is client-side support, particularly in web browsers. Server-side upgrades alone are not sufficient – if the user's browser does not support hybrid handshakes or post-quantum extensions, the connection will fall back to classical cryptography. As of today, mainstream browsers like Chrome and Firefox do not yet support PQC-enabled TLS handshakes out of the box. However, experimental builds and developer tools from projects like Open Quantum Safe (e.g., oqs-client) allow organizations to test client-server interoperability with hybrid key exchanges.

Organizations should begin validating browser compatibility in controlled environments. This includes using test clients that simulate browser behavior, monitoring for handshake fallbacks, and checking which curve negotiation options are accepted. For enterprise-controlled environments, such as managed desktops or kiosk systems, IT teams can selectively deploy browsers or browser extensions that support PQC-aware cipher suites for high-sensitivity applications. In the long run, client support will depend on upstream integration from browser vendors, so tracking development roadmaps from Google, Mozilla, Microsoft, and Apple is important.

Until full browser support becomes standard, PQC implementations should focus on dual-stack resilience, ensuring that PQC is used where supported but classical handshakes remain functional for clients that are not yet quantum-ready. Logging handshake behavior and negotiating cipher preferences can help measure real-world client adoption and inform future enforcement policies.

11.2.2 Step-by-step: how to upgrade TLS for post-quantum readiness

Step 1: Assess and inventory TLS usage
Begin by identifying all systems, services, and applications that rely on TLS for secure communication. This includes web servers, load balancers, internal APIs, microservices, and embedded devices. Document the current TLS version in use, supported cipher suites, and certificate sources. This should be done during Phase 1 – Discovery/Step 1 – Inventory as discussed in Chapter 5.

Step 2: Upgrade to TLS 1.3
Transition every eligible system to TLS 1.3. Most modern operating systems, including recent versions of Linux, Windows Server, and cloud-hosted infrastructure, support TLS 1.3 natively. This transition removes outdated cryptographic mechanisms and enables hybrid key exchange extensions required for PQC.

Step 3: Integrate hybrid key exchange
Implement TLS 1.3 hybrid key exchange using libraries that support quantum-safe cryptography. OpenSSL 3.0 with the Open Quantum Safe fork or BoringSSL with PQC patches enables Kyber integration alongside ECDH. These configurations allow dual key exchanges: classical for compatibility and Kyber for quantum resistance.

11.2.2.1 Example configuration with OpenSSL (simplified)

```
scss
CopyEdit
SSL_CTX_set_cipher_list(ctx, "TLS_AES_256_GCM_SHA384:TLS_CH
ACHA20_POLY1305_SHA256");
SSL_CTX_set1_curves_list(ctx, "X25519:kyber512");
```

Step 4: Replace or reissue certificates
Update certificates to hybrid or quantum-safe versions where supported. Vendors like DigiCert offer hybrid certificates that bundle classical and post-quantum signatures. Although Windows TLS stacks are not yet fully integrated with these standards, test environments using OpenSSL and nginx or Apache can validate early configurations.

Step 5: Update certificate lifecycle and monitoring
Adjust your certificate lifecycle management to accommodate PQC. This includes ensuring visibility into expiration, renewal automation, and compliance logging for hybrid certificate use. Tools like Venafi, Keyfactor, and AppviewX are beginning to support PQC and can provide centralized visibility across environments. This topic is discussed further in Chapter 18.

Step 6: Validate and monitor
Conduct penetration testing and monitoring against your updated TLS infrastructure. Validate hybrid handshakes using test clients, such as OpenSSL's s_client, or browser-based inspection tools. Ensure that logs and metrics accurately reflect the use of the handshake algorithm, key sizes, and certificate paths.

TLS upgrades should begin in internet-facing systems, especially those serving login pages, APIs, or sensitive customer data. Domains at the top-level (TLD) such as *.com, *.bank, *.gov, or any handling long-lived data like financial records, health data, or intellectual property should be prioritized. These systems face the highest risk from quantum-enabled adversaries and are the most likely targets for harvesting. Internal environments, especially microservices and legacy applications, should follow closely once TLS 1.3 is broadly adopted. Hybrid key exchanges can bridge compatibility gaps while laying the foundation for future upgrades.

11.2.2.2 Example of TLD remediation

An e-commerce company operating under www.retailsecure.com could begin by:

- Migrating all edge TLS termination at their content delivery network (CDN) to TLS 1.3.

- Replacing their current certificate with a hybrid certificate from a vendor like Digicert.
- Deploying OpenSSL 3.0 in their application servers with Kyber-enabled cipher suites.
- Verifying handshake behavior in Chrome and Firefox, ensuring compatibility and fallback paths.
- Monitoring for errors, handshake renegotiation issues, or performance degradation.

By approaching TLS upgrades as a structured rollout rather than a one-time patch, organizations can strengthen their cryptographic posture while maintaining availability and performance. PQC in TLS is not a hypothetical future; it is a near-term necessity that can and should begin today.

11.2.3 VPN security

For virtual private networks, the primary vulnerability does not lie in the encryption algorithm used to protect the data stream itself, but in how the encryption keys are exchanged. Most VPNs today rely on asymmetric key exchange mechanisms such as Diffie-Hellman (DH) or Elliptic Curve Diffie-Hellman (ECDH). These methods have served well in the classical era, but quantum computing, through Shor's Algorithm, threatens to break them entirely. If an attacker records today's encrypted key exchanges, they could decrypt them later once quantum capabilities become available. This is the heart of the "Harvest Now, Decrypt Later" threat.

A VPN tunnel is a secure, encrypted connection between two endpoints, typically between a user's device and a private network, or between two networks across the public internet. The tunnel acts like a private conduit through which data travels, shielding it from external visibility or interception. It encapsulates, encrypts, and routes traffic securely, making it appear as though the remote device is operating within the local network. Tunnels are typically established using protocols such as IPsec or SSL/TLS, in combination with Internet Key Exchange (IKE), for negotiating encryption keys.

While TLS also encrypts data in transit, it typically protects individual sessions between browsers, apps, and servers. VPN tunnels, by contrast, secure all traffic at the network layer, often including DNS queries, application data, and other traffic not directly controlled by the user. This makes VPNs essential for protecting traffic across untrusted networks, such as public Wi-Fi, or for enabling secure remote access to internal systems. VPN tunnels are especially useful in corporate environments where full network-level encryption and access control are needed.

Fortunately, symmetric encryption algorithms such as AES and hash functions like SHA-384 are not broken in the same way by quantum attacks. Grover's Algorithm weakens their effective security by roughly half, but they remain viable if key sizes are increased. For this reason, it is critical that organizations using VPNs immediately transition to AES-256 for encryption and SHA-384 or higher for hashing. If your current VPN configuration still relies on 128-bit AES or any use of SHA-1 or MD5, you are exposing yourself to unnecessary risk.

To move toward a post-quantum VPN posture, you must address the key exchange layer. NIST's chosen replacement, Kyber, is the lattice-based key encapsulation mechanism (KEM) choice for this. Several emerging standards define how Kyber and similar mechanisms can be integrated into VPN protocols. Chief among them are:

RFC 8784: Post-quantum IKEv2 with Hybrid Key Exchange
This RFC outlines how to perform IKEv2 key exchanges using both classical and post-quantum algorithms in tandem. It allows VPNs to negotiate dual key pairs, providing backward compatibility while adding quantum-resistant protection.

RFC 9242: More Efficient Hybrid Key Exchange
Building on RFC 8784, this specification introduces performance improvements to hybrid exchanges by optimizing how the cryptographic materials are structured and transmitted. It also simplifies interoperability across vendor platforms.

RFC 9370: Guidance for Secure Deployment of Hybrid Key Exchange in IKEv2
This document provides deployment best practices, guidance on fallback mechanisms, and recommendations for securing the post-quantum portion of hybrid negotiations. It helps reduce implementation risk and increases the resilience of the overall key agreement.

These standards are critical to transitioning existing VPN infrastructure toward quantum resistance. And they are ready for adoption today.

Here are several steps you can take immediately to harden your VPN connections and begin preparing for post-quantum migration:

1. Adopt Suite B GCM-based cipher suites using AES-256, as defined in RFC 6379. This ensures strong encryption that holds up even under Grover's Algorithm.
2. Replace any 2048-bit RSA VPN certificates with 4096-bit equivalents. While still classical, these longer keys provide greater resistance to brute-force attacks in the interim.
3. Ensure all hashing functions used for integrity and signing are at least SHA-384. Retire SHA-1 and MD5 completely.
4. Begin implementing RFCs 8784, 9242, and 9370 to support hybrid key exchanges in your IKEv2 configurations.

5. Review all TLS connections and upgrade them to TLS 1.3 with Perfect Forward Secrecy (PFS) ciphers. Pair them with hardened VPN tunnels and support them with up-to-date certificate management tools.

11.2.4 Updating IKE to quantum-safe key exchange

The Internet Key Exchange (IKE) protocol, particularly IKEv2, is responsible for negotiating secure parameters between VPN clients and gateways. To upgrade IKE for post-quantum security, follow these steps:

Step 1: Adopt post-quantum key exchange mechanisms
Replace traditional DH or ECDH exchanges with NIST-approved algorithms such as Kyber. This can be done in a hybrid format, where both classical and quantum-safe materials are exchanged simultaneously.

Step 2: Use hybrid configurations during transition
Hybrid key exchange ensures compatibility with older clients while adding quantum resistance. This also enables phased rollouts across large networks without requiring an all-or-nothing upgrade.

Step 3: Update gateways and clients
Ensure your VPN software and firmware support these hybrid algorithms. Vendors such as Quantum Xchange and PQShield offer transitional solutions and integration libraries for Kyber and other PQC algorithms.

Step 4: Modify your IKEv2 configuration
Update your configuration policies to reflect hybrid cryptographic suites. A sample configuration line might read:

```
ini
CopyEdit
ike=aes256-sha512-kyber512
```

Verify that clients and gateways can negotiate this configuration without errors, and ensure fallback support for devices that may not yet be PQC-capable.

Step 5: Verify compatibility and monitor performance
Test your updated VPN configuration in controlled environments. Validate both connectivity and performance. Ensure logs and alerts are configured to detect negotiation failures, downgrade attempts, or unexpected performance degradation.

Transitioning VPNs to quantum-safe configurations is not just a future-state objective. With standards in place and vendor support emerging, it is an actionable step for any organization looking to protect long-lived or highly sensitive network traffic. The critical takeaway is that while symmetric encryption, such as AES-256 and SHA-384, remains safe, the doorway through which keys are negotiated must be closed to quantum threats. The earlier you begin, the fewer retroactive compromises you will have to face later.

11.3 HYBRID CERTIFICATES AND DUAL STACKS

Hybrid certificates are designed to bridge the gap between today's classical cryptography and tomorrow's quantum-safe systems. These certificates combine a traditional digital signature algorithm, such as RSA or ECDSA, with a post-quantum algorithm, such as CRYSTALS-Dilithium or Falcon. When deployed, they enable systems to validate signatures using either or both components, depending on the capabilities of the client or server. This dual compatibility helps organizations transition incrementally, reducing the need for a full-scale cryptographic overhaul in a single step.

Hybrid certificates differ from dual certificates. A dual certificate strategy involves issuing separate classical and post-quantum certificates, typically served together in a chain or using protocol negotiation to determine which to use. Hybrid certificates, on the other hand, embed both algorithms into a single certificate object, streamlining deployment and simplifying trust relationships.

Recent research and testing, especially by NIST, NCCoE, and IETF contributors, has introduced new hybrid and composite certificate formats that go beyond basic dual signatures. These structures are designed to support flexible deployment scenarios, enhance performance under constrained conditions, and facilitate the management of certificate chain compatibility across diverse environments. Notable formats include:

11.3.1 Chameleon

The *Chameleon* format enables interoperability by embedding both classical and quantum-safe public key and signature data within the same X.509 certificate using well-structured Object Identifiers (OIDs). It supports multiple algorithm types and enables backward compatibility by presenting the classical signature as the primary signature, while preserving the post-quantum component as a secondary structure. This format is particularly useful when supporting legacy systems alongside modern clients that can interpret post-quantum extensions.

How it works: Chameleon certificates preserve compatibility by layering signature types with the classical one prioritized in standard fields, and the post-quantum signature encoded in an extension or alternate structure. The validation logic can then adapt based on the client's capabilities.

When to use it: Use Chameleon when broad backward compatibility is essential, such as in public web environments, third-party integrations, or transitional enterprise settings with mixed device support.

11.3.2 Catalyst

The *Catalyst* format is a space and performance-optimized hybrid structure intended for bandwidth-constrained or latency-sensitive environments, such as IoT, mobile, or embedded systems. It minimizes overhead by encoding a single logical signature from a composite of classical and quantum-safe keys, designed to be validated efficiently.

How it works: Catalyst certificates reduce duplication by using a single composite public key that internally contains both classical and quantum-safe components. Signatures are encoded compactly to avoid redundancy and reduce certificate size.

When to use it: Use Catalyst in environments with strict performance or payload limits, such as smart cards, mobile apps, or sensor networks that still require quantum readiness.

11.3.3 AltPublicKey

The *AltPublicKey* format introduces an experimental method of including multiple public key types within a certificate by adding one or more alternate public keys through custom X.509 extensions. This enables multi-algorithm negotiation at the certificate level, allowing clients to select which key to use for verification based on supported cryptographic stacks.

How it works: AltPublicKey extensions hold additional public keys (e.g., one RSA, one Dilithium), and the application layer or cryptographic library selects the appropriate key to verify based on local capabilities or policy.

When to use it: Use AltPublicKey in exploratory or lab environments to test multi-key negotiation, or in vendor ecosystems where control over client and server stacks enables custom parsing and verification logic.

These certificate profiles are actively being tested within the context of IETF drafts, NIST interoperability labs, and commercial pilot programs. While not yet standardized, they represent likely directions for future hybrid certificate schemes and should be evaluated as part of any cryptographic migration strategy.

Today, most commercial PKI vendors are actively developing support for hybrid or dual-stack certificate authorities. Providers like DigiCert, ISARA, Keyfactor, and Entrust have pilot programs and test environments available. While full production-grade deployment remains limited due to pending standardization from the IETF, experimentation and staged rollouts are strongly encouraged.

DigiCert, for example, has released a Post-Quantum Cryptography Toolkit specifically built for early adopters. This toolkit allows engineers to generate and install hybrid certificates using RSA alongside CRYSTALS-Dilithium, one of the NIST-selected algorithms for post-quantum digital signatures. It includes setup instructions for configuring OpenSSL and Apache on a Linux system, making it ideal for technical teams who want to test compatibility and performance in a lab or pre-production environment. Designed for architects and solution designers across financial services, utilities, government, and manufacturing, the toolkit helps demystify the deployment process and exposes organizations to the operational realities of quantum migration. Although experimental, the certificates are cryptographically valid today and are designed to remain useful in a quantum future. DigiCert encourages feedback from these test programs to inform future iterations of their toolkits and services.

Hybrid certificates should be introduced during major PKI upgrade cycles, especially when refreshing infrastructure, migrating workloads to the cloud, or modernizing authentication architectures. They are particularly valuable for systems with long-lived data, such as financial transaction records, personal identity data, and intellectual property archives.

To manage hybrid certificates at scale, organizations should lean on certificate lifecycle management (CLM) platforms. Solutions from Venafi, Keyfactor, and AppviewX offer visibility, automation, and policy enforcement for certificate issuance, renewal, and revocation. These platforms are beginning to support post-quantum metadata and algorithm detection, making them essential tools for future-ready PKI governance.

For Microsoft environments, the core cryptographic engine is SymCrypt, an open-source library that underpins Windows Server, Azure, Microsoft 365, and other key services. In December 2024, Microsoft added support for the Leighton-Micali Signature Scheme (LMS) and ML-DSA (CRYSTALS-Dilithium, now standardized as FIPS 204). This is a strong indication that Microsoft is preparing for PQC integration. However, as of today, Microsoft's Certificate Authority (MS CA) and Azure Key Vault do not yet support hybrid certificates or keys. They continue to rely on pseudo-random number generators (PRNGs) for key generation and offer no native interface for hybrid algorithms. We will discuss key generation further in the next chapter. Organizations using Microsoft CA must explore third-party integrations or standalone tools for PQC testing. Alternatively, they can prepare environments to be compatible with hybrid certs issued externally, storing keys and certificates in managed key vaults once Microsoft updates its ecosystem.

In contrast, Amazon Web Services (AWS) has moved more aggressively. AWS Key Management Service (KMS) supports some post-quantum capabilities, including integration with third-party quantum-safe key exchange and digital signature providers. AWS has not yet fully embedded PQC into its native certificate authority or Secrets Manager services, but it offers more experimental flexibility than Microsoft's tooling at present.

11.3.4 Step-by-step: setting up a certificate authority for PQC testing

To fully explore or adopt hybrid and quantum-ready certificates, organizations must understand how to configure and manage the infrastructure that supports them. This process begins with setting up a certificate authority, establishing a proper trust chain, and issuing certificates that incorporate quantum-safe algorithms. Even if production use is not yet feasible across all systems, this foundational work allows teams to experiment safely and prepare for broader adoption.

Step 1: Choose your CA architecture

Decide whether you will use an internal CA (such as Microsoft CA or a Linux-based OpenSSL CA) or partner with an external vendor that offers PQC-ready services (like DigiCert or ISARA). For most organizations starting with internal testing, a Linux-based CA using OpenSSL offers flexibility and full control.

Step 2: Build a root CA

Set up a root certificate authority on a secured system. This CA will sign intermediate certificates and should be kept offline for security. Generate a root certificate using OpenSSL or a tool like HashiCorp Vault. For hybrid support, configure the root to include both a classical and post-quantum signature. You may use the Open Quantum Safe (OQS) version of OpenSSL, which allows for hybrid certificate generation.

Example (OpenSSL with OQS patch):

```
bash
CopyEdit
openssl req -new -x509 -newkey rsa:3072 -keyout root.key
-out root.crt -days 3650 -sigalg rsa-sha256
```

Once PQC support is integrated:

```
bash
CopyEdit
oqs-openssl req -new -x509 -newkey dilithium2 -keyout root
_pqc.key -out root_pqc.crt -days 3650
```

Step 3: Create an intermediate CA with hybrid capabilities

Generate an intermediate certificate and sign it with the root. Use a hybrid certificate format that chains classical and PQC algorithms. This intermediate CA will issue certificates to systems and services.

DigiCert's toolkit provides templates and example command-line workflows to help with this process. You'll also need to configure the CA to recognize hybrid signatures using supported tools.

Step 4: Configure certificate policies

Define the parameters for certificate issuance, such as key lengths, approved algorithms (e.g., RSA 3072 + Dilithium3), expiration times, and usage constraints (e.g., TLS server and client authentication, code signing). Include quantum-safe options in the policy file, particularly when using experimental or hybrid algorithms.

Step 5: Establish a trust chain

Once the root and intermediate CAs are configured, create a certificate chain file that links them. This allows clients and systems to verify the authenticity of issued certificates, even if they do not yet recognize PQC formats.

```
bash
CopyEdit
cat intermediate.crt root.crt > full_chain.pem
```

Step 6: Issue hybrid certificates

Use your intermediate CA to issue hybrid certificates for test servers, internal applications, or client systems. These certificates will include both RSA or ECDSA and a post-quantum signature (e.g., Dilithium3 or Falcon). Tools from vendors like ISARA and Open Quantum Safe include command-line utilities and documentation for creating hybrid certificates.

When using the DigiCert toolkit, follow the instructions provided to generate and install hybrid certificates on a test Linux system using Apache and OpenSSL. The toolkit guides you through enabling Dilithium within the OpenSSL build and using it in conjunction with classical cryptography.

Step 7: Deploy to test systems

Install the hybrid certificates on test servers and verify functionality. Ensure clients can negotiate connections using either signature type. Monitor for compatibility issues and performance changes.

Testing scenarios should include:

- TLS handshakes with modern browsers
- VPN tunnels using quantum-safe IKE policies
- Code-signing of internal applications
- Certificate validation through CLM systems or trust stores

Step 8: Integrate with lifecycle management

Connect your test CA and hybrid certs with a certificate lifecycle management platform if available. Use Keyfactor, AppviewX, or Venafi to automate renewals, monitor expirations, and enforce cryptographic policy. This concept is discussed at length in Chapter 18.

Step 9: Document and review

Keep a detailed record of each step, including certificate formats used, configurations, and test outcomes. This documentation becomes the basis for broader deployment planning, executive briefings, and audit preparedness.

11.4 CODE SIGNING AND SOFTWARE INTEGRITY

While standards for PKCS#11 integration are still catching up, version 3.2 defines LMS and HSS for use in hardware security modules. These hierarchical signatures allow for quantum-safe firmware and code signing, especially in environments where software updates must remain valid for years.

Signed code often has a long shelf life, so organizations should begin the transition now, even if they are years from adopting post-quantum key exchanges elsewhere. Hybrid signature schemes or composite formats can help ensure backward compatibility during the migration period. Code signing is one of the most critical components of modern software supply chain security. It ensures that the software a user downloads or installs has not been modified, tampered with, or corrupted. If these signatures are forged, attackers can distribute malware disguised as legitimate updates. At its core, code signing confirms that the software originates from a verified source and that the code's integrity remains intact from signing to execution.

Traditionally, most code signing relies on algorithms like RSA or ECDSA. These schemes are widely supported and deeply embedded in development pipelines, signing tools, operating systems, and firmware validators. However, both RSA and ECDSA can be broken by quantum attacks. A powerful enough quantum computer running Shor's Algorithm could fake digital signatures, making it possible for attackers to push out malicious updates that look completely legitimate to users and devices.

This risk is compounded by the long lifespan of signed code. Firmware updates in critical infrastructure, operating systems, and IoT devices may remain in the field for a decade or more. Even if a quantum computer capable of real-time attacks is still years away, code signed today will still be vulnerable when those machines arrive. That's why quantum-resistant digital signatures must be adopted early in the migration journey.

11.4.1 Quantum-safe digital signature algorithms

The most promising post-quantum digital signature algorithms include:

- *CRYSTALS-Dilithium*: A lattice-based digital signature algorithm offering strong security with efficient performance. Now standardized as FIPS 204.
- *Falcon*: A lattice-based algorithm that provides compact signatures and is well-suited for bandwidth-constrained environments.
- *Leighton-Micali Signature Scheme (LMS)* and *Hierarchical Signature System (HSS)*: Stateless hash-based signature algorithms suited for one-time or limited-use signing tasks. These are ideal for firmware and embedded system updates and are now supported in *PKCS#11 v3.2*, the industry standard for cryptographic interface specifications.

11.4.2 What is PKCS#11?

PKCS #11, also known as Cryptoki, is a cryptographic token interface standard that defines an API for applications to access cryptographic services from hardware devices. This allows applications to interact with cryptographic hardware, such as Hardware Security Modules (HSMs), smart cards, and secure tokens, without needing to know the specifics of the underlying hardware. We will discuss HSMs further in the next chapter.

With version 3.2, PKCS#11 introduced support for post-quantum signature schemes such as LMS and HSS, allowing organizations to begin signing code in a quantum-safe way using existing secure hardware infrastructure. These enhancements make it possible to issue and verify digital signatures in high-assurance environments such as:

- Critical infrastructure firmware updates
- Industrial control systems
- Smart meters and utility software
- Network hardware appliances

11.4.3 Step-by-step: preparing code signing for a post-quantum world

Step 1: Inventory your signing processes

Begin by identifying where code signing happens across your environment. This may include:

- Software development build pipelines
- DevOps and CI/CD environments
- Device firmware update workflows
- Third-party code and libraries integrated into your systems

Document which keys are used, what algorithms are in place (RSA-2048, ECDSA, etc.), and the shelf life of the signed software. This should be done during Phase 1 – Discovery/Step 1 – Inventory as discussed in Chapter 5.

Step 2: Choose a post-quantum signature strategy

Decide whether your use cases require immediate support for quantum-safe algorithms (e.g., for long-lived firmware) or hybrid or composite signing formats to maintain backward compatibility during the transition.

Use cases like IoT or embedded firmware may be best served by LMS or HSS with constrained key usage limits and stateless design. More general software updates might adopt Dilithium or Falcon, which are seeing wider toolchain support.

Step 3: Upgrade toolchains and libraries

Use updated cryptographic libraries that support PQC digital signatures. Options include:

- *PQShield*: Lightweight, quantum-safe signing libraries and hardware integration tools.
- *Open Quantum Safe*: Extensions to OpenSSL that support PQC signing algorithms.
- *QuintessenceLabs*: Secure key management platforms that include quantum-safe modules.
- *ISARA*: Composite and hybrid signing SDKs that support co-signing with RSA or ECC for compatibility.

Install the updated libraries in development environments and ensure support across build servers, CI/CD platforms, and automated deployment pipelines.

Step 4: Configure a signing policy

Define how and when PQC signatures will be used. For example:

- Firmware images longer than five years in production must be signed with LMS or Dilithium.
- Internal development builds may retain classical signatures but log readiness.
- Public releases after 2027 must include hybrid or quantum-safe digital signatures.

Include the allowed algorithms, certificate authorities, expiration rules, and key management protocols in this policy.

Step 5: Issue quantum-safe signing certificates

Obtain a PQC-capable code signing certificate from a vendor such as DigiCert, ISARA, or PQShield. Alternatively, create your own internal test CA and issue hybrid certificates using tools like OpenSSL with Open Quantum Safe extensions.

If using PKCS#11-compatible Hardware Security Modules (HSMs), configure them to support LMS or HSS keys and integrate these into your signing workflows. Many vendors now support firmware signing using these stateless hash-based algorithms.

Step 6: Update and sign your code

Using your updated libraries or HSMs, generate new signatures using PQC algorithms. For example:

```
bash
CopyEdit
oqs-openssl dgst -sign dilithium3.key -out firmware.sig
firmware.bin
```

Or, in hybrid mode:

```
bash
CopyEdit
oqs-openssl dgst -sign hybrid.key -out app.sig app.exe
```

Store the signatures alongside the application or firmware. Use manifest files or metadata headers to link the signature to the code, enabling downstream verification.

Step 7: Verify compatibility and signature validation

Ensure that your endpoints, bootloaders, or OS-level components can verify PQC signatures. For firmware, this may require an update to the device's trust store or secure boot configuration.

In development, integrate signature validation into pre-deployment checks. In production, monitor logs for signature failures or mismatches.

Step 8: Monitor and adjust

Track adoption and monitor performance. PQC signature sizes and verification times may vary, so test under real-world conditions. Watch for emerging standards related to PKCS#11 support, particularly as LMS and HSS adoption increases.

Document your configuration choices and share test results across the security team to support broader rollout planning.

Adopting post-quantum digital signatures is not just a technical milestone; it is a strategic move to preserve the integrity of your codebase and digital assets in the years to come. Even if full adoption across your pipeline is still on the horizon, beginning with low-risk use cases and long-lived software helps build familiarity and protect your most persistent artifacts. The earlier you begin testing, the smoother your transition to quantum-safe signing will be.

11.5 PQC IN APIS AND APPLICATIONS

Modern applications and APIs depend on cryptography to protect everything from authentication tokens to data in transit and at rest. As quantum computing advances, these cryptographic foundations will need to evolve. Ensuring APIs and applications are quantum-ready means rethinking how cryptographic libraries are used, how keys are generated and exchanged, and how secure communications are established.

Start by identifying where cryptographic functions exist within your application. This includes TLS connections, API tokens, digital signatures, password hashing, and encrypted storage. Prioritize areas that handle sensitive user data, financial transactions, or persistent credentials. Key generation, encryption, and authentication flows should be mapped to understand where traditional public-key algorithms, such as RSA, DSA, or ECDSA, are currently used.

From there, select the appropriate post-quantum cryptographic algorithms. This decision will depend on your performance constraints and interoperability needs. As previously discussed, Kyber is a leading candidate for key encapsulation, while Dilithium and Falcon offer strong options for digital signatures.

To implement these algorithms, developers can turn to open-source libraries such as OpenSSL and BoringSSL, both of which can be extended with support from the Open Quantum Safe (OQS) project and liboqs. These libraries provide wrappers and APIs for working with post-quantum algorithms, eliminating the need to build low-level cryptographic routines from scratch. Commercial SDKs, such as those from PQShield and ISARA, offer more tailored support for enterprise needs, including hardware acceleration and documentation suited for production environments. Sandbox AQ, for example, delivers enterprise-grade toolkits with support for both open-source integration and proprietary deployment requirements. Libraries and SDKs play a few key roles in the application stack. They simplify complex cryptographic tasks, make sure key sizes and certificate formats are handled correctly, and help developers steer clear of common mistakes.

Choosing libraries that are actively maintained and follow NIST's roadmap can also save you trouble down the line by reducing the risk of compatibility problems as standards change.

When integrating PQC into applications, it is best to start small. Focus first on internal services that are easier to test and roll back. Once you have confidence in the integration and performance impact, expand to external-facing APIs and production systems. Ensure your development environment includes hybrid testbeds, where PQC and classical algorithms are run in parallel, allowing for graceful fallback and better diagnostics.

Different application platforms have different needs. Web applications often rely heavily on TLS for secure communication, making them a natural starting point for PQC adoption via hybrid certificates and updated TLS stacks. Enterprise desktop applications may depend on more complex certificate chains and identity management integrations, requiring updates to local certificate stores and authentication flows. Mobile apps have unique performance and compatibility constraints, especially when dealing with limited compute resources or third-party SDKs. PQShield, for example, provides lightweight, hardware-optimized cryptographic libraries that are ideal for mobile and IoT applications. In all cases, developers must assess the specific ecosystem dependencies and plan accordingly. Post-quantum algorithms may require additional compute resources or memory. Developers may also need time to get up to speed with key size implications, signature verification logic, and hybrid configurations. Support this with training, documentation, and clear architectural guidance.

To guide both developers and security teams through this process, consider the following steps:

1. *Map cryptographic dependencies*
   Perform a thorough review of your application architecture to locate cryptographic touchpoints. Document where encryption, digital signatures, and key exchange mechanisms are used. You can create CBOMs for this as discussed in Chapter 5.
2. *Choose PQC-compatible libraries*
   Select a PQC-supporting cryptographic library suited to your environment. If you're using OpenSSL or BoringSSL, look into adding liboqs support. For commercial platforms, evaluate SDKs from vendors like Sandbox AQ, ISARA, and PQShield.
3. *Integrate and isolate*
   Introduce PQC in a controlled segment of your application or API. This could be a single microservice, a feature flag-controlled module, or a staging environment.
4. *Test in real conditions*
   Use performance benchmarks and regression testing to compare PQC and classical cryptography side by side. Measure handshake latency,

data size overhead, and compatibility with client applications or browsers.

5. *Enable hybrid mode*
   Where possible, use hybrid key exchange and signature mechanisms to support backward compatibility. This allows legacy clients to continue functioning while modern ones can benefit from PQC enhancements.
6. *Educate and support developers*
   Provide internal documentation, code samples, and architectural patterns that explain how PQC should be used across your environment. Create a channel for developers to ask questions or report issues during the integration process.
7. *Monitor and iterate*
   Once in production, monitor the behavior of PQC-enabled components. Look for error rates, performance bottlenecks, and unanticipated compatibility issues. Use this data to refine your rollout plan.

As the software landscape becomes increasingly interconnected, the importance of quantum-resilient APIs and applications continues to grow. Taking deliberate, well-documented steps now ensures that your systems will continue to function securely when quantum computing capabilities eventually become a reality.

11.6 PQC FOR DATA ENCRYPTION

For all the attention given to securing data in motion, many of the most sensitive and persistent digital assets live at rest. Customer records, financial reports, source code, backups, and trade secrets all reside in storage systems that, although encrypted, are often protected by cryptographic tools no longer suitable for the quantum age. Transitioning to post-quantum cryptography for data at rest is not simply about upgrading encryption libraries. It requires a systemic review of how data is stored, how it is encrypted, and especially how encryption keys are generated, protected, and managed over time.

Symmetric encryption algorithms, such as AES-256, remain largely secure even in the face of quantum threats, provided they are used correctly. The true vulnerability lies not in the data encryption itself, but in how the encryption keys are handled. Many systems today use asymmetric encryption to wrap or protect symmetric keys, particularly in cloud object storage, database encryption, and backup systems. These public key algorithms are directly threatened by quantum computing, making the key management layer the weakest link in what might otherwise appear to be a strong encryption scheme.

Most modern systems use envelope encryption, where the data is encrypted with a unique symmetric key, often called a Data Encryption Key

(DEK), and that DEK is then encrypted using a Key Encryption Key (KEK). The most commonly used algorithms for KEKs are symmetric options like AES, but asymmetric algorithms like RSA-OAEP are still occasionally used to wrap symmetric keys. For example, a file stored in Amazon S3 might be encrypted with AES-256. Still, if the key protecting it is wrapped using RSA-2048, then it is only a matter of time before that envelope becomes vulnerable to quantum decryption. Replacing or augmenting this layer with quantum-resistant key encapsulation mechanisms such as CRYSTALS-Kyber could be a good idea.

11.6.1 Discovering cryptographic dependencies

The first step in migrating data-at-rest protection to PQC is understanding what you have. Discovery and inventory are foundational. Start by identifying where your data resides. This includes not only file servers and databases, but also backups, archives, object stores, and virtual machines. Examine how that data is encrypted. Is it protected using full-disk encryption, such as BitLocker or LUKS, transparent database encryption like Oracle TDE or SQL Server, or application-layer cryptography implemented directly in your code? What algorithms are in use? How are keys stored and rotated? What KMS or HSM platforms are involved?

You should also understand the cryptographic libraries and interfaces used by each system. OpenSSL, Bouncy Castle, and custom cryptography code should be reviewed to determine where classical algorithms are still in play. Automated tools can support this process, especially in complex or distributed environments. Platforms like Venafi, Fortanix, and SandboxAQ offer crypto inventory and discovery capabilities tailored to encryption at rest. Cloud-native security platforms, including those in CNAPP suites like Palo Alto Prisma Cloud and Wiz, can help map encryption status across S3 buckets, Azure Blob Storage, and other object stores.

These efforts should align with the broader discovery methodology outlined in Phase 1. The steps described here mirror and extend the processes in Chapters 5, 6, and 7, which focus on inventorying cryptographic assets, assessing algorithmic exposure, and prioritizing systems based on risk and operational value. Use that guidance to structure your data-at-rest analysis. Apply the same frameworks for sensitivity classification, attack surface evaluation, and business impact to your encryption landscape.

Once the inventory is complete, classify the data based on sensitivity and longevity. Pay particular attention to high-value or regulated information with long retention periods. Medical records, financial statements, patent filings, and engineering data all fall into this category. Even if the data is encrypted today, a future compromise of the key layer could expose it years from now. Delayed quantum attacks do not care about your retention schedule; they only care that the encrypted data was once valuable and still is.

11.6.2 Designing quantum-resistant architectures for data at rest

If your current storage environment does not use AES-256 or a stronger encryption standard, your first priority should be to upgrade your encryption standards. Many systems still rely on AES-128 or even weaker schemes for data at rest. In the face of emerging quantum threats, that baseline is no longer sufficient. AES-256 remains the most reliable and widely supported symmetric encryption standard, offering practical protection against brute-force and quantum-assisted attacks. Key size matters, and anything less than 256 bits will not hold up in the long run.

Once AES-256 is in place, the next step is to examine how your keys are managed. The encryption algorithm might be solid, but if the keys that secure it are wrapped or exchanged using vulnerable asymmetric methods like RSA or ECC, your data remains exposed. This is especially common in systems that use envelope encryption or key wrapping, where a strong symmetric key protects the data, but that key itself is encrypted using RSA or ECC. If a quantum adversary can break the key wrapping, the strength of AES becomes irrelevant.

To move toward quantum readiness, organizations should begin adopting quantum-safe key encapsulation mechanisms. NIST's selected algorithm for this purpose, CRYSTALS-Kyber, provides a strong replacement for RSA and ECC in key wrapping and exchange. Initially, hybrid wrapping schemes may be necessary. These combine both classical and post-quantum algorithms in a single operation, allowing legacy systems to maintain compatibility while newer clients begin validating the quantum-safe layer.

In practical terms, this might involve wrapping an AES-256 key with both RSA-3072 and Kyber-512, then storing the wrapped keys alongside the encrypted data in a format your systems can recognize. Alternatively, some modern key management services allow direct integration of PQC algorithms. Whether you use an internal key vault or a cloud-native KMS, verify that post-quantum algorithms are supported and begin testing their implementation in lower-risk environments.

Key size and key wrapping are foundational. Strong symmetric encryption must be paired with resilient key exchange and management. Without both, the protection around your data at rest remains incomplete. Use this opportunity to audit the entire encryption pipeline, not just the algorithm settings. Look closely at how keys are generated, how they're stored, and how they're recovered. Then ask whether any part of that process still relies on cryptographic assumptions that are known to be vulnerable in a post-quantum world. That is where your attention should turn next.

11.6.3 Implementing PQC in real-world storage systems

The transition to PQC for data at rest will look different depending on the system involved. In file storage systems, quantum-safe encryption can be applied using libraries like OpenSSL extended with the Open Quantum Safe (OQS) plugin. AES-256 can continue to encrypt the data, but the key used for AES should be wrapped using a PQC mechanism such as Kyber. These keys can be stored alongside the file or in a secure key vault, depending on your architecture.

For example:

```
bash
CopyEdit
# Encrypt file
openssl enc -aes-256-cbc -in confidential.docx -out
confidential.enc -pass file:./aes.key
# Wrap AES key using Kyber
openssl pqc-wrap -alg kyber512 -in aes.key -pubkey pub.pem
-out aes.key.pqc
```

In database environments, some vendors are beginning to support PQC directly, especially in custom implementations. If your organization manages encryption manually at the application level, consider replacing RSA key wrapping with PQC KEMs using LibOQS or other supported libraries. Transparent database encryption systems will require vendor alignment, but in many cases, hybrid solutions can be layered to begin migration.

In cloud storage, look to envelope encryption. Services like AWS KMS are beginning to support PQC through BYOK (Bring Your Own Key) and integrations with third-party tools. Ensure that the key wrapping layer uses a quantum-safe algorithm and that the key material is tracked with appropriate metadata.

11.6.4 Testing, monitoring, and migration strategy

Migrating to PQC for data at rest is best approached incrementally. Start with pilot programs in development or test environments. Select one or two use cases where you can test performance, compatibility, and operational fit. Use dual-wrapped keys or hybrid certificates where needed to maintain continuity.

Pay particular attention to the ability to decrypt and access archived data. This is a good time to evaluate how long you need to retain access to encrypted files and whether the decryption process is documented, auditable, and resilient.

Build telemetry and monitoring into your migration. Track the performance of PQC algorithms, the success of key wrapping and unwrapping operations, and any anomalies in decryption or validation. Consider tagging data and keys based on their cryptographic properties so that you can create policies and reports for PQC readiness.

Applying post-quantum cryptography to your data at rest may not be the first step in your PQC journey. However, in the long run, it will be an important step to ensure long-term confidentiality and resilience.

11.7 SHARED RESPONSIBILITY MODEL

Adopting post-quantum cryptography is not a solitary effort. Just like in cloud computing, PQC implementation will follow a shared responsibility model. Some tasks will fall squarely on the organization, others will be fulfilled by vendors, and many will require coordination between both. Understanding who owns what ensures that nothing slips through the cracks and that both sides are aligned in maintaining cryptographic resilience.

At the organizational level, it's up to the enterprise to handle things like discovery, classification, and governance internally. That includes managing your cryptographic inventory, assessing risk, and deciding which vulnerabilities to tackle first, whether you do it in-house or bring in outside help. These tasks rely on institutional knowledge of data flows, application architecture, and operational dependencies. Only the business itself can determine which systems are most critical and where legacy algorithms pose the greatest risk.

Vendors, on the other hand, are responsible for building PQC support into their products and services. This includes integrating standardized algorithms, such as Kyber and Dilithium, into TLS stacks, VPN clients, code signing platforms, and certificate authorities. If your cloud provider, software vendor, or appliance manufacturer does not yet support post-quantum upgrades, your ability to migrate may be limited. Holding vendors accountable means choosing partners who are actively investing in quantum readiness and offering roadmaps with clear timelines.

In many areas, responsibility is shared among various parties. For example, lifecycle management of hybrid certificates depends on the vendor supplying a compatible product and the enterprise configuring and operating it correctly. Revocation readiness requires tools that support rapid updates, as well as governance processes that trigger revocation in a timely manner. Logging, monitoring, and alerting must be enabled by vendors, but tuned and interpreted by the enterprise (Table 11.1).

Table 11.2 outlines these relationships using a RACI framework: Responsible, Accountable, Consulted, and Informed.

To illustrate:

- For *cryptographic asset discovery and inventory*, the enterprise is both responsible and accountable. The vendor may be consulted if discovery tools are provided as part of a managed service.

Table 11.1 Shared responsibility model

Post-Quantum Activity	*Enterprise Responsibility*	*Shared Responsibility*	*Vendor Responsibility*
Cryptographic Asset Discovery & Inventory	✓		
Risk Assessment	✓		
Risk Prioritization	✓		
Data Classification for Post-Quantum Readiness	✓		
Quantum Vulnerability Assessment	✓		
Cryptographic Bill of Materials (CBOM)		✓	
Supply Chain & Vendor Cryptography Assessment		✓	
Regulatory & Compliance Gap Analysis	✓		
Quantum Risk Roadmap Development	✓		
Stakeholder Engagement & Policy Updates	✓		
Compensating Controls Deployment	✓		
Hybrid Cryptographic Strategy		✓	
Post-Quantum Cryptographic Research & Benchmarking		✓	
Regulatory & Audit Preparation	✓		
Application & System Dependencies Mapping		✓	
Algorithm Migration & Replacement		✓	
Quantum-Safe SSL/TLS Implementation		✓	

(Continued)

Table 11.1 (Continued) Shared responsibility model

Post-Quantum Activity	*Enterprise Responsibility*	*Shared Responsibility*	*Vendor Responsibility*
Post-Quantum VPNs & Secure Communication		✓	
Post-Quantum Secure Software Development Kits (SDKs) and Libraries Integration		✓	
Hardware Security Module (HSM) Upgrades			✓
Quantum-Resistant Code Signing		✓	
Certificate Lifecycle Management (CLM) Updates		✓	
Key Management & Distribution Overhaul		✓	
Zero Trust & Identity Management Adaptation	✓		
Application & API Cryptographic Modernization		✓	
ICS, OT, IoT & Embedded Systems PQC Readiness			✓
Post-Quantum Cryptographic Testing		✓	
Real-Time Quantum Threat Monitoring		✓	
Penetration Testing & PQC Validation		✓	
Compliance Audits & PQC Certification		✓	
Incident Response & Recovery Plan Updates	✓		
Cryptographic Resilience Exercises		✓	
Crypto-Agility Framework Adoption		✓	

(*Continued*)

Table 11.1 (Continued) Shared responsibility model

Post-Quantum Activity	*Enterprise Responsibility*	*Shared Responsibility*	*Vendor Responsibility*
Certificate Renewal & Automation		✓	
Workforce Training & PQC Awareness	✓		
Threat Intelligence & PQC Monitoring		✓	
Long-Term Infrastructure & Hardware Modernization		✓	
Cross-Vendor Cryptographic Coordination		✓	

- For the *Cryptographic Bill of Materials (CBOM)*, responsibility and accountability fall to the vendor, especially when delivered as part of a software package or hardware appliance. However, the enterprise must still be informed and know how to validate the CBOM.
- In *Post-Quantum Algorithm Configuration*, responsibility may be shared. A vendor supplies PQC support through configuration options, but the enterprise must enable them, enforce policy, and ensure that applications are tested before deployment.

This RACI alignment helps establish clear expectations and prevents duplication or omission. For successful post-quantum migration, these boundaries should be codified into your vendor management programs, product evaluations, and internal governance charters. Ultimately, shared responsibility means shared trust. PQC success depends not only on deploying the right algorithms but on coordinating human processes, technology choices, and operational maturity across multiple teams and organizations. It is a team sport, and clarity of roles is the playbook.

11.8 CONCLUSION

Replacing vulnerable cryptographic algorithms is ultimately a series of deliberate, phased actions that must be woven into the broader fabric of your IT and security operations. Fortunately, opportunities for integration are everywhere. Every time you renew a TLS certificate, update a VPN client, or roll out a new microservice, you've got an opportunity to add

Table 11.2 Shared responsibility RACI

Post-Quantum Activity	*Enterprise (R/A/C/I)*	*Shared (R/A/C/I)*	*Vendor (R/A/C/I)*
Cryptographic Asset Discovery & Inventory	**R,A**		**C**
Risk Assessment & Prioritization	**R,A**		**C**
Data Classification for Post-Quantum Readiness	**R,A**		**C**
Quantum Vulnerability Assessment	**R,A**		**C**
Cryptographic Bill of Materials (CBOM)		**R,A**	
Supply Chain & Vendor Cryptography Assessment	**C**	**R,A**	**I**
Regulatory & Compliance Gap Analysis	**R,A**		
Quantum Risk Roadmap Development	**R,A**		
Stakeholder Engagement & Policy Updates	**R,A**		
Compensating Controls Deployment	**R,A**		
Hybrid Cryptographic Strategy	**C**	**R,A**	**I**
Post-Quantum Cryptographic Research & Benchmarking	**C**	**R,A**	**I**
Regulatory & Audit Preparation	**R,A**		
Application & System Dependencies Mapping		**R,A**	
Algorithm Migration & Replacement		**R,A**	
Quantum-Safe SSL/TLS Implementation		**R,A**	
Post-Quantum VPNs & Secure Communication		**R,A**	
Hardware Security Module (HSM) Upgrades	**I**	**C**	**R,A**
Quantum-Resistant Code Signing	**R,A**	**I**	**I**
Certificate Lifecycle Management (CLM) Updates	**C**	**R,A**	**C**
Key Management & Distribution Overhaul	**C**	**R,A**	**C**
Zero Trust & Identity Management Adaptation	**R,A**		**C**
Application & API Cryptographic Modernization	**C**	**R,A**	**C**
IoT & Embedded Systems PQC Readiness	**I**	**C**	**R,A**

(Continued)

Table 11.2 (Continued) Shared responsibility RACI

Post-Quantum Activity	*Enterprise (R/A/C/I)*	*Shared (R/A/C/I)*	*Vendor (R/A/C/I)*
Post-Quantum Cryptographic Testing		**R,A**	
Real-Time Quantum Threat Monitoring	**I**	**R,A**	
Penetration Testing & PQC Validation	**C,I**	**R,A**	
Compliance Audits & PQC Certification	**C,I**	**R,A**	
Incident Response & Recovery Plan Updates	**R,A**		**C**
Cryptographic Resilience Exercises	**C,I**	**R,A**	
Crypto-Agility Framework Adoption	**C,I**	**R,A**	
Certificate Renewal & Automation	**C,I**	**R,A**	
Workforce Training & PQC Awareness	**R,A**		
Threat Intelligence & PQC Monitoring	**C,I**	**R,A**	
Long-Term Infrastructure & Hardware Modernization	**I**	**R,A**	**C**
Cross-Vendor Cryptographic Coordination	**I**	**R,A**	**C**

post-quantum protections. The trick is to plan for it in advance, work it into your existing processes, and keep a clear eye on the results.

Hybrid deployments offer a practical first step. They allow you to combine classical and quantum-safe algorithms within the same protocol negotiation, making it possible to upgrade without breaking compatibility. These approaches are already supported in many leading cryptographic libraries and are being tested by vendors across the security ecosystem. If you wait for pure post-quantum implementations to be production-ready everywhere, you may find yourself falling behind. Starting with hybrid configurations allows you to build confidence, collect performance data, and identify integration challenges early.

Progress must be measured, not assumed. Establish KPIs that reflect your organization's crypto-agility, such as the percentage of TLS endpoints using hybrid key exchange or the number of applications signed with PQC algorithms. Use visual dashboards to track migrations, flag lingering vulnerabilities, and report progress to governance bodies. These indicators will help drive accountability and unlock budget, especially when competing against other modernization efforts.

Most importantly, treat PQC implementation as part of your normal rhythm. Like patching, versioning, or compliance testing, the work of cryptographic modernization must become routine. Bake algorithm reviews into your build pipelines. Include quantum readiness in architecture reviews. Document decisions, test outcomes, and fallback paths. The organizations that navigate this transition successfully won't do so by racing at the last minute, but by making continuous, incremental progress today.

The algorithms have been selected. The standards are maturing. The tools are here. The threat is real. What remains is execution.

In the next chapter, we turn our attention to key management. From generation and rotation to storage and recovery, the cryptographic keys at the heart of your systems must be just as future-ready as the algorithms that protect them. Replacing algorithms is only part of the equation. Securing and managing the keys themselves is where quantum resilience truly takes shape.

Chapter 12

Enhance key distribution and generation

The future of encryption doesn't hinge solely on algorithms. It also depends on how securely keys are created, exchanged, and managed. Even the strongest cryptographic system can fail if its keys are weak, predictable, or poorly handled. In a quantum-threatened world, this challenge takes on new urgency. The building blocks of key generation and distribution must evolve to withstand the computational capabilities of quantum adversaries.

This chapter explores three foundational shifts. First, the move from deterministic pseudo-random number generators to entropy-rich quantum random number generators. Second, the standardization of new post-quantum key encapsulation mechanisms, such as ML-KEM, which are critical for secure key establishment. Third, the emergence of quantum key distribution networks, which utilize the laws of physics to protect keys in transit. Each of these changes represents an opportunity to strengthen the cryptographic lifecycle and future-proof your security infrastructure.

12.1 FROM PRNG TO QRNG: BUILDING KEYS WITH TRUE ENTROPY

Most cryptographic keys in use today are generated using *pseudo-random number generators (PRNGs)*. These generators rely on deterministic algorithms and system entropy sources, such as clocks, network activity, or CPU timing. While effective for many use cases, PRNGs have limitations. Given enough time and computational power, a determined attacker could model or predict their output.

To understand why this matters, it's important to first understand what cryptographic keys are and why we need random numbers to create them. A cryptographic key is a secret value used to encrypt and decrypt data, verify digital signatures, or establish secure communication channels. Just as a physical key unlocks a lock, a cryptographic key grants access to protected information. If someone else can guess or recreate your key, they can unlock that information.

DOI: 10.1201/9781003685760-17

Keys aren't just any numbers; the numbers have to be completely unpredictable. If an attacker can guess how a key was generated, the system's security is compromised. That's why random number generators are used to create keys that are impossible to predict. The more randomness (also known as entropy) behind a key, the stronger it is.

PRNGs simulate randomness by using complex algorithms seeded with bits of unpredictable system data, such as mouse movements or network delays. But because they're still based on mathematical formulas, their output is only as secure as the secrecy and variability of their inputs. Over time, if the algorithm or the seed becomes predictable, so does the key.

Quantum random number generators (QRNGs) take a fundamentally different approach. Instead of relying on algorithms, they generate randomness by measuring truly unpredictable physical events. A common example involves sending a single photon, a particle of light, toward a beam splitter. The photon can randomly go one way or another, and the outcome is not determined by any prior condition. This randomness comes from the laws of quantum mechanics, which say the result is not just unknown, it is unknowable until it happens. Because these outcomes are fundamentally unpredictable, QRNGs produce high-quality entropy that cannot be modeled or recreated, not even by a quantum computer. This makes them especially valuable for generating cryptographic keys in systems that demand the highest levels of trust and security.

In short, random number generators are the foundation for creating secure cryptographic keys. The better the randomness, the stronger the key. And in a post-quantum world, the quality of that randomness becomes even more important. Vendors like QuintessenceLabs now build QRNGs directly into hardware, giving you plug-and-play entropy sources that feed straight into your key generation process. These devices can either replace or boost your existing entropy sources, strengthening cryptographic security at the foundation.

For organizations upgrading their infrastructure or deploying new security systems, QRNGs should be considered essential. They provide a quantum-safe foundation for generating symmetric keys, session tokens, initialization vectors, and other cryptographic elements. The sooner they are adopted, the less likely today's keys will become tomorrow's vulnerability.

However, quantum safety doesn't stop at generation. Once a key is created, it has to be stored securely, rotated regularly, revoked when necessary, and eventually destroyed. If key management breaks down at any point, even the strongest encryption can fall apart. That risk only gets bigger as systems become more distributed and complex.

Rotation is the process of periodically replacing cryptographic keys with new ones. In classical systems, this is often done annually or after a specific number of uses. In quantum-safe systems, rotation becomes even more important, particularly for hybrid configurations. A compromised classical key, even if combined with a post-quantum component, could still be exploited. Frequent key rotation reduces the window of exposure and ensures that even if an old key is eventually broken, the data it protects is no longer useful.

Revocation is equally critical. Whether due to a suspected compromise, policy violation, or lifecycle expiration, there must be a clear mechanism to invalidate keys across systems and environments. For post-quantum readiness, revocation systems must be able to handle new certificate formats, support composite or hybrid identifiers, and scale across hybrid and cloud environments.

Key management systems (KMS) must evolve to accommodate the expanding demands of post-quantum cryptography. Traditional KMS platforms were designed to handle RSA, ECC, and symmetric keys using well-established lifecycle practices, but supporting quantum-safe cryptography requires a new level of agility. A modern KMS must be capable of recognizing and storing next-generation key types, such as those based on Kyber or Dilithium. It should support hybrid key material that combines classical and post-quantum components, automatically enforce rotation schedules, integrate with certificate lifecycle systems, and consistently propagate revocation events across both on-premises and cloud-native architectures.

A well-designed KMS not only stores hybrid or post-quantum keys but also enforces policy-based usage restrictions, tracks access and utilization, enables cross-environment replication, and supports dual-stack cryptographic workflows. It should be able to rotate a composite key containing both RSA and Dilithium signatures, monitor its application across workloads, and revoke or replace that key with minimal service interruption when necessary. Several leading KMS providers are beginning to incorporate quantum-safe capabilities into their platforms:

Amazon Web Services (AWS) KMS has made the most progress to date, offering early support for post-quantum experimentation through integrations with third-party libraries. While native support for NIST-approved PQC algorithms has not yet been rolled out to production customers, AWS continues to work with quantum research partners and provides flexibility for hybrid key management via Lambda functions and open-source tooling.

Google Cloud KMS supports strong automation, key versioning, and integration with BoringSSL and other components of the Open Quantum Safe ecosystem. While PQC key types are not yet available out of the box, Google has demonstrated a clear commitment to quantum readiness through its contributions to hybrid TLS implementations and cryptographic research.

Azure Key Vault has not yet introduced native support for quantum-safe algorithms or hybrid certificates. However, Microsoft's cryptographic roadmap includes planned support for ML-DSA and LMS through SymCrypt, and Azure customers can prepare by experimenting with external CAs and manual hybrid certificate deployment in conjunction with their key vault policies.

HashiCorp Vault provides a highly flexible and extensible open-source KMS platform and has seen experimental PQC integrations via plugins and community projects. Organizations running Vault in hybrid environments may be able to prototype PQC support sooner than on managed cloud platforms. However, full lifecycle automation for quantum-safe keys is still a work in progress.

Thales CipherTrust and *Entrust KeyControl* represent enterprise-grade KMS solutions that offer strong compliance support and tight integration with hardware security modules (HSMs). Both vendors have begun rolling out quantum-ready enhancements, including support for QRNGs and plans to support NIST-standardized algorithms once integration with PKCS#11 is finalized.

As the standards mature and adoption accelerates, KMS platforms will be pivotal in translating cryptographic policy into practice. Their ability to store, rotate, distribute, and retire both classical and post-quantum keys will determine whether organizations can deploy PQC at scale or remain exposed to long-term cryptographic risk.

Finally, secure logging and audit trails are essential. As organizations transition to PQC, the ability to demonstrate control over key generation, rotation, and revocation becomes a core part of governance. This is especially true in regulated environments, where proving compliance with cryptographic policies may determine eligibility for contracts, partnerships, or certifications.

Quantum safety begins with better randomness, but it's built on end-to-end key discipline. By moving from PRNG to QRNG and integrating modern key lifecycle management practices, organizations can lay a solid foundation for cryptographic integrity that will hold up against even the most advanced adversaries.

12.2 ML-KEM AND THE SHIFT IN KEY EXCHANGE

Creating a strong key is only half the battle. Securely distributing that key across a network, especially over untrusted channels, is just as critical. In classical cryptography, this has traditionally been accomplished through asymmetric algorithms, such as RSA or elliptic-curve Diffie-Hellman (ECDH). These systems rely on mathematical problems that quantum computers are expected to solve efficiently, rendering them obsolete once large-scale quantum hardware becomes available.

Recognizing this risk, NIST has prioritized the development of quantum-resistant key exchange methods. In late 2024, it finalized the standard for *ML-KEM*, a new Key Encapsulation Mechanism (KEM) based on lattice cryptography. ML-KEM enables two parties to securely agree on a shared secret over a public channel, even in the presence of quantum adversaries.

For those familiar with Diffie-Hellman, it helps to compare the two. In a traditional DH handshake, both parties generate private and public keys. They exchange the public keys and use them, along with their private keys, to compute the same shared secret. The security of this process relies on the difficulty of solving discrete logarithm problems, which is an approach that quantum computers can break.

ML-KEM takes a different path. Instead of both sides contributing key material, only the server generates a public-private key pair. The client uses the server's public key to create a shared secret and a ciphertext, referred to as the "encapsulation". The client sends the ciphertext to the server. The server, using its private key, decapsulates the message to recover the same shared secret. This one-way encapsulation process eliminates the need for back-and-forth negotiation and avoids the requirement for both parties to perform complex calculations based on each other's keys.

To put it more simply:

- In Diffie-Hellman, both sides mix ingredients to bake the same cake.
- In ML-KEM, the client bakes the cake using the server's public recipe, then sends it back. The server uses a special tool, its private key, to extract the secret ingredient.

This makes ML-KEM particularly efficient for modern applications, such as TLS and VPNs. It is compact, fast, and designed to be secure against both classical and quantum attacks. The structure of ML-KEM also simplifies session setup, reducing the attack surface and minimizing the number of round trips between endpoints.

We are still waiting for the Internet Engineering Task Force (IETF) to finalize standards for quantum-safe key exchange mechanisms. These include both *Hybrid Key Exchange (Hybrid KEX)* and *pure Post-Quantum Cryptographic Key Exchange (pure PQC KEX)*, which are anticipated to be finalized by late 2025 or early 2026. Consequently, those will likely be in place prior to you reading this book.

Hybrid KEX refers to a transitional approach that combines both classical and post-quantum algorithms during the key exchange process. The goal is to combine the well-tested strength of current classical cryptography, such as Elliptic Curve Diffie-Hellman (ECDH), with the emerging protection of quantum-safe algorithms like ML-KEM. If one component of the hybrid scheme is ever broken, the remaining component can still provide security. In practice, a client and server will each generate key shares using both classical and post-quantum methods, then combine those to derive a shared secret. This strategy provides backward compatibility while mitigating the risk of complete compromise if either scheme proves vulnerable in the future.

Pure PQC KEX, in contrast, abandons classical methods entirely and relies solely on quantum-resistant algorithms to establish secure keys. This approach simplifies the exchange and removes potential attack surfaces related to classical algorithm vulnerabilities. However, it assumes a mature ecosystem that can fully support these new algorithms across clients, servers, and network infrastructure – a state we have not yet fully achieved.

Until the IETF publishes stable standards for both approaches, implementations remain experimental or limited to test environments. In the meantime, organizations can prepare by adopting cryptographic libraries that support hybrid configurations and by building cryptographic agility into their systems. When finalized, these key exchange standards will shape the foundation of secure communications in a post-quantum world.

For security architects, ML-KEM represents a practical way to begin replacing vulnerable key exchange mechanisms. Organizations can adopt it incrementally by updating VPN configurations, refreshing TLS stacks, or integrating support into embedded devices and APIs. Vendors like PQShield and Sandbox AQ offer libraries and SDKs that help teams implement these changes with minimal disruption.

12.3 QUANTUM KEY DISTRIBUTION (QKD): PHYSICS OVER MATH

While PQC algorithms, such as ML-KEM, rely on the difficulty of certain mathematical problems, quantum key distribution (QKD) takes a different approach altogether. Instead of protecting data through mathematical complexity, QKD secures it by exploiting the physical properties of quantum particles.

In a typical QKD system, one party (often called Alice) sends a series of quantum states, such as polarized photons, through a quantum channel to another party (Bob). The measurement of these states is subject to the uncertainty principle, which means any attempt to intercept or measure them introduces detectable anomalies. After the quantum transmission, Alice and Bob use a classical channel to compare a portion of their results and discard mismatches. What remains is a shared secret that can be used as a cryptographic key.

QKD offers a level of security that, in principle, is unbreakable. However, this power comes with trade-offs. QKD requires specialized hardware, such as photon detectors, trusted nodes, and secure transmission media, including fiber-optic cables, free-space optics, or satellites. The cost, complexity, and physical limitations of this infrastructure mean that QKD is not suitable for every use case.

Today, QKD is most viable in high-assurance environments such as government networks, financial data centers, or intercontinental communications between critical institutions. Quantum Xchange's Phio TX is an example of a solution that integrates QKD into existing systems, utilizing an overlay network to deliver keys out-of-band. QuintessenceLabs provides tools that allow QKD-generated keys to be used within conventional key management systems, bridging the gap between classical and quantum architectures.

For organizations exploring QKD, preparation begins with understanding the infrastructure requirements. This includes identifying secure facilities for quantum transmitters and receivers, establishing quantum channels, and integrating with existing encryption and key management systems. Staff must also be trained in the maintenance and monitoring of quantum devices, which behave differently from traditional network equipment.

Though expensive and logistically intensive, QKD can offer unparalleled security for specific high-value scenarios. Its ability to detect eavesdropping in real time and ensure perfect forward secrecy based on physical principles makes it an attractive option for sectors where confidentiality is non-negotiable. The core advantage lies in the principles of quantum mechanics. When a third party attempts to intercept quantum key material, such as polarized photons, the act of observation irreversibly alters their state. This phenomenon, grounded in the Heisenberg uncertainty principle, introduces detectable errors in the transmission. During the reconciliation phase, Alice and Bob compare portions of their received and measured bits over a classical channel. If the error rate exceeds a certain threshold, they know the transmission has been compromised and discard the key. This built-in intrusion detection makes QKD unique; the very laws of physics enforce security, not assumptions about computational difficulty (Table 12.1).

12.4 HARDWARE SECURITY MODULES AND KEY VAULTS FOR PQC

Hardware Security Modules (HSMs) and key vaults sit at the center of the PQC evolution. These systems are responsible for generating, storing, and protecting keys across a wide range of enterprise functions, including TLS and VPNs, code signing, and database encryption. Without meaningful upgrades to these components, any organization attempting a post-quantum migration will eventually run into bottlenecks that limit scalability, automation, or compliance.

Table 12.1 QKD table

Aspect	*Post-Quantum Cryptography (PQC)*	*Quantum Key Distribution (QKD)*
Definition	Cryptographic algorithms resistant to quantum and classical attacks, based on mathematical problems.	A method of securely transmitting encryption keys using quantum mechanics principles.
Foundation	Software-based, using advanced mathematical constructs (e.g., lattices, hashes).	Physics-based, leveraging quantum states like photons.
Key Security	Relies on computational hardness of quantum-resistant algorithms.	Relies on the laws of quantum mechanics to ensure key security.
Implementation	Replaces existing cryptographic algorithms in software (e.g., TLS, VPNs, certificates).	Requires specialized quantum hardware and infrastructure (e.g., fiber-optics, satellites).
Compatibility	Works within classical communication networks.	Requires a separate quantum network alongside classical infrastructure.
Cost	Relatively low; mainly software upgrades.	High; involves deploying quantum channels and equipment.
Eavesdropping Detection	Does not inherently detect eavesdropping.	Detects eavesdropping by observing quantum state disturbances.
Scalability	Easily scalable in existing IT environments.	Limited by distance and infrastructure requirements.
Standards	NIST is standardizing PQC algorithms (e.g., Kyber, Dilithium).	No universally adopted standards yet, but protocols like BB84 are widely used.
Scalable Security Needs	Enterprise-wide encryption replacement (e.g., PKI, VPNs, IoT).	Small-scale high-security communications (e.g., military).
Budget Constraints	Cost-effective, software-only solutions.	High-value assets where cost is less of a concern.
Existing Infrastructure	Works with existing IT and communication networks.	Requires dedicated quantum infrastructure.
Immediate Deployment	Readily available through NIST-approved algorithms.	Emerging technology with ongoing standardization.

12.4.1 Hardware Security Modules (HSMs)

HSMs are specialized devices that protect cryptographic keys in isolated environments, shielding them from extraction or misuse. They are widely used in both on-premises and cloud environments to secure private keys used for signing, decryption, or authentication. However, the HSM landscape is still catching up to the demands of post-quantum cryptography.

Most current-generation HSMs use pseudo-random number generators (PRNGs) to create key material. Quantum-ready HSMs are beginning to adopt quantum random number generators (QRNGs) in place of traditional random number generators. Vendors such as QuintessenceLabs, PQShield, and Thales now offer QRNG-augmented HSMs that can generate high-entropy keys with greater assurance.

Despite this progress, full support for NIST-approved post-quantum algorithms is still limited. The challenge lies in the PKCS#11 standard, also known as the Cryptographic Token Interface Standard, which was discussed in the previous chapter. Version 3.2 of PKCS#11 introduced support for post-quantum digital signature schemes, such as LMS and HSS, enabling quantum-safe firmware signing and select code signing workflows. However, it does not yet offer comprehensive support for all of NIST's draft post-quantum algorithms, including key encapsulation mechanisms like ML-KEM. As a result, the ability to implement PQC in an HSM today depends heavily on the specific vendor's roadmap and willingness to support experimental features.

When to deploy quantum-ready HSMs will depend on the organization's infrastructure timeline. The ideal moment is during a hardware refresh cycle or the implementation of a new cryptographic service. In these windows, replacing legacy HSMs with quantum-capable models can future-proof the architecture without significant disruption.

Leading vendors include:

- *PQShield*, which offers quantum-safe silicon IP designed for secure embedded hardware
- *QuintessenceLabs*, which integrates QRNGs into HSMs for enhanced key generation and management
- *Thales*, which supports hybrid cryptographic schemes and is adding PQC readiness to its product portfolio

Until PKCS#11 evolves further and more vendors adopt support for the full range of post-quantum algorithms, most enterprise deployments will require customization or interim solutions.

12.4.2 Key vaults

While HSMs are hardware-centric, key vaults manage key material across systems and environments, on-premises, in the cloud, or within hybrid architectures. Services like Azure Key Vault, AWS Key Management Service (KMS), and Google Cloud KMS provide a secure interface for storing keys, secrets, and certificates. These tools help automate lifecycle management, enforce access controls, and integrate with DevOps pipelines.

In a post-quantum context, key vaults will need to handle new cryptographic materials that may have longer key sizes, different serialization formats, and hybrid certificate structures. They will also need to support both classical and PQC algorithms during the transition period.

However, native support from cloud providers is still evolving. As of now, most key vault services do not offer full support for hybrid certificates or quantum-safe algorithms. This poses a challenge for organizations that want to begin testing PQC in production-like settings. One workaround is to use OpenSSL with PQC extensions to generate hybrid keys and store them in existing vaults, either as secrets or wrapped using classical encryption. These configurations are not ideal, but they offer a bridge while vendors finalize their PQC roadmaps.

For enterprises looking to bridge this gap more robustly, platforms like Keyfactor's EJBCA offer a promising solution. EJBCA is an open-source, enterprise-grade Certificate Authority that now includes built-in support for NIST's PQC algorithms, including Kyber and Dilithium. It provides a PQC-ready public key infrastructure (PKI) that can issue hybrid certificates and integrate with modern vault services, including Azure Key Vault. This capability allows organizations to test and deploy quantum-safe certificates while maintaining centralized control over key lifecycle management. EJBCA supports flexible policy enforcement, automated certificate workflows, and robust logging, all of which are essential for auditability and compliance.

Operationalizing PQC without vault support at scale would be extremely difficult. Vaults are essential for automation, auditability, disaster recovery, and compliance with regulatory frameworks that require key escrow or detailed logging. That is why key vault upgrades should be prioritized alongside algorithm and hardware transitions.

Organizations planning a PQC migration should:

- Assess their current vault capabilities and limitations
- Identify whether vaults support hybrid key formats and certificate chaining
- Begin working with vendors to track upcoming PQC support and influence roadmap prioritization

In the meantime, early pilots and test environments using vendor toolkits and open-source libraries can help teams prepare. For example, issuing a hybrid certificate with a PQC-enabled OpenSSL build and storing it in a simulated vault environment builds familiarity with new formats and workflows. These exercises are not just technical experiments; they lay the foundation for organizational readiness and reduce the likelihood of rushed or poorly planned rollouts when industry-wide PQC mandates are enforced.

Key vaults and HSMs are not often the headline features of cryptographic modernization, but they are the foundation on which everything else rests.

Without quantum-capable versions of both, no amount of algorithmic readiness will be enough. Integrating PQC into your infrastructure begins with securing the roots.

12.4.3 FIPS modules and compliance in a PQC environment

For many organizations, especially those operating in regulated industries or government sectors, Federal Information Processing Standards (FIPS) compliance is not optional. FIPS 140-3 outlines the security requirements for cryptographic modules, and it plays a central role in validating that cryptographic operations are performed securely within both software and hardware systems.

A FIPS-validated cryptographic module ensures that key operations such as generation, encryption, decryption, and signing are handled using approved algorithms and implemented with a high level of rigor. These modules are used within HSMs, software libraries like OpenSSL, and cryptographic toolkits built into operating systems. Any change to a FIPS module, such as adding support for post-quantum algorithms, requires revalidation or updated module certification through NIST's Cryptographic Module Validation Program (CMVP).

As NIST standardizes post-quantum algorithms through publications like FIPS 204 (CRYSTALS-Dilithium) and other upcoming standards, cryptographic vendors are beginning the process of integrating these into their FIPS modules. However, as of today, very few modules have been validated to include post-quantum algorithms. This creates a lag between the availability of new cryptography and its use in FIPS-compliant systems.

Organizations that rely on FIPS modules will need to plan carefully to ensure PQC upgrades align with regulatory expectations. This includes the following steps:

1. *Monitor NIST's CMVP listings* for new FIPS-validated modules that support post-quantum algorithms. Vendors such as Microsoft, Thales, and PQShield are expected to submit updated modules for validation over the next one to two years.
2. *Engage with your cryptographic vendors* to determine their roadmap for FIPS module upgrades. Many vendors are working toward FIPS 140-3 compliance with post-quantum capabilities, but may only support specific algorithms, such as LMS or Dilithium, in the early stages.
3. *Use hybrid configurations* where post-quantum algorithms are layered on top of FIPS-approved classical mechanisms. In many cases, FIPS modules can still be used for classical operations. In contrast, post-quantum operations are handled by a companion module in a non-FIPS mode until validation is complete.

4. *Isolate and test post-quantum operations* in non-production environments until FIPS validation is available. You may use separate key stores or cryptographic boundaries for these functions, allowing the rest of your system to remain FIPS-compliant.
5. *Prepare your compliance documentation* to reflect these transitional configurations. Regulators will want to see that quantum readiness is being pursued responsibly, even if full FIPS validation is not yet possible.

The FIPS validation process is rigorous and often time-consuming, but it is progressing. As post-quantum cryptographic algorithms mature and more are finalized through the FIPS 203–206 series, validated modules will follow. Early adopters who prepare their architecture today will be in a much better position to certify updated systems and meet compliance expectations when the new modules arrive.

In short, PQC upgrades in FIPS environments require a dual-track approach that includes support for classical security rigor through current FIPS modules while building the testing, documentation, and vendor relationships needed to integrate quantum-safe components once formally validated. For many federal and critical infrastructure operators, this path will be the only viable route toward a trusted post-quantum future.

12.5 CONCLUSION

Quantum-safe cryptography begins long before a message is sent or a handshake is completed. It starts with the generation, protection, and distribution of the cryptographic keys that underpin all secure systems. As this chapter illustrates, true post-quantum readiness means evolving every layer of key infrastructure, from the randomness that seeds entropy to the vaults that safeguard secrets over time.

Upgrading from PRNGs to QRNGs is more than a technical improvement. It is a shift toward unpredictability that quantum computers cannot model. ML-KEM and related key encapsulation mechanisms introduce a new era of secure exchange, designed to operate even when classical assumptions fail. Quantum Key Distribution, although more niche, represents a powerful safeguard for environments where physical assurance is more important than mathematical probability.

These advances require planning, architecture, and the modernization of HSMs, key vaults, and management platforms. They demand compliance strategies that align with evolving standards and audit frameworks, such as FIPS, and ask organizations to think beyond encryption alone, focusing instead on the full lifecycle of cryptographic trust.

Quantum resilience is not achieved through a single upgrade or vendor purchase. It is built step by step, across systems, over time. By focusing now on key generation, distribution, and lifecycle management, organizations can establish the foundations of cryptographic strength that will remain intact, regardless of what comes next.

The next chapter turns to IoT and embedded systems, which are the most complex and overlooked frontiers in the quantum migration journey. These devices often operate with limited resources, long lifecycles, and fragmented update processes, yet they must be secured against future threats. Chapter 13 explores how to integrate PQC into constrained environments, adapt firmware signing for post-quantum assurance, and overcome the unique challenges of industrial control systems and long-lived hardware.

Chapter 13

Integrate PQC into IoT and embedded systems

When most people think about cybersecurity, they imagine firewalls, cloud infrastructure, and enterprise applications. Rarely does the conversation begin with sensors on a pipeline, programmable logic controllers at a power station, or the firmware running on a hospital ventilator. Yet these embedded systems form the backbone of critical infrastructure, and their long life cycles, geographic sprawl, and physical inaccessibility make them one of the most difficult domains for post-quantum migration.

In operational environments, cryptographic agility is often an afterthought. Unlike IT systems that can be patched overnight or upgraded quarterly, industrial control systems (ICS) and embedded Internet of Things (IoT) devices are designed to last for decades. When their cryptographic protections are compromised, whether by aging algorithms or emerging quantum threats, replacing them is not a matter of weeks or months; it could take years. That delay leaves a growing window in which encryption may quietly erode, risking tampered data, unauthorized access, or silent manipulation of national critical functions.

13.1 LONG-LIFECYCLE HARDWARE AND ICS CHALLENGES

Many embedded systems and industrial control devices are built to last. Unlike enterprise laptops or cloud instances, these components often remain in service for a decade or more. That longevity becomes a vulnerability in the quantum era. If a device installed today is still in use after large-scale quantum computers become practical, any cryptographic protections it relies on may be fundamentally broken. In such cases, secure channels, firmware integrity, and authenticated commands could all be rendered invalid.

This is where the Mosca Model, introduced in Chapter 3, becomes especially useful. The model frames post-quantum risk in terms of three variables: x, the time it will take to replace or upgrade the system; y, the time the system or data must remain secure; and z, the estimated time until

DOI: 10.1201/9781003685760-18

quantum computers are capable of breaking today's encryption. If $x + y > z$, the system is at risk. In the case of industrial control systems and embedded hardware, y might be ten years or longer, and x, the time required to fully refresh hardware fleets, could easily add another five to ten years. When you run those numbers, it's clear that long-lifecycle infrastructure is already brushing up against the limits of that inequality. Waiting to act may mean running straight into a post-quantum failure window with no easy escape.

Many industries will deprioritize post-quantum cryptography for embedded systems simply because the risks seem distant, but for sectors like energy, transportation, water management, oil and gas, and healthcare, the consequences of cryptographic failure are too significant to ignore. In August 2022, the Cybersecurity and Infrastructure Security Agency (CISA) issued a memo urging Industrial Control System (ICS) operators to begin planning for quantum threats. Their message was clear: upgrades will be hard, slow, and expensive, but the cost of inaction could be far worse.

The risks aren't just hypothetical. A post-quantum adversary wouldn't need to break into every facility. They would only need to break the right cryptographic link between command and control systems and field devices. At the same time, asymmetric encryption is present in more ICS and embedded systems than some assume. While the volume may be lower than in IT networks, asymmetric cryptography underpins secure VPN connections for remote access, certificate-based authentication for software and device communication, and digital signatures used in firmware validation. If these protections fail, attackers could intercept updates, inject malicious code, or hijack control mechanisms.

For example, programmable logic controllers (PLCs), which manage critical operations in sectors like manufacturing, water treatment, and energy distribution, often rely on asymmetric cryptography for both firmware validation and device authentication. Signed firmware ensures that only trusted updates can be installed, while certificate-based authentication confirms that commands or configurations originate from an authorized source. If a quantum-capable adversary can break the digital signature scheme or compromise certificate-based authentication, they could not only install malicious firmware but also impersonate trusted administrators or control systems. That means an attacker could send commands that appear to come from a legitimate operator console, disabling alarms, bypassing safety limits, or reprogramming logic to create subtle, cascading failures.

In a manufacturing environment, this could lead to robotic systems operating outside design tolerances, increasing the risk of defective products or worker injury. In a water treatment facility, if an attacker compromises the VPN channel used to transmit control commands, they could forge cryptographically validated instructions that adjust chlorine levels or divert wastewater into clean supply lines. The system would accept the command as legitimate, putting public health and safety at immediate risk. In a power grid, the ability to spoof authenticated control messages could lead to load imbalances, false fault signals, or even rolling blackouts.

In healthcare, the stakes are just as high. IoT medical devices, such as infusion pumps, heart monitors, and insulin systems, depend on encrypted communication and secure firmware updates to function safely within hospital networks. If an attacker were to use quantum-powered decryption to tamper with those updates or intercept messages, they could install rogue software that changes dosages or silences alerts, putting patient safety in real danger. These devices often run in environments where keeping systems up and running takes priority over locking them down, which makes strong cryptographic protection even more critical.

In the energy sector and other critical infrastructure environments, PQC adoption isn't just about cybersecurity; it's about national resilience. Oil pipelines, electrical substations, and water systems rely on industrial control systems and field-deployed devices that may stay in operation for 20 years or more. These systems often have limited processing power and strict bandwidth constraints, making PQC integration especially difficult. Lightweight algorithms are only part of the answer. Vendors must also deliver firmware updates, cryptographic agility, and compatibility with constrained environments. For these sectors, the pressure to modernize comes not from innovation cycles, but from geopolitical risk and federal mandates.

Industrial equipment is rarely centralized. Devices are deployed across cities, rural networks, and offshore facilities. Replacing them involves physical labor, scheduling outages, coordinating with third parties, and securing budgets that compete with more visible priorities. Even then, many of these systems rely on legacy components that vendors no longer support, and those vendors cannot develop quantum-safe replacements until the standards are finalized.

While the ecosystem catches up, mitigating controls will be necessary. Organizations should assess whether PQC-enabled gateways or cryptographic proxies can be deployed in front of legacy equipment. These devices can terminate connections, handle post-quantum handshakes, and forward communications internally using legacy protocols. Although this introduces operational complexity, it helps extend the security envelope without requiring immediate replacement.

Other mitigation options include network segmentation to isolate critical devices, strict access controls to prevent unauthorized changes, enhanced monitoring to detect suspicious activity, and stronger operational discipline around key management. Firmware update processes should be locked down, ideally with cryptographic signing using hybrid or post-quantum schemes. In cases where updates are infrequent, organizations may even consider manually verifying updates in highly critical environments to prevent supply chain tampering.

The financial impact of early upgrades adds another layer of complexity. Industrial equipment is typically treated as a capital expenditure, amortized over a period of many years. Replacing these assets before the end of their depreciation cycle reduces the organization's ability to fully capitalize on them. This creates friction between the security imperative and the financial model. In many cases, cybersecurity leaders will need to collaborate closely with finance and procurement to build a business case that supports early replacement. This often means multi-year budgeting, coordination with existing refresh schedules, and executive, if not board-level, endorsement.

To get ahead of these challenges, organizations can begin by opening a dialogue with key vendors. Ask direct questions about timelines for PQC support in future firmware or hardware releases. Request written commitments or public roadmaps. Work together to define interface specifications that can accommodate future PQC algorithms, even if the vendor cannot yet commit to full implementation. For newer deployments, explore whether modular components, swappable cryptographic chips, or firmware updatability can be factored into purchasing decisions.

With these challenges in mind, the goal right now isn't to tear everything out and start over; it's to build a roadmap. Organizations must inventory their ICS and embedded assets, determine where cryptography is present, and incorporate post-quantum requirements into their hardware refresh planning. That means aligning procurement with expected IETF and NIST milestones, preparing for the computational demands of PQC, and beginning conversations with vendors now, before the clock runs out.

Migration won't be fast. It will require patience, planning, and pressure on both internal stakeholders and external vendors. However, with each step, organizations move closer to ensuring that their most vital systems remain trusted, even as quantum threats become a reality. Long-lifecycle hardware presents one of the most stubborn roadblocks in the journey to post-quantum security, but it also offers one of the most strategic opportunities. By taking action now, organizations can avoid being forced into reactive decisions later, when the stakes are much higher and the options more limited.

13.2 LIGHTWEIGHT CRYPTOGRAPHY FOR CONSTRAINED DEVICES

One of the biggest challenges in IoT and embedded systems is that many devices operate with minimal processing power, limited memory, and strict energy budgets. Post-quantum algorithms, particularly lattice-based ones, tend to require larger key sizes and greater computational resources than their classical counterparts. In an embedded system, this can be a showstopper.

To address this, some vendors are exploring lightweight implementations of PQC algorithms or hybrid approaches that use a classical outer layer with quantum-safe elements tucked inside. Others are experimenting with hardware acceleration, including quantum-enhanced HSMs that offload the computational burden from the device itself. Still, it's not yet clear which strategies will scale across tens of thousands of constrained devices, especially those deployed in hard-to-reach locations.

For many organizations, this will be a balancing act. Some devices may be candidates for replacement, particularly those already nearing end-of-life or deployed in high-risk environments. Others may require firmware updates that incorporate PQC support through optimized libraries or by reusing existing cryptographic co-processors. In select cases, organizations may deploy intermediary gateways that handle the heavy lifting of PQC operations on behalf of lightweight endpoints.

One promising solution just mentioned was intermediary gateways, which act as cryptographic proxies between constrained devices and the broader network. These gateways perform quantum-safe operations on behalf of endpoints that cannot support PQC natively. In practice, the gateway terminates the secure connection from the outside world using post-quantum algorithms, then relays the communication to the embedded device using its legacy protocol stack. This allows organizations to extend a protective post-quantum boundary without requiring immediate replacement or full upgrades of legacy devices.

For example, a smart meter deployed in a rural grid may continue using its existing symmetric or RSA-based protocols. At the same time, a nearby edge gateway handles all external-facing TLS connections using Kyber for key exchange and Dilithium for signatures. From the outside, the device appears PQC-ready. Internally, it continues functioning with minimal disruption.

Gateways can also be designed to enforce policies, validate firmware signatures, or act as a secure update distribution point. Many are deployed as ruggedized hardware appliances, ARM-based edge nodes, or virtual machines that sit between device networks and cloud platforms.

Vendors such as Fortanix, Thales, and WolfSSL offer products or software development kits (SDKs) that support this type of intermediary role. Fortanix provides edge-integrated key management and crypto services through its Runtime Encryption platform. Thales Luna HSMs can be deployed at the edge to centralize and accelerate cryptographic workloads. WolfSSL, widely used in embedded environments, now supports post-quantum ciphers via integration with liboqs, making it easier to build proxy functions into IoT gateway software.

For teams building their own solution, a typical design might include:

- An embedded Linux or RTOS device running a lightweight TLS stack (e.g., WolfSSL or mbedTLS) integrated with liboqs
- A VPN or secure tunnel endpoint that accepts PQC-enabled connections using OpenSSL 3.0 with hybrid key exchange
- An internal relay process that translates traffic between PQC protocols and legacy device communications (e.g., Modbus, MQTT, CoAP)
- Logging, authentication, and certificate validation logic to monitor and control access

This approach buys time. It enables organizations to prioritize which devices get full PQC upgrades, while ensuring that all external-facing communications are protected against quantum-era threats.

For many organizations, this will be a balancing act. Some devices may be candidates for replacement, particularly those already nearing end-of-life or deployed in high-risk environments. Others may require firmware updates that incorporate PQC support through optimized libraries or by reusing existing cryptographic co-processors. In select cases, intermediary gateways may be the most practical and cost-effective option.

It is also worth noting that this migration won't be uniform. Not every device needs full PQC support today. As encryption lifecycles shrink and attackers grow bolder, every unpatched endpoint becomes a liability. The key is to build in agility now, so future upgrades are measured in weeks rather than years.

13.3 PQC-AWARE FIRMWARE UPDATES

Firmware updates are one of the few opportunities to retrofit post-quantum security into embedded devices without replacing them outright. For this to work, organizations must modernize their signing and validation pipelines.

Many current systems rely on RSA or ECC signatures to verify that firmware comes from a trusted source. These signatures are baked into bootloaders, hardware roots of trust, and update protocols. Once a quantum computer can forge those signatures, malicious firmware can masquerade as legitimate, leaving no warning until a system fails or is compromised.

The solution lies in adopting post-quantum digital signature schemes, such as Dilithium or LMS, and in creating hybrid or composite signing mechanisms during the transition. This allows devices to validate both classical and quantum-safe signatures, ensuring backward compatibility while moving forward with stronger security guarantees.

Organizations must also prepare their build systems and firmware update infrastructure to support new certificate formats and larger signatures. Testing for performance impacts and validation failures will be critical, especially in systems that cannot tolerate long boot times or unexpected errors. Just as important is having a clear revocation strategy. If a quantum-safe signature key is compromised, devices must be able to identify and reject updates signed with that key and roll back to a known good state.

The firmware update process, often overlooked, becomes a central component of the post-quantum journey. It is the lever through which thousands of devices can be upgraded in parallel, with little downtime and relatively low cost; however, only if the infrastructure around those updates is ready for the challenge.

13.4 BUILDING PQC INTO HARDWARE AND SOFTWARE PRODUCTS

Companies that develop hardware and software products sit at the core of post-quantum preparedness. Their decisions will directly shape how organizations across various industries adopt, deploy, and secure post-quantum cryptography over the coming decade. Yet, the path for implementing PQC into product lines is not always clear, especially for companies that balance legacy support, constrained development cycles, and long-term customer relationships.

While the primary focus of this book is to guide enterprises through the migration to post-quantum cryptography, many of those same enterprises also develop and maintain products that will themselves need to be quantum-resistant. Whether those products are embedded controllers, cloud applications, mobile platforms, or network appliances, the responsibility for building in PQC lies squarely with the vendor. Although this book is not a comprehensive product development guide, this section outlines key considerations and starting points for integrating PQC into your product development lifecycle.

The introduction of PQC affects both product development and product security. From a development perspective, engineers must evaluate how new algorithms affect system performance, memory usage, and interoperability with third-party libraries. From a security standpoint, PQC represents both an upgrade to modernize cryptographic strength and a risk if implemented poorly or inconsistently across firmware, communications protocols, and device identity frameworks.

For vendors, the first step is to assess product exposure and identify which components rely on vulnerable algorithms. This typically includes key exchange in TLS stacks, code signing mechanisms, device authentication, and VPN or encrypted communication channels. Once the risk surface is understood, organizations can prioritize products based on lifecycle stage, customer impact, and cryptographic dependency.

For some products, especially newer ones with modular firmware architectures, PQC can be introduced via a software or firmware patch. This might involve replacing a TLS library with one that supports hybrid key exchange or adding a post-quantum signature check during the firmware validation routine. These updates are typically faster to develop, less disruptive to users, and easier to roll back if compatibility issues arise.

In other cases, particularly for embedded or resource-constrained products, a patch may not be feasible. Devices with limited memory, CPU, or network capabilities may require a full redesign to support PQC. In these situations, manufacturers should build a new version of the product that includes hardware-based cryptographic acceleration, larger buffers, or native support for QRNG-based key generation. This development cycle could take 12 to 36 months, depending on complexity, regulatory requirements, and supply chain constraints.

To begin integrating PQC into your product development lifecycle, consider launching a formal R&D track dedicated to the modernization of cryptography. Start with prototypes using libraries like liboqs or OpenSSL with PQC extensions. Test hybrid certificate support in internal builds and evaluate how signature size or key negotiation latency affects your application under realistic loads. Embed crypto-agility principles from the outset, treat cryptography as a pluggable module, not a hard-coded component. To treat cryptography as a pluggable module, rather than a hard-coded component, means designing your product so that cryptographic algorithms, libraries, and protocols can be easily replaced, upgraded, or reconfigured without requiring the rewriting of large sections of application code or rebuilding the entire system. It also means that you establish design patterns that support algorithm substitution, version tracking, and rollback.

In many legacy products, cryptographic functions, such as key generation, encryption, or signature verification, are embedded directly into the application logic. Developers may call specific algorithms (like RSA-2048 or SHA-1) directly, hard-code key sizes, or tightly couple the cryptographic routines to the application's core workflows. This makes future changes extremely difficult and high-risk. Suppose a vulnerability is discovered or a new standard, such as a post-quantum algorithm, must be adopted. In that case, those cryptographic pieces are difficult to isolate and replace without breaking the surrounding code.

By contrast, a *pluggable cryptographic architecture* relies on:

- *Abstraction layers*: Instead of calling an algorithm directly, the application calls an interface, such as "encrypt(data, key)", and the underlying crypto provider handles the implementation.
- *Configuration-driven design*: Algorithms, key sizes, and cipher suites are selected through configuration files or environment variables rather than being hard-coded.
- *Modular libraries*: Cryptographic functionality is separated into dedicated modules or services, often using well-maintained libraries like

OpenSSL, BoringSSL, WolfSSL, or commercial SDKs. These modules can be updated or replaced independently.
- *Clear separation of concerns*: Business logic, user workflows, and application features remain separate from cryptographic mechanics, allowing them to evolve independently.

Just as important is building crypto-agility into the product design from the beginning. As we've discussed repeatedly, PQC is not a one-time fix. The algorithms standardized today may need to be replaced or updated if new cryptanalytic breakthroughs emerge. Vendors must prepare for the possibility that future attacks or research could weaken a PQC algorithm, triggering the need to switch cipher suites rapidly. Products should be architected to allow for algorithm substitution without firmware reinstallation, including configurable cipher suites, updatable cryptographic libraries, and the separation of cryptographic logic from core application code. Failure to build crypto-agility now could result in painful and expensive retrofits later. Vendors that offer this flexibility from day one will not only reduce their own maintenance burden but also become more valuable to customers who want assurances that their investments will remain secure over time. It also simplifies testing, reduces the risk of introducing new bugs during upgrades, and future-proofs your product against evolving standards.

As a general rule, product manufacturers should consider firmware updates for devices released in the last three to five years that already include sufficient cryptographic flexibility and hardware headroom. For older products nearing end of life or running outdated stacks, full product refreshes may offer a more sustainable long-term solution.

Throughout this process, collaboration across engineering, product management, and legal teams is essential. Developers need support in selecting and integrating new cryptographic libraries. Security teams must evaluate potential side-channel risks or implementation flaws. Legal and compliance staff should be involved early, especially when targeting regulated markets where FIPS validation or government certifications may be required.

Product vendors must also engage with their customers. This involves publishing roadmaps for PQC adoption, providing interim mitigations where necessary, and aligning new features with customer refresh cycles. For example, an industrial equipment vendor might announce that future versions of its control unit will support hybrid TLS within the next 18 months, while offering a hardened gateway module with crypto-agility features as a stopgap.

Customers, especially those managing critical infrastructure, increasingly expect this level of transparency. Vendors that can demonstrate leadership on PQC will gain a competitive advantage, while those that delay may find themselves locked out of security-conscious markets.

Finally, manufacturers should consider joining standards groups and collaborative initiatives, such as the IETF, NIST working groups, and the Open Quantum Safe project. These communities offer access to the latest guidance, reference implementations, and interoperability testing environments, which can accelerate development and reduce risk.

The era of quantum-resilient products has already begun. Whether through software updates or hardware redesigns, vendors have an essential role to play in building the infrastructure of a secure post-quantum future. Waiting for customers to demand change may be too late. Leading with proactive integration, well-communicated roadmaps, and secure-by-design development will separate the trusted suppliers from those left behind.

13.4.1 The Q-Ready Framework for product development

Although the Q-Ready Framework presented in this book is primarily designed to help enterprises migrate their internal infrastructure to post-quantum cryptography, many of its core concepts also apply to the development of commercial hardware and software products. If your organization manufactures devices, platforms, or applications that rely on cryptographic protections, the same stages – discovery, planning, implementation, validation, and maintenance – can be adapted to guide quantum readiness within the product lifecycle.

Here's how product teams can map the Q-Ready phases to their work:

- *Discovery* aligns with the inventory of cryptographic dependencies across the product stack. This involves scanning codebases, firmware, libraries, protocols, and toolchains to identify where vulnerable algorithms, such as RSA, ECC, or SHA-1, are used. For product teams, this also includes assessing third-party SDKs, open-source libraries, and vendor components that may be embedded in your product. Creating a "crypto bill of materials" (CBOM) is a crucial first step.
- *Planning* informs product roadmap prioritization, helping organizations decide which product lines, models, or firmware branches to upgrade first. It supports strategic decisions such as whether to issue a firmware update or initiate a full product redesign. Planning also involves selecting vendors for cryptographic libraries or hardware components and building up internal capability through training or hiring. At this stage, security architects should work closely with product managers and R&D leads to align PQC adoption with development timelines and go-to-market strategies.
- *Implementation* overlaps with the integration of post-quantum algorithms into product code, whether by enabling hybrid TLS in a network module, switching to Dilithium for firmware signing, or embedding a

PQC-capable cryptographic library. It also includes refactoring code to support crypto-agility, making cryptographic functions modular and replaceable. If the product targets regulated industries, this is also the phase where teams must begin preparing for FIPS 203–206 validation, testing against standards, and documenting cryptographic behaviors for audit readiness.

- *Validation* translates to QA testing, fuzzing, interop trials, and side-channel resistance evaluation. For product teams, this involves creating controlled environments to validate post-quantum algorithms against expected behaviors, measuring performance impact, verifying fallbacks in hybrid configurations, and ensuring PQC updates don't break legacy compatibility. Cryptographic validation should also extend to integration testing with cloud services, mobile apps, or firmware update infrastructure, as well as product penetration testing.
- *Maintenance* becomes a roadmap for ongoing support, algorithm agility, and future updates. This includes creating patch pipelines, monitoring NIST and IETF developments, and preparing to rotate algorithms if vulnerabilities are discovered. For product vendors, maintenance also means providing tools and documentation for customers to update cryptographic settings, manage keys, and apply secure firmware updates over the device's lifespan.

However, there are important limitations. The Q-Ready Framework does not fully address product-specific concerns that exist outside of traditional enterprise IT environments. For example, hardware certification and compliance testing introduce complexities for embedded cryptographic modules that must meet regulatory or sector-specific standards. Field-deployed devices, such as those used in industrial or consumer IoT, often require bootstrapping trust without the benefit of centralized management systems. This creates challenges in securely establishing device identity and cryptographic baselines in uncontrolled environments.

Another concern involves the secure delivery of software updates. Over-the-air (OTA) update frameworks must support post-quantum signing mechanisms while also providing robust rollback protections in case of update failure or compromise. Ensuring the integrity of these updates becomes especially difficult when working with constrained devices or legacy protocols. What makes things even more complicated is the wide range of customer configurations vendors have to support. Products often end up in very different environments, each with its own cryptographic setup, different key structures, certificate chains, or algorithm preferences. A one-size-fits-all approach usually falls short, which means flexibility has to be built in from the start.

Finally, supply chain integration becomes a major factor. Product development often depends on coordination with contract manufacturers, silicon vendors, firmware authors, and other third parties. Many of these partners must also become post-quantum ready before a complete product solution can be secured. This dependency introduces timing and quality assurance risks that must be carefully managed.

Because of these unique challenges, product teams should treat the Q-Ready Framework as a foundational reference and extend it with product-aware processes drawn from the secure development lifecycle (SDL). That means embedding cryptographic architecture reviews in early design phases, updating threat models to account for quantum-capable attackers, and establishing cryptography-specific requirements in product specifications and test plans.

Where possible, organizations should create a parallel crypto-agility plan for their product portfolio, just as they would for enterprise infrastructure. That plan should include:

Which products support modular cryptography today?
Which libraries or APIs are PQC-capable?
Where can PQC support be added via an update?
Where is a full hardware redesign needed?
Where may end-of-life decisions be more cost-effective?

By combining the structure of the Q-Ready Framework with product-centric practices, engineering teams can chart a deliberate, defensible course toward PQC adoption. Doing this now, before customers, regulators, or adversaries force the issue, will reduce future disruptions and build long-term trust in the cryptographic integrity of your products.

13.5 MANAGING IRREPLACEABLE LEGACY SYSTEMS

While much of this chapter has focused on pathways to integration and modernization, the reality is that some systems cannot be upgraded. These legacy systems may lack vendor support, cryptographic agility, or even the processing power to accept modern algorithms. In many industrial and embedded environments, this is not the exception; it's the rule. From SCADA devices in rural substations to medical imaging systems still in active use after 20 years, truly non-upgradable systems present one of the most stubborn roadblocks on the journey to quantum readiness.

The goal in these situations isn't perfection; it's containment. That means applying compensating controls, isolating cryptographic dependencies, and formally documenting the risk in a way that balances security, safety, and operational continuity.

One of the most effective strategies is cryptographic isolation. This involves placing a modern, PQC-capable intermediary between the legacy system and the broader network. That proxy, whether it's an edge gateway, secure appliance, or hardened virtual machine, terminates external connections, performs all cryptographic operations using post-quantum algorithms, and relays traffic to the legacy system using its original protocol stack. From the outside, the system appears quantum-resistant. Internally, it continues functioning exactly as it did before.

In environments like oil and gas pipelines or industrial robotics, this middlebox approach is often the only realistic option. For instance, a turbine controller running a decades-old firmware image might communicate over Modbus without authentication or encryption. Instead of tearing out the turbine, an intermediary gateway could be installed to enforce access control, wrap the traffic in a PQC-secure tunnel, and log all interactions. The system itself hasn't changed, but its exposure is drastically reduced.

In addition to isolation, compensating controls must be deployed to reduce the risk. These may include segmenting the network to isolate legacy systems from internet-facing infrastructure, installing unidirectional gateways or data diodes to limit data flow and prevent command injection, and enforcing strict allowlists and role-based access controls to manage communication and user permissions. Organizations may also require manual approval workflows for firmware changes or operational adjustments, especially in safety-critical systems. Where digital safeguards are lacking, physical security enhancements, such as tamper-evident seals, locked enclosures, or surveillance, can serve as additional barriers against compromise.

Even with these controls in place, legacy systems will never be truly quantum-resistant. When technical remediation is not feasible, the only remaining path is formal governance. This requires creating and maintaining a risk acceptance framework that explains the trade-offs involved in maintaining these systems. A structured review process should be implemented to identify impacted systems, explain why they cannot be upgraded, and quantify the business, safety, or regulatory consequences of replacing them. The framework should also detail what compensating controls are in place and how effective they are likely to be in reducing the exposure window. This assessment must then be presented to senior leadership or governance bodies, such as the CISO, Chief Risk Officer, or operational lead, for formal sign-off and periodic review.

These reviews should not be treated as one-time exceptions. They must be revisited regularly, at least annually, or whenever threat models, regulations, or feasibility change. Some organizations may fold these reviews into an existing exception management system used to track unsupported software, hardware nearing end-of-life, or known vulnerabilities across the enterprise.

To put this into perspective, consider a legacy MRI machine in a regional hospital. It runs on an outdated operating system with no ongoing support, and the manufacturer went out of business a decade ago. Replacing it would cost millions and disrupt clinical services for months. Instead, the hospital may install an isolated update server on-site that uses PQC-secure communication protocols, restrict the MRI's network access to a dedicated VLAN, and require dual-operator approval before any software change is made. These steps don't modernize the cryptography on the device, but they do contain the risk in a way that makes sense for patient safety and operational constraints.

Ultimately, cryptographic remediation is not a binary state; it's a spectrum. Some systems will leap ahead with firmware updates and cryptographic agility. Others will lag behind. The responsibility of the security team is not to force immediate upgrades but to ensure that even the laggards are visible, managed, and contextualized within a larger enterprise risk strategy.

Quantum readiness doesn't require every system to be modernized. It requires every system to be known, protected to the extent possible, and accounted for in the organization's security and governance posture. Legacy assets may never be upgraded, but they should never be ignored.

13.6 CONCLUSION

Integrating post-quantum cryptography into IoT and embedded systems is not a matter of flipping a switch. It is a methodical, often painstaking process shaped by physical constraints, extended life cycles, and complex stakeholder ecosystems. As this chapter has illustrated, these limitations are not excuses; they are planning variables. The longer a device is expected to live, the more urgent it becomes to account for cryptographic decay over time. That urgency grows as standards harden and threat actors prepare for Q-Day.

Across industrial control systems, constrained IoT deployments, firmware pipelines, and the product supply chain, PQC readiness requires deep collaboration between engineers, product managers, procurement teams, and security architects. It demands practical compromise, forward-looking architecture, and a commitment to crypto-agility. Vendors and end users alike must build infrastructure that is ready to adapt because cryptography will not remain static for the next 20 years, and neither will the threats.

Long-lived devices, unpatchable firmware, and hard-to-reach systems cannot wait for the market to be ready. They must be accounted for now, through careful planning, vendor engagement, and smart mitigations that reduce risk while the ecosystem catches up. If we ignore these hidden systems, we risk allowing quantum compromise to begin in the shadows, at the edge of the network, where trust is hardest to enforce and failure is most difficult to detect.

In the next chapter, we move into the Validation Phase, where planning turns into proof. We'll examine how to test your deployed post-quantum solutions for functionality, beginning with interoperability, regression, and performance evaluation. We'll also explore emerging toolkits from PQShield, PQSim, and others that help verify post-quantum configurations under real-world conditions. This is the moment when your crypto strategy meets reality, and the results will determine whether your organization is truly ready or just hopes to be.

Section V

Phase 4

Validation

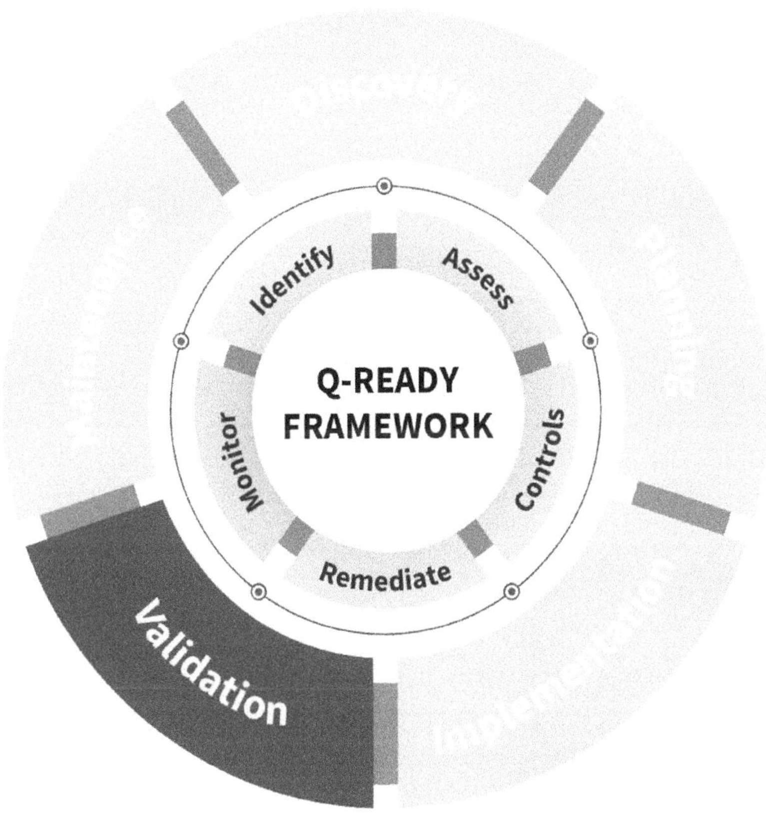

Figure SV.1 Validation Phase.

DOI: 10.1201/9781003685760-19

Chapter 14

Test deployed solutions for functionality

By the time organizations reach this phase in their post-quantum cryptography (PQC) journey, the easy decisions are behind them. The algorithms have been selected, the infrastructure updated, and the code deployed, but all of that means very little if the changes don't work under real conditions. This chapter marks the beginning of the Validation Phase, where strategies and upgrades must prove their worth not in theory, but in action.

This step returns us to the testing concepts introduced in Chapter 8. There, we mapped out a lab-based testing framework and outlined how to create proof-of-concept environments. Now, we revisit that work so we can execute against it. The focus has shifted from planning to practice. Your PQC implementations are no longer hypothetical; at this point, they should be live or nearly so. The question now is whether they hold up to the scrutiny of integration, performance, and real-world use.

14.1 INTEROPERABILITY TESTING

One of the most overlooked aspects of post-quantum deployment is how well systems interact once PQC is introduced. A cryptographic scheme that performs flawlessly in isolation may fail completely when placed in a network of hybrid systems, legacy protocols, and third-party integrations.

Interoperability testing ensures that your PQC-enabled services can communicate effectively with each other and with external parties. This includes internal microservices, APIs, partner systems, cloud platforms, and legacy clients. These systems may have different levels of PQC support or varying implementations of hybrid key exchange. The goal is to validate handshake processes, key negotiation, certificate parsing, and fallback logic across the entire environment.

To perform this testing, organizations should simulate full end-to-end communication chains. For example, verify that a client using hybrid TLS can establish a secure connection with a server that utilizes a post-quantum-enabled OpenSSL stack. Confirm that both sides validate the certificate

DOI: 10.1201/9781003685760-20

chain, negotiate keys correctly, and can encrypt and decrypt messages without data loss.

In mixed environments, it is critical to test downgraded negotiation paths. If a server receives a request from a client that does not support PQC, will it respond appropriately or drop the connection? If fallback is permitted, does the log accurately reflect that the session was not quantum-safe?

This phase of testing should also include validation of certificate formats and hybrid chains. For example, test whether your systems can parse and trust hybrid certificates generated by third-party certificate authorities, such as DigiCert or ISARA. Confirm that intermediate and root certificates support mixed algorithms where needed, and that revocation checks (e.g., OCSP or CRL) function correctly in both PQC and hybrid contexts.

14.1.1 Protocols and components to test

The following systems and interfaces are particularly vulnerable to PQC-related interoperability issues and should be prioritized for testing:

- *TLS 1.3*: Test hybrid key exchange and authentication using combinations like ML-KEM with Dilithium or Falcon.
- *SSH*: Validate Kyber-based hybrid key exchange and client/server handshake compatibility.
- *QUIC (UDP)*: Ensure low latency and reliability in handshake negotiation with PQC-enabled endpoints.
- *X.509 Certificates*: Confirm parsing, trust validation, and compatibility of hybrid and composite certificates across operating systems and applications.
- *Hardware Security Modules (HSMs)*: Test support for post-quantum key generation, encapsulation, and signing workflows.

To support this testing, several tools and frameworks are available:

- *OpenSSL with liboqs*: The Open Quantum Safe (OQS) fork of OpenSSL supports many of the leading post-quantum algorithms and hybrid TLS configurations. It is widely used for prototyping and early integration tests.
- *BoringSSL PQC branch*: Google's fork of OpenSSL includes experimental PQC support and is particularly useful for testing Android and Chrome-related stacks.
- *WolfSSL + liboqs*: For embedded or resource-constrained environments, WolfSSL offers lightweight TLS libraries with post-quantum support via liboqs.
- *Wireshark*: Useful for inspecting TLS handshakes and confirming key exchange parameters in live traffic captures.

- *TestSSL.sh* or *SSLyze*: These tools can probe TLS endpoints and report which ciphers are offered, which are accepted, and how servers respond to different negotiation scenarios.
- *PQ-TLS test suites* from Open Quantum Safe or NIST interoperability events: These curated environments provide test cases and known-good configurations to validate your stack against.

14.1.2 Building a robust testing plan

Enterprises should create test environments that mimic production as closely as possible. A well-rounded interoperability testing plan should begin with environment setup, including the deployment of dual-stack TLS and SSH endpoints that support both classical and post-quantum algorithms. This allows teams to replicate real-world conditions and validate how cryptographic systems will behave once PQC is introduced.

Next, functional testing should be conducted using known-good test vectors to confirm the success of key exchanges, signature validation, and full end-to-end encryption across services. These functional checks establish a baseline of expected behavior under ideal conditions.

Performance benchmarking is another critical component. Teams should measure handshake latency, monitor PQC key generation and signing times, and assess the impact on payload size and transport overhead. These metrics help identify bottlenecks or resource constraints that could affect deployment viability in production.

Negative testing should also be included to expose failure modes. This involves intentionally using unsupported or misconfigured PQC options to observe how systems handle errors, fallback scenarios, or protocol mismatches.

In addition, certificate compatibility must be verified. Enterprises should test whether PQC-enabled or hybrid X.509 certificates are properly recognized and trusted by browsers, enterprise applications, and mobile platforms. This ensures the user-facing components of the system function as expected.

Finally, make vendor compatibility testing a priority. Be sure to include things like certificate authorities, APIs, and cloud-native services in your staged tests so you can spot any issues with third-party systems or shared infrastructure early on. These edge cases are often where integration problems show up first.

14.1.3 Common issues observed in NIST PQC testing

In large-scale interoperability evaluations led by NIST and its collaborators, several recurring challenges were observed that could impede the successful deployment of post-quantum cryptography. One of the most prominent issues involved *ASN.1 and DER encoding mismatches*, resulting in certificate parsing failures. ASN.1 (Abstract Syntax Notation One) is a standard interface description language used to define data structures for representing, encoding, transmitting, and decoding data. DER (Distinguished Encoding Rules) is a binary encoding format for ASN.1, commonly used in X.509 certificates. When implementations deviate from strict encoding rules, such as including unnecessary leading zeros in integers or misordering certificate fields, receiving systems may reject certificates outright. For example, suppose a certificate uses a non-canonical DER encoding for a public key or digital signature. In that case, a cryptographic library may fail to parse or validate it even if the underlying data is correct.

Another common problem was *OID registry conflicts*. OIDs (Object Identifiers) are globally unique numeric identifiers used to specify cryptographic algorithms, certificate policies, and other protocol elements. Each algorithm must have a registered Object Identifier (OID) so that software can recognize and process it correctly. However, in PQC adoption, some systems were found to reject new or unrecognized OIDs, either because their software lacked updates or because they relied on hardcoded OID mappings. For instance, if a certificate includes an OID for CRYSTALS-Dilithium that a browser or server stack does not recognize, it may fail validation, even if the signature itself is correct. This creates friction during early adoption, especially in environments that depend on consistent algorithm negotiation and certificate validation.

In addition to encoding and identifier challenges, teams also ran into issues with *payload size limits*. Post-quantum digital signatures are much larger than traditional ones, and in some legacy systems, those larger sizes pushed past buffer limits or protocol field constraints. That led to dropped packets, cut-off payloads, or failed handshakes during secure communications. These problems showed up most often in embedded systems, mobile apps, and low-bandwidth environments where memory and packet size are already stretched thin.

Another challenge stemmed from *gaps in the TLS stack*. Not all TLS libraries currently support hybrid key exchange, and some fail to handle fallback mechanisms properly. When a PQC-enabled client attempts to negotiate a secure session with a server that only supports classical algorithms, or vice versa, the connection may silently fail or default to an insecure configuration without properly logging the downgrade. These silent failures are dangerous because they may go unnoticed in production environments.

Finally, *limitations in PKCS#11* interfaces were identified as a critical barrier, particularly in hardware security modules (HSMs). PKCS#11 is a standard API used to communicate with cryptographic tokens such as HSMs and smart cards. Many current implementations do not support the digest-then-sign model required by several PQC algorithms, which prevents them from processing quantum-safe signatures. Without updated vendor support for new signing workflows and algorithms, organizations relying on HSMs for secure key management may struggle to adopt PQC without significant architectural changes.

14.1.4 Best practices and enterprise recommendations

Interoperability testing should begin early, ideally in parallel with algorithm evaluation and pilot integration efforts. Waiting until late in the migration process to validate interoperability increases the risk of architectural surprises and deployment delays.

Whenever possible, organizations should use hybrid configurations. Supporting both classical and post-quantum cryptography in a dual-stack setup helps ensure everything keeps working smoothly, even in environments that aren't fully ready to make the leap to PQC just yet.

It is also essential to track the evolution of standards. Regularly monitor updates from NIST, IETF, and the CA/Browser Forum regarding PQC profiles, certificate structures, algorithm identifiers, and validation behaviors. These evolving standards will directly impact how interoperability is maintained across cryptographic ecosystems.

Enterprise teams must coordinate closely with vendors. This includes working with software providers, HSM vendors, and certificate authorities to confirm their level of PQC support, validate compatibility across systems, and understand timelines for upcoming updates or patches.

This is also the time to engage vendors and external partners. Many PQC issues emerge not within your own systems, but at the boundaries, where your architecture interfaces with someone else's. Identify those seams and test them early. Reach out to critical partners and cloud providers to understand what PQC support they offer, and under what conditions. Where possible, schedule joint testing windows or set up shared staging environments to validate compatibility.

Finally, document all interoperability findings and build automated regression tests into your deployment pipeline. Every new cryptographic library version, firmware patch, or software release should trigger compatibility testing across your supported configurations to ensure that future changes do not silently reintroduce PQC-incompatible behavior. Integrating these tests into CI/CD workflows allows cryptographic readiness to evolve in step with your environment. If two systems cannot agree on how to protect the data they exchange, then neither can guarantee the result. As PQC adoption accelerates, testing for that agreement, clearly, thoroughly, and repeatably, becomes one of the most important steps in securing the path forward.

14.2 REGRESSION TESTING

Once PQC is in place, your systems must continue to do everything they did before and do it well. Regression testing is what confirms that newly integrated post-quantum cryptographic code has not disrupted core functionality, broken existing services, or introduced unexpected side effects. It ensures that your system remains stable, secure, and user-friendly after the transition.

The scope of regression testing includes far more than just cryptographic operations. It spans authentication flows, certificate validation, data encryption and decryption, database transactions, API traffic, third-party integrations, load balancing, and user-facing behavior such as session persistence and redirects. If your web application uses client certificates for authentication, can it still complete a login under PQC? If your APIs sign and validate tokens, are those tokens still recognized under hybrid signature formats?

The first step in regression testing is simple but critical; just run the exact same automated test suite that you used before the cryptographic upgrade. This provides a baseline for identifying behavioral changes. Look for failed assertions, increased error rates, unexpected re-authentication prompts, broken session cookies, or redirects that no longer land correctly. Small anomalies may hint at larger compatibility issues with certificates, key handling, or TLS negotiations.

Regression testing must also be thorough and environment-aware. Cryptographic operations are deeply embedded in the infrastructure stack. Bugs introduced during PQC migration are often not inherent to the cryptographic libraries themselves, but rather in the systems that rely on them. A legacy identity provider may struggle with the new signature format in a hybrid certificate. A client-side JavaScript library may fail to parse a token signed with a post-quantum algorithm. A network appliance may time out during handshake negotiation due to longer PQC signature verification or key generation.

You must test across realistic environments, including cloud workloads, edge devices, and mobile platforms, if applicable. Don't limit testing to development builds or staging servers. For accurate results, test using the same configurations, DNS routing, and certificate chains you expect in production.

There are several categories of regression testing that organizations should consider when validating post-quantum cryptography implementations.

Functional testing involves confirming that all features continue to work as intended after PQC integration. This includes testing key workflows such as user login, purchases, data uploads, and API calls. Even minor cryptographic changes can affect authentication, session handling, or application routing, so it is critical to verify that each function behaves as expected.

Cryptographic integrity testing focuses on validating that core cryptographic operations, such as encryption, decryption, digital signing, and signature verification, perform correctly using the newly adopted algorithms. This helps ensure that data remains protected and that trust mechanisms continue to function across the system.

Performance testing compares the responsiveness and throughput of the application before and after the PQC upgrade. Post-quantum algorithms may introduce longer handshake times or additional processing overhead, especially in high-volume environments. Testing should target areas like TLS negotiation, digital signature processing, and key exchange performance to understand any latency introduced.

UI/UX testing assesses how these changes impact the user experience. Testers should monitor for delayed responses, authentication timeouts, broken redirects, or interface issues that may arise from cryptographic delays or unexpected errors. These issues, while rooted in backend changes, can quickly erode user trust if not caught early.

Security testing ensures that new cryptographic behavior aligns with security policies and controls. This includes validating that fallback logic (such as reverting to classical algorithms when PQC is not supported), logging mechanisms, and error handling continue to operate securely and predictably. Recovery paths should be tested to confirm that the system can handle failure states without exposing sensitive data or increasing risk.

By covering all these dimensions, teams can detect unintended consequences early, maintain continuity of service, and uphold both user experience and security assurances.

Popular tools to support these testing efforts include:

- *Selenium/Playwright*: For browser-based UI and end-to-end flow testing. Useful to catch regressions in login behavior or TLS certificate warnings.
- *Postman/Insomnia*: For automated API testing and contract validation across PQC-enabled endpoints.
- *JMeter/Locust/k6*: For load testing and performance benchmarking before and after PQC rollout.
- *pytest + Hypothesis (Python)*: For unit and property-based testing of cryptographic logic or business rules.
- *JUnit/TestNG (Java)*: For backend services where crypto libraries are updated.
- *Wireshark*: To inspect network behavior during TLS handshakes or VPN sessions and identify failed negotiations.
- *OpenSSL CLI tools*: To validate cert chains, simulate TLS handshakes, or test hybrid cipher suites directly.

Equally important is testing rollback procedures. No matter how well-planned the deployment is, your team must be prepared to revert to classical crypto configurations if a PQC implementation fails in production. This includes switching out libraries, re-issuing classical certificates, or disabling PQC cipher suites in TLS settings. Regression testing should cover these recovery paths. Practice rolling back and restoring a service, and confirm that functionality and data integrity remain intact.

Finally, document all regression results and include them in your change control processes. Treat cryptographic updates like any other critical infrastructure change, worthy of tracking, review, and cross-functional validation. Only after thorough regression and rollback testing should a PQC implementation be considered production-ready. Post-quantum cryptography changes the mathematics, but regression testing ensures you haven't changed the experience or broken the system in the process.

14.3 LATENCY TESTING

Post-quantum algorithms come with some real performance trade-offs. They typically use larger keys, create longer handshake messages, and generate bigger digital signatures compared to classical algorithms. That can mean more strain on your systems, extra network traffic, and noticeable slowdowns during important operations. Latency testing helps you pinpoint where those delays happen, measure their impact, and figure out whether any of them could affect how usable or reliable your system really is.

Start by isolating the handshake process for protocols like TLS or IKEv2. Measure the time it takes to complete a handshake using classical methods such as RSA or ECDH. Then perform the same handshake using hybrid configurations that incorporate ML-KEM or Kyber, NIST's post-quantum key encapsulation mechanisms. Repeat these tests under various load conditions to observe how latency scales. Look not only at connection time but also at how CPU and memory usage vary between classical and post-quantum operations. For web applications and APIs, this may also include timing the impact of verifying hybrid certificates or parsing PQC-enabled Java Web Tokens (JWTs).

When conducting latency tests, it is important to evaluate both average performance and tail latency, the worst-case delays experienced under peak load or degraded conditions. Average performance can provide a broad overview, but it's the outliers that typically break user trust. Users might tolerate a small delay, but not sporadic multi-second lags or broken connections. This is especially relevant in use cases like online banking, video streaming, or VoIP, where trust, security, and responsiveness must coexist without compromise.

In embedded systems or IoT devices, performance measurement should extend to factors like battery consumption, initial handshake time on device boot, and peak memory usage during cryptographic operations. Some devices may appear compatible with PQC in theory, but only function acceptably with hardware acceleration or cryptographic offloading. For battery-powered devices, even modest increases in computation time can result in measurable reductions in battery life.

Latency testing should mirror real-world conditions as closely as possible. Simulate actual user behavior, including API request patterns, login flows, certificate validation, or device boot sequences. Include network conditions that match production, including variable latency, packet loss, and jitter. Monitor not just system-level metrics, but also user-experience indicators, such as perceived response time, timeout rates, or interface responsiveness.

Several tools can support latency and performance testing in post-quantum environments:

- *OpenSSL with OQS extensions*: Use command-line tools to initiate handshakes using PQC-enabled configurations and time each negotiation (time openssl s_client -connect). The OQS fork supports ML-KEM, Kyber, and other algorithms.
- *Wireshark*: Inspect packet captures to analyze the duration of TLS handshakes, the size of handshake messages, and the negotiation process in detail.
- *Apache Benchmark (ab)/wrk/k6*: Generate high-throughput HTTP request traffic to test API response times and server-side TLS performance.
- *iperf3*: Measure raw network throughput and latency with and without PQC-enabled tunnels (e.g., VPNs or TLS proxies).
- *Locust/JMeter*: Simulate realistic user behavior, including login flows or transactions, and measure system latency under concurrent load.
- *Valgrind/perf/Intel VTune*: Profile CPU performance and memory usage during cryptographic operations to pinpoint hotspots.
- *Battery Profiler Tools (e.g., Android Battery Historian or TI EnergyTrace)*: For embedded and mobile devices, track power consumption during handshake execution.

In production-facing systems, latency results should also feed into service-level objective (SLO) reviews. For example, if a PQC-enabled handshake increases TLS connection time from 50 ms to 250 ms, determine whether that change breaks existing performance targets. For cloud-native services, consider testing cold-start behavior in serverless functions or container-based workloads, where startup time can be critical.

In short, latency testing is about striking a balance between security and speed. Post-quantum cryptography is essential for future-proofing your infrastructure, but if it degrades performance enough to disrupt services or frustrate users, it can backfire. Measure carefully, optimize where possible, and make data-driven decisions about when and how to deploy PQC in performance-sensitive environments.

14.4 SECURITY TESTING

Security testing is the fourth and equally vital category of post-quantum validation. It ensures that the cryptographic migration has not introduced vulnerabilities, weakened existing controls, or created exploitable edge cases.

This testing should be led by the security team and coordinated with engineering, DevOps, and compliance stakeholders. It should be performed before a system goes live and after any cryptographic changes, library upgrades, or infrastructure modifications. In high-assurance and regulated environments, security testing should also occur on a recurring schedule, such as quarterly or after every major release.

Start with *penetration testing* to simulate real-world attacks against your PQC-enabled infrastructure. Use both internal red teams and external ethical hackers to focus on downgrade attacks, handshake hijacking, certificate parsing anomalies, insecure fallbacks, and unintentional leaks caused by hybrid protocol confusion. Red team exercises are especially valuable for identifying edge-case behavior not covered by normal regression tests.

Follow this with *smoke testing* for critical controls. Test basic scenarios, such as login, certificate verification, and token validation, to ensure that switching to hybrid or quantum-safe algorithms does not bypass core security checks. This can catch implementation oversights before they become serious issues.

Implement *Static Application Security Testing (SAST)* to analyze source code for errors introduced by PQC-related changes. This includes improper error handling, insecure key management logic, or misuse of PQC libraries. Tools such as SonarQube, Fortify, and Checkmarx can help catch these flaws early in the development lifecycle.

Run *Dynamic Application Security Testing (DAST)* against running applications to detect vulnerabilities in live environments. These tools simulate attacks such as malformed certificate injection or protocol fuzzing. OWASP ZAP, Burp Suite, and Veracode are commonly used to identify issues in TLS configurations, endpoint behavior, or cryptographic workflows.

Software Composition Analysis (SCA) is another vital component. It scans for known vulnerabilities in third-party libraries and SDKs, including those that implement or wrap PQC functions. This helps prevent supply chain risks and ensures you are not importing outdated or flawed cryptographic components. Tools like Snyk or Black Duck offer automated tracking of open-source and commercial dependencies.

Additional forms of testing include:

- *Fuzz testing (Fuzzing)*: Feed malformed, semi-random, or intentionally corrupted data to APIs, libraries, or certificate parsers to discover crash conditions, memory leaks, or logic flaws. Tools like AFL (American Fuzzy Lop), LibFuzzer, and Peach Fuzzer are effective in this context, particularly when targeting cryptographic decoding and certificate validation routines.
- *Side-channel analysis*: For systems involving hardware cryptographic modules or constrained devices, test for timing, power, or electromagnetic leakage that could reveal secrets during PQC operations. This requires specialized tools and labs but is increasingly relevant for embedded and mobile applications.
- *Credential and secrets scanning*: Use tools like TruffleHog, GitLeaks, or GitGuardian to scan repositories, builds, and environments for hardcoded PQC keys, test credentials, or sensitive materials introduced during migration.
- *Audit logging verification*: Confirm that key events, such as failed PQC handshakes, fallback usage, or certificate validation failures, are logged correctly and that these logs are ingested by SIEM tools. They must be alertable, retained according to policy, and structured enough for incident investigation.

Security testing should also include audit logging verification. Ensure that failed PQC handshakes, certificate parsing errors, and algorithm fallbacks are logged, monitored, and alertable. Logs must be usable for incident response, forensic investigation, and compliance. Security testing should be treated as a continuous lifecycle activity. Cryptographic upgrades touch the heart of authentication, trust, and data protection mechanisms. Even a minor flaw can have cascading consequences. Regular revalidation, peer review of test coverage, and the inclusion of security tests in continuous integration/continuous deployment (CI/CD) pipelines are best practices. By performing robust and layered security testing, organizations can ensure that their PQC upgrades are not only mathematically secure but operationally resilient and safe under fire. Cryptography may be theoretical, but attacks are practical, and testing is the bridge between the two.

14.5 A FRAMEWORK FOR FUNCTIONAL TESTING

A sound testing strategy combines all four types of testing: interoperability, regression, latency, and security into a repeatable framework. Here's a structured approach for executing functionality testing:

1. *Prepare the environment*: Use the proof-of-concept lab from Chapter 8. Include PQC-enabled endpoints, legacy systems, and tools like OpenSSL with liboqs, PQShield SDKs, or PQSim test clients.
2. *Define the scope*: Identify systems that have been upgraded or modified to support PQC. Prioritize those with user-facing components or compliance obligations.
3. *Develop test cases*: For each system, define a series of test cases that cover known functionality, expected PQC behavior, edge cases, and failure paths.
4. *Automate the execution*: Integrate testing into your CI/CD pipelines. Include unit tests for PQC libraries, integration tests for applications, and system tests for end-to-end behavior.
5. *Log and validate*: Record handshake times, CPU utilization, success and failure rates, and cryptographic negotiation details. Validate outputs against known-good baselines.
6. *Review and document*: Analyze failures, unexpected latencies, or protocol mismatches. Update documentation and prepare reports for risk and compliance teams.
7. *Schedule retests*: As standards evolve or vendor libraries are updated, retest periodically. PQC validation is a continuous process.

Functional testing of PQC implementations should not be left solely to developers or cryptographers. It requires collaboration across several teams. Security engineers validate the cryptographic correctness. QA engineers ensure application functionality is preserved. DevOps teams monitor performance, latency, and service reliability. Risk and compliance teams ensure documentation is maintained and controls are aligned with policy.

In high-assurance environments, third-party validation may also be warranted. External testing firms, red teams, or academic partners can provide objective assessments of your implementation's resilience, especially when deploying in regulated or public-facing contexts.

The most effective testing is integrated into the release cycle. Functional validation should happen:

- After initial deployment to the test environment
- Before any production rollout
- After vendor library upgrades
- During system-wide audits or annual reviews
- Following any cryptographic incident or failure

In short, testing should be an ongoing process. Every major cryptographic change demands a full revalidation. Even minor version bumps may introduce breaking changes or performance regressions.

14.6 TOOLS AND VALIDATION SUITES

Several toolkits can support post-quantum functionality testing:

- *PQShield* offers hardware-compatible SDKs and validation suites that simulate quantum-safe deployments across TLS, VPNs, and embedded systems.
- *PQSim* is designed to mimic post-quantum conditions and validate application behavior under hybrid or pure PQC configurations.
- *liboqs* provides a reference implementation of NIST PQC algorithms and can be used with OpenSSL or BoringSSL for live handshake testing.
- *QuintessenceLabs* offers entropy testing and key generation tools that validate the strength of QRNGs and key lifecycle processes.

These tools should be integrated into your lab and used during each testing cycle. Combined with manual validation and integration testing, they form a comprehensive toolkit for measuring success.

14.7 CONCLUSION

Functional testing is where theory meets reality. It confirms whether your PQC investments translate into meaningful protection or whether they introduce unintended risks. Without it, you are operating on faith rather than evidence.

As organizations deploy PQC across their systems, functionality and security testing becomes the new standard of assurance. It ensures that upgraded cryptographic protections don't come at the cost of broken workflows, degraded performance, or silent incompatibilities. By investing in structured, continuous testing now, organizations reduce the risk of failure later and build the operational muscle needed for cryptographic change that is never really finished.

In the next chapter, we enter the second step of the Validation Phase, where we focus not on testing, but on monitoring. Chapter 15 explores how to measure, monitor, and certify the security properties of your post-quantum systems through auditability, transparency, and formal validation methods.

Chapter 15

Monitor for new threats and issues

As I've said throughout this book, deploying post-quantum cryptography is not something you do once and forget. It marks the beginning of an ongoing process where every component, from key generation to protocol enforcement, must be closely monitored. As quantum-safe systems begin to scale across an enterprise, the need to monitor them for new threats becomes as critical as the migration itself.

This chapter outlines what that monitoring should look like in practice. It builds on the functional testing discussed in Chapter 14 and turns attention to continuous operations. Now that systems are deployed and validated, the job is to ensure they stay that way. In a post-quantum world, which means new classes of risk, novel failure modes, and the emergence of hybrid threats that blend legacy vulnerabilities with cryptographic misconfigurations.

15.1 MONITORING POST-QUANTUM CRYPTOGRAPHY IN PRODUCTION

The goal of PQC monitoring is not only to detect traditional security events, but also to identify cryptographic drift, entropy issues, misuse of algorithms, and breakdowns in certificate validation. This requires more than standard logging. It demands visibility into cryptographic operations, as well as integrations with the security operations center (SOC) that allow for real-time threat detection and response.

Monitoring should be implemented as soon as PQC is introduced into production. Waiting for failures or compliance audits leaves little room for recovery. Organizations should treat PQC like any other mission-critical system. Logs must be collected, parsed, and correlated across devices, services, and user behaviors. Certificates should be tracked for expiration, revocation, and format inconsistencies. Key usage patterns should be baselined and anomalies investigated.

 DOI: 10.1201/9781003685760-21

15.1.1 What to monitor: key events and signals

The first step in building a PQC monitoring strategy is understanding what needs to be observed. Unlike traditional threats that focus on access control, data exfiltration, or endpoint compromise, cryptographic monitoring focuses on the proper usage and behavior of security primitives.

Key events to monitor include:

- *Certificate failures*: These include unsupported or invalid hybrid certificates, unexpected algorithm downgrades, or mismatch errors during TLS handshakes.
- *Signature verification anomalies*: Detection of failed or bypassed signature checks, which could indicate tampering or misconfiguration.
- *Entropy pool exhaustion*: A drop in entropy quality, especially from quantum random number generators (QRNGs), which could weaken key material.
- *Unexpected cipher negotiation*: Instances where a system negotiates a non-PQC algorithm, either due to fallback or misconfigured preferences.
- *Key usage patterns*: Unusual frequency or distribution of key operations, which might suggest misuse or key leakage.
- *Cryptographic library errors*: Failures or warnings from OpenSSL, BoringSSL, liboqs, or other libraries supporting post-quantum protocols.

The goal is to catch failures in cryptographic behavior before they evolve into breaches. A system issuing dozens of PQC-signed certificates per hour is not necessarily secure if those certificates are invalid, unverified, or improperly distributed.

15.1.2 Entropy validation and QRNG health

Entropy is the foundation of secure key generation. A system may pass all performance tests and still be fundamentally insecure if the keys it generates are predictable. That is why entropy validation should be a regular part of cryptographic health monitoring.

If you are using a QRNG, its status must be tracked with the same rigor as other hardware sensors. Check for throughput drops, signal degradation, or firmware bugs that affect the quality of entropy. Vendors such as QuintessenceLabs provide APIs that expose QRNG health, allowing you to integrate those checks into centralized dashboards or security monitoring tools.

Entropy anomalies should trigger alerts. These might include sudden changes in entropy pool statistics, fallback to PRNG sources without notification, or failure to meet randomness thresholds. In cryptography, poor randomness is not a nuisance; it's a direct vulnerability.

15.2 SOC INTEGRATION AND MONITORING TOOLS

To effectively monitor post-quantum cryptography, organizations must extend their Security Operations Center (SOC) tooling to understand and ingest cryptographic telemetry. This is not always native to existing platforms, so extensions and custom parsing may be required.

Tools and platforms that support PQC monitoring include:

- *IBM Guardium*: Offers deep visibility into cryptographic events and data activity. Can be configured to alert on certificate anomalies, algorithm downgrades, or entropy issues.
- *Sandbox AQ*: Provides advanced cryptographic monitoring, including post-quantum algorithm tracking and quantum risk assessments. Supports integration with SIEM platforms and includes analytics dashboards for visualizing cryptographic health.
- *QRNG dashboards*: Hardware vendors, such as QuintessenceLabs, often provide monitoring portals for QRNG status. These can be connected to telemetry aggregation tools using API hooks.
- *PKI and certificate management tools*: Vendors such as Venafi or Keyfactor offer capabilities to track the lifecycle of hybrid and PQC certificates, detect usage drift, and alert on failures.

The SOC team should be trained to understand the meaning of these alerts. A spike in failed Dilithium signature verifications may be more than a bad patch. It could be an indication of a misconfigured certificate authority, a failed firmware signing chain, or an attempted downgrade attack. Monitoring should not be treated as a project because it is a continuous responsibility. PQC systems should be monitored from the moment they enter a test environment and then throughout their production lifecycle.

Just as important, monitoring ownership must be clear. Cryptographic monitoring often falls between teams. Security operations may not understand the details of key exchange protocols. Developers may not be aware of certificate lifecycle dependencies. Cryptographic events must be treated as first-class security signals, and responsibility for tracking them should be assigned to the platform security teams in collaboration with the SOC.

Set baselines during testing. Define what normal PQC behavior looks like for your environment. Use those baselines to build alerts that capture deviations, whether they involve expired hybrid certificates, missing entropy, or failed algorithm negotiations.

15.3 A FRAMEWORK FOR PQC MONITORING

To guide implementation, organizations can adopt a five-part framework for PQC monitoring:

1. *Baseline your cryptographic environment*: Inventory where PQC is deployed, the algorithms in use, and the systems that depend on them.
2. *Instrument key components*: Enable logging and telemetry on libraries, endpoints, certificate authorities, QRNGs, and middleware.
3. *Integrate into central monitoring systems*: Feed data into SIEMs, SOC dashboards, or security analytics tools. Normalize formats where needed.
4. *Define and tune alerts*: Start with entropy drops, certificate errors, unexpected fallback to classical algorithms, or key usage anomalies. Tune to minimize false positives.
5. *Review and respond*: Include PQC events in security incident reviews. Confirm that detections result in real-time action, remediation, or triage.

15.4 THE EVOLVING ROLE OF INCIDENT RESPONSE IN A POST-QUANTUM WORLD

As cryptographic systems evolve to defend against quantum threats, so too must the teams responsible for responding when things go wrong. Post-quantum cryptography changes the nature of failure. It introduces new technologies, new failure modes, and new attack vectors, many of which fall outside the traditional scope of incident response. That's why the Incident Response (IR) team must evolve alongside the rest of the organization.

In a PQC-enabled environment, IR teams must become fluent not only in identifying and responding to traditional threats (e.g., credential theft, ransomware, exfiltration) but also in understanding cryptographic behavior. This includes certificate validation logic, key lifecycle dependencies, QRNG entropy health, and hybrid negotiation failures. While these signals may originate in infrastructure or cryptographic tooling, it is the IR team that will be expected to investigate, explain, and resolve them or at least be able to triage and route alerted issues to the appropriate teams for remediation.

15.5 NEW SKILLS FOR A NEW ERA

Incident response (IR) analysts will require deeper technical knowledge in several domains to effectively handle post-quantum cryptographic incidents. First, they must develop familiarity with post-quantum algorithms and protocols, including ML-KEM, Dilithium, and Falcon, as well as their applications in TLS, VPNs, and code signing workflows. Understanding how these algorithms function in practice will allow analysts to recognize valid behavior, identify anomalies, and detect signs of tampering or misconfiguration.

In addition, IR teams must become proficient in certificate and key debugging. This includes the ability to analyze hybrid certificates, trace trust chain failures, and troubleshoot signature mismatches caused by format incompatibility or misaligned cryptographic expectations between systems. As hybrid deployments proliferate, these skills will become increasingly essential.

While not a security incident per se, entropy and randomness analysis is another critical area. QRNG telemetry can be monitored for anomalies to detect fallback to pseudo-random number generators (PRNGs), and the implications of weak entropy on key security. A compromised entropy source can lead to predictable keys and serious vulnerabilities that may not be evident through conventional logging. Consequently, someone needs to understand how to triage these types of alerts, and while this is likely an IT problem, monitoring alerts for this vulnerability could easily fall to a security analyst.

Finally, library-level diagnostics will become a routine part of PQC incident response. Analysts must be comfortable interpreting error traces from cryptographic libraries such as OpenSSL, BoringSSL, and liboqs. They need to correlate these errors with system-level behaviors and assess whether they reflect benign misconfigurations or signs of exploitation.

That said, it's important to recognize the boundaries of responsibility. A certificate validation failure, for instance, might indicate an attack and should be flagged for investigation by the SOC. However, it can just as easily result from a misconfigured hybrid deployment. SOC teams must be careful not to overwhelm themselves with noise from overly aggressive alerting. The IR team is not responsible for debugging broken PQC implementations; that responsibility should fall to infrastructure or application owners. The goal is to detect security-relevant failures without turning the SOC into a cryptography help desk.

To support this shift, training programs should incorporate these subject areas into incident response onboarding curricula. Additionally, cryptographic subject matter experts (SMEs) should be made available to assist with complex investigations during the early phases of adoption, ensuring that knowledge gaps do not hinder a timely and accurate response.

Post-quantum systems will generate alerts that differ from traditional threat indicators. Some will represent misconfiguration, while others may signal active exploitation or precursor behavior.

IR teams must develop new triage flows for:

- *Certificate validation failures*: Is the failure due to unsupported algorithms, expired components, or a malformed hybrid structure? Has it occurred before? Is it localized or systemic?
- *Unexpected algorithm fallback*: Did a system negotiate RSA or ECDH when PQC was configured? Was this expected behavior for a legacy client, or did it indicate a downgrade attempt?
- *Entropy exhaustion or degradation*: Has the QRNG failed? Was a PRNG used as a backup? Are any keys generated during the affected period still in use?
- *Library exceptions*: Do signature mismatches or key generation errors point to implementation flaws, version mismatches, or corruption?

These events must be logged with sufficient granularity to support IR investigations. Alerts should be enriched with context, including affected hosts, cryptographic settings, timestamps, and associated users or systems.

15.5.1 New types of PQC-related investigations

As PQC deployment expands, IR teams can expect to investigate a number of new and unfamiliar incident types. One common case will involve hybrid handshake failures, where compatibility gaps between systems with uneven PQC readiness cause negotiation breakdowns. These failures can interrupt service and mask deeper issues related to cryptographic configuration drift.

Another emerging scenario is certificate spoofing or rejection attacks. These occur when attackers exploit ambiguity in hybrid certificate parsing to bypass verification logic or cause legitimate certificates to be rejected by incompatible systems. As hybrid chains become more common, the risks of parsing inconsistency and mismatched trust anchors will grow.

IR teams may also confront code-signing trust breaks, where firmware or update packages fail PQC signature validation. These issues can arise from mismatched cryptographic libraries, outdated verification modules, or improperly issued keys. The result may be halted deployments, failed patches, or increased risk of supply chain tampering.

Entropy-based key prediction will also require attention, particularly in environments relying on low-quality or emulated quantum random number generators (QRNGs). If key material is reused or generated from insufficient entropy sources, attackers may be able to infer or replicate cryptographic secrets, undermining the very protections PQC was meant to ensure.

Finally, downgrade campaigns are likely to emerge, in which adversaries intentionally coerce systems to fall back to classical algorithms that are still present in hybrid stacks. These attacks can exploit legacy support paths and misconfigured negotiation logic to undermine quantum safety without triggering obvious alarms.

These cases may involve unfamiliar logs, cross-team coordination, and a level of cryptographic forensics that few incident response (IR) teams have previously encountered. Responding effectively will require close collaboration with platform security engineers, PKI architects, and compliance analysts. As these investigations grow in frequency and complexity, preparation and communication will be critical to resolving them quickly and thoroughly.

15.5.2 New playbooks, exercises, and IR strategy

To prepare for these scenarios, IR teams should develop and maintain PQC-specific playbooks tailored to the new classes of incidents they will face. These playbooks should outline procedures for investigating and recovering from handshake negotiation failures, including how to isolate affected systems, validate configuration consistency, and determine whether the issue stems from misaligned cryptographic stacks or unexpected fallback behavior. In cases where poor entropy is suspected, the playbooks should also guide the rotation of cryptographic keys and outline how to assess the health and integrity of QRNG sources.

Additionally, clear steps should be provided for reissuing PQC certificates that fail verification, especially when dealing with hybrid formats that may encounter parsing or compatibility issues. Playbooks must also account for how to handle compromised or revoked hybrid certificates, ensuring revocation propagates properly across environments and does not introduce new points of failure. Forensic review procedures should be included to support the investigation of cryptographic fallbacks or anomalies, with emphasis on identifying intentional downgrade attempts or unexplained shifts in algorithm negotiation.

Equally important, playbooks must define clear escalation paths to cryptography and infrastructure teams. These stakeholders bring the necessary context and expertise to interpret cryptographic signals and implement recovery plans that preserve both operational continuity and cryptographic integrity. Playbooks should not remain static documents; they must be actively maintained and tested, and they should be considered in scope for any security exercise or readiness audit.

To that end, organizations are encouraged to develop new tabletop exercises that simulate quantum-adjacent events. These scenarios may include outages in QRNG hardware, expired PQC certificates across partner integrations, or the detection of malformed PQC-signed JWTs in a public API. Tabletop exercises serve a dual purpose: they train the IR team on technical response and also familiarize platform owners, developers, compliance professionals, and executive stakeholders with their roles in a coordinated response. By testing assumptions and surfacing gaps in coordination, these exercises strengthen the organization's overall resilience. Additional guidance on creating tabletop exercises and updating playbooks is provided in Chapter 19.

The first time a hybrid certificate fails in production is not the time to decide how your team will respond. IR readiness must match cryptographic readiness. While libraries and standards bodies may handle the mathematics of PQC, the operational burden of responding to cryptographic incidents lies squarely with your people.

By embedding PQC awareness into IR strategy, through training, tooling, simulations, and proactive playbook development, security teams can help ensure that their organizations are prepared not just to deploy quantum-safe algorithms but to defend them.

15.6 CONCLUSION

Quantum threats may still be emerging, but PQC systems are already being deployed. That means the time to begin monitoring those systems is now. Cryptographic health cannot be assumed. It must be measured, validated, and watched continuously.

Post-quantum monitoring requires a shift in mindset. It expands the security perimeter from access and identity to include entropy, key material, and cryptographic behavior. It demands collaboration between engineers, operators, and security professionals who may not have worked closely before.

Monitoring does not eliminate risk, but it transforms your ability to detect, respond, and improve. It gives you the visibility needed to confirm that your cryptographic systems are working as intended and the confidence to evolve them as standards change.

In the next chapter, we move to the final step in the Validation Phase: Auditability. Chapter 16 will explore how to validate the integrity of your PQC environment through independent verification, formal attestation, and compliance-ready logging. Now that your systems are working and monitored, it's time to prove it.

Chapter 16

Readiness assessments and compliance audits

For many organizations, cryptographic migration will not be considered complete until it has passed the scrutiny of a formal audit. Security teams can deploy quantum-safe algorithms, validate their performance, and monitor their operation in real time. However, unless those efforts are aligned with external guidance and demonstrable to oversight providers, the organization may still be exposed to compliance risk.

In the final step of the validation phase, the focus shifts from implementation to verification. This chapter explores how to prepare for post-quantum cryptographic (PQC) compliance audits, what auditors will expect to see, and how to align your environment with guidance from key regulatory bodies, including the National Institute of Standards and Technology (NIST), the Cybersecurity and Infrastructure Security Agency (CISA), and the Payment Card Industry (PCI) Security Standards Council.

16.1 WHY AUDITS MATTER IN PQC ENVIRONMENTS

In classical cryptography, compliance audits have long been a fixture of risk and governance programs. They confirm whether keys are rotated properly, whether encryption meets policy, and whether controls are being enforced consistently. Post-quantum cryptography introduces new complexity to this process. Algorithms are new, standards are evolving, and vendors are still racing to implement support.

Auditors will need to understand not just what algorithms you use but how and where you use them. They will ask how you maintain interoperability with legacy systems, whether your keys are generated with verified entropy, and what your fallback plan is if a PQC algorithm is deprecated. In regulated industries, such as finance, healthcare, energy, or government contracting, this level of scrutiny is already on the horizon.

Conducting internal audits ahead of regulatory deadlines not only builds confidence but also reduces the risk of rushed compliance when requirements become mandatory. They also help security teams identify blind spots and resolve implementation drift early before it becomes an issue.

DOI: 10.1201/9781003685760-22

16.2 ALIGNING WITH NIST, CISA, AND PCI DSS

A successful PQC audit starts with clear alignment to authoritative guidance. Today, a few sources stand out.

NIST SP 1800-38: This special publication provides practical guidance on transitioning to post-quantum cryptography. It offers a full implementation example and recommends approaches to cryptographic inventory, readiness assessments, and hybrid deployment models. Auditors will expect organizations to use these recommendations as a baseline, especially those working in the public sector or federally aligned industries.

NIST IR 8547: This internal report lays out a risk-based approach for prioritizing systems and assets based on cryptographic sensitivity, lifecycle duration, and replacement difficulty. It introduces the idea of "crypto inventory" and mapping cryptographic components to business processes. For audit readiness, being able to produce this inventory and demonstrate how it was created will be essential.

CISA PQC **readiness guidance**: The Cybersecurity and Infrastructure Security Agency has issued detailed advisories on PQC migration, particularly for industrial control systems and national critical functions. Their recommendations focus on beginning early, understanding hardware constraints, and working closely with vendors. CISA guidance is particularly important for operators in utilities, manufacturing, transportation, and healthcare.

PCI DSS 4.0: For organizations in payment processing and retail, the latest PCI standard introduces requirements for strong cryptographic key management and emerging technology considerations. While it does not yet mandate PQC, PCI DSS 4.0 includes language encouraging awareness of quantum threats and proactive measures for maintaining encryption resilience.

Aligning with these frameworks means adopting not only technical controls but also effective documentation practices, internal accountability, and measurable KPIs for cryptographic health. It is no longer enough to deploy a new algorithm. You must be able to prove that it works, that it is in policy, and that it was deployed systematically.

16.3 WHAT INTERNAL AUDITORS SHOULD REVIEW

This section is written specifically for internal compliance officers, risk managers, and audit teams who will be responsible for evaluating the organization's post-quantum cryptography (PQC) program. However, it also serves as a practical guide for CISOs, platform owners, and security teams who must prepare for these audits. Understanding what internal auditors will be looking for allows technical and operational stakeholders to align early, reduce friction, and ensure a smooth validation process.

As PQC transitions from a future risk to an active part of the security stack, internal audits will play a critical role in validating that cryptographic changes are both secure and aligned with enterprise policy and regulatory expectations.

The goal of any internal PQC audit is to determine whether the program is well-governed, securely implemented, and positioned for long-term resilience. At a high level, auditors should focus on three core questions: Does the organization have a clear and rational policy for cryptographic transition? Have technical and operational controls been implemented in alignment with that policy? And are those controls measurable, repeatable, and consistent with recognized industry frameworks?

To answer those questions, auditors should review several types of documentation and operational evidence. When assessing the PQC program, you should begin by verifying that your organization has a formal, clearly documented policy governing cryptographic transition. This policy should outline why the organization is moving to post-quantum algorithms, what standards are being followed (e.g., NIST SP 1800-38, CISA guidance), and how risk is being managed during the migration.

Next, confirm that operational controls match the stated policy. Review whether the organization has a comprehensive cryptographic asset inventory that includes algorithm types, key lengths, usage contexts (e.g., TLS, VPN, code signing), expiration timelines, and ownership details. Ask where this inventory resides, how it was built, and how frequently it is updated.

Internal auditors should also evaluate the transition plan itself. Is there a step-by-step roadmap? Does it prioritize systems according to cryptographic sensitivity or business impact? Does the plan account for hybrid deployments, key rotation schedules, and vendor dependencies? This plan should be specific enough to guide implementation, yet flexible enough to adapt to evolving standards.

Assess whether cryptographic testing has been conducted and documented. Review logs from interoperability testing, regression testing, performance benchmarks, and security testing. Look for evidence that the testing was thorough, repeatable, and updated as new algorithms or software versions were introduced.

You should examine records of key generation to ensure that proper entropy sources were used. If quantum random number generators (QRNGs) are in use, confirm that they are monitored and validated. Investigate certificate management logs for issuance of hybrid certificates, renewal behavior, and revocation events. Confirm that fallback behaviors, where systems revert to classical cryptography, are logged and alertable.

Monitoring and incident response procedures should be another focal point. Evaluate whether the organization has defined thresholds and alerts for PQC-related anomalies, such as signature validation failures, algorithm downgrade attempts, and entropy pool exhaustion. Confirm that alert data is routed to the security operations center (SOC), or relevant teams in real time, and that IR playbooks include steps for triaging cryptographic incidents.

Review whether there are audit trails for firmware signing, code release validation, and secure boot verification. These controls are especially important in environments like IoT, OT, and regulated industries.

Request documentation of vendor attestations and third-party library assessments. If PQC algorithms are being sourced from open-source or commercial providers, ensure that those components have been reviewed for security, licensing, and compatibility.

Lastly, verify that the PQC program is integrated into daily operations. Check that policies are reflected in DevOps pipelines, infrastructure-as-code scripts, key vault usage, and CI/CD workflows. Ask whether cryptographic upgrades can be performed without breaking production services, and whether contingency plans exist if a PQC algorithm must be deprecated or replaced.

In short, the internal audit process should not simply ask "Is PQC deployed?". It should ask whether that deployment is intentional, controlled, documented, and resilient. A strong internal audit provides the confidence that the cryptographic foundations of the organization are ready for quantum risk and ready to evolve when the standards inevitably shift again (Table 16.1).

16.4 PREPARING FOR THE AUDITOR'S VISIT

Whether a formal audit is coming next quarter or next year, preparation should begin now. Start by reviewing the audit trails your systems produce today. Are cryptographic events logged in a manner that aligns with business processes? Can you trace a certificate from issuance through usage to expiration? Are your hybrid deployments clearly documented?

Leverage tools like IBM Guardium, which offers cryptographic event tracking and compliance-ready reporting. Extend those capabilities with custom dashboards that reflect post-quantum telemetry, such as algorithm usage trends, key rotation logs, and fallback detection.

Assign internal owners for cryptographic policy and audit preparation. Involve your compliance, engineering, and infrastructure teams early in the process. Do not wait for the auditor to raise questions that you have not yet asked yourself.

Table 16.1 Audit worksheet

Audit Category	*Audit Question*	*Evidence Required*
Governance and Policy	Is there a documented policy for cryptographic transition to PQC?	PQC transition policy document
Governance and Policy	Does the policy reference NIST SP 1800–38 and other relevant frameworks?	Policy references to NIST and CISA frameworks
Governance and Policy	Is there executive sponsorship and cross-functional ownership of the PQC program?	Meeting notes, org charts, executive endorsements
Cryptographic Inventory	Is there a current inventory of cryptographic assets by algorithm, key length, and usage?	Crypto inventory report with metadata
Cryptographic Inventory	Is the inventory stored in a centralized, regularly updated system?	Inventory system access and update logs
Cryptographic Inventory	Are asset owners clearly assigned for each cryptographic item?	Asset owner mapping or documentation
Transition Planning	Does the transition plan include prioritized systems based on business risk?	Risk-based migration roadmap
Transition Planning	Are timelines and milestones clearly defined for migration phases?	Timeline and Gantt chart or implementation plan
Transition Planning	Does the plan account for vendor dependencies and hardware refresh cycles?	Vendor engagement records, risk register
Testing and Validation	Have interoperability tests been performed with hybrid and PQC algorithms?	Interoperability test results, tool output
Testing and Validation	Are regression tests documented and automated across environments?	Test automation reports or CI logs
Testing and Validation	Is latency tested across representative traffic and device types?	Latency benchmark reports
Testing and Validation	Has the security testing covered PQC-specific risks like fallback and downgrade attacks?	Security test results, red team findings
Key Management	Are key generation methods documented with entropy source validation?	Key generation logs, entropy audit trails
Key Management	Are QRNGs monitored and health checked regularly?	QRNG health reports or alerts
Key Management	Are key rotation schedules defined and followed?	Rotation logs, scheduled task configs
Monitoring and Alerting	Are alerts configured for failed PQC handshakes and entropy anomalies?	Alert rule configs, recent alert logs

(Continued)

Table 16.1 (Continued) Audit worksheet

Audit Category	*Audit Question*	*Evidence Required*
Monitoring and Alerting	Are logs from crypto libraries, key vaults, and QRNGs routed to the SOC?	SIEM ingestion records, SOC dashboard screenshots
Monitoring and Alerting	Is there a dashboard or SIEM integration that tracks PQC-specific signals?	Real-time dashboard output, alert history
Incident Response	Do IR playbooks include PQC-specific incident types and triage steps?	IR playbooks, incident postmortems
Incident Response	Have tabletop exercises included scenarios involving PQC certificate or key failures?	Exercise scripts, participation records
Firmware and Software Integrity	Is firmware signing using PQC or hybrid algorithms documented and auditable?	Firmware signing records, audit trails
Firmware and Software Integrity	Are secure boot and OTA update mechanisms updated for PQC validation?	Secure boot config, OTA validation results
Third-Party Components	Have third-party crypto libraries been assessed for PQC readiness and security?	SCA results, SBOM reports
Third-Party Components	Are vendor attestations or software bill of materials (SBOMs) available?	Vendor security review or attestation letters
Operational Integration	Are PQC policies embedded in DevOps pipelines and infrastructure-as-code?	Pipeline configs, policy enforcement code
Operational Integration	Do CI/CD processes include crypto-agility validation steps?	CI job logs with PQC integration steps
Fallback and Agility	If a PQC algorithm is deprecated, can the environment be updated without major disruption?	Algorithm update procedures, change management docs
Fallback and Agility	Is there a documented procedure for removing classical algorithms from hybrid stacks?	Hybrid policy documents, configuration scripts

16.4.1 Internal, external, and self-assessments

Audit readiness is not a one-size-fits-all process. Different types of assessments serve different purposes and timelines.

Internal audits are conducted by the organization itself, often through its security, compliance, or internal audit teams. They are most effective when done before a formal external audit is scheduled. Internal audits allow the organization to test its preparedness, surface weak points, and resolve discrepancies without external pressure.

External audits are conducted by third-party assessors or regulatory agencies. These audits may be required for certifications, contractual obligations, or regulatory filings. They tend to focus on compliance, documentation, and evidence. Organizations should treat internal audits as dress rehearsals for these more formal assessments.

Self-assessments are often the starting point. They help teams understand the scope of PQC exposure, review standards like SP 1800-38 or IR 8547, and begin compiling inventories and documentation. These reviews do not carry legal weight, but they are essential for building awareness and aligning stakeholders.

16.4.2 A PQC audit readiness framework

To streamline the process, organizations can adopt a four-part framework for PQC audit readiness:

1. *Discover and document*: Create a full inventory of cryptographic assets. This includes protocols, algorithms, keys, certificates, signing mechanisms, and dependencies. Classify them by criticality, lifecycle, and quantum risk exposure. This should be done as part of Phase 1: Discover/Step 1 Inventory
2. *Plan and align*: Develop a documented PQC migration strategy. Reference NIST, CISA, and PCI DSS guidelines. Include timelines, priorities, risk mitigation strategies, and vendor coordination plans. This should be done as part of Phase 1: Discover/Steps 2 and 3: Assess and Prioritize.
3. *Implement and measure*: Deploy quantum-safe components according to the strategy. Collect logs, validate performance, and record implementation artifacts. Ensure that everything from entropy sources to certificate authorities is auditable.
4. *Verify and adapt*: Run internal audits and simulate third-party reviews. Address gaps, update documentation, and refine controls. Incorporate audit feedback into ongoing risk and compliance reviews.

16.5 CONCLUSION

Compliance in a post-quantum world is about proving trust, not just declaring it. Audits provide the structure and accountability that ensure cryptographic transitions are more than theoretical. They turn policy into evidence, and evidence into assurance.

By aligning with trusted frameworks such as NIST SP 1800-38, IR 8547, and PCI DSS 4.0, and by preparing clear documentation and implementing measurable controls, organizations can demonstrate that their security posture is both forward-looking and defensible.

As with any complex migration, the work does not end when the system is deployed. It ends when you can prove to an external assessor that your system will stand up to scrutiny.

In the next chapter, we shift from validation to planning for longevity. Chapter 17 begins the Maintenance Phase, focusing on sustaining cryptographic resilience, adapting to new standards, and embedding crypto-agility into every layer of your enterprise.

Section VI

Phase 5

Maintenance

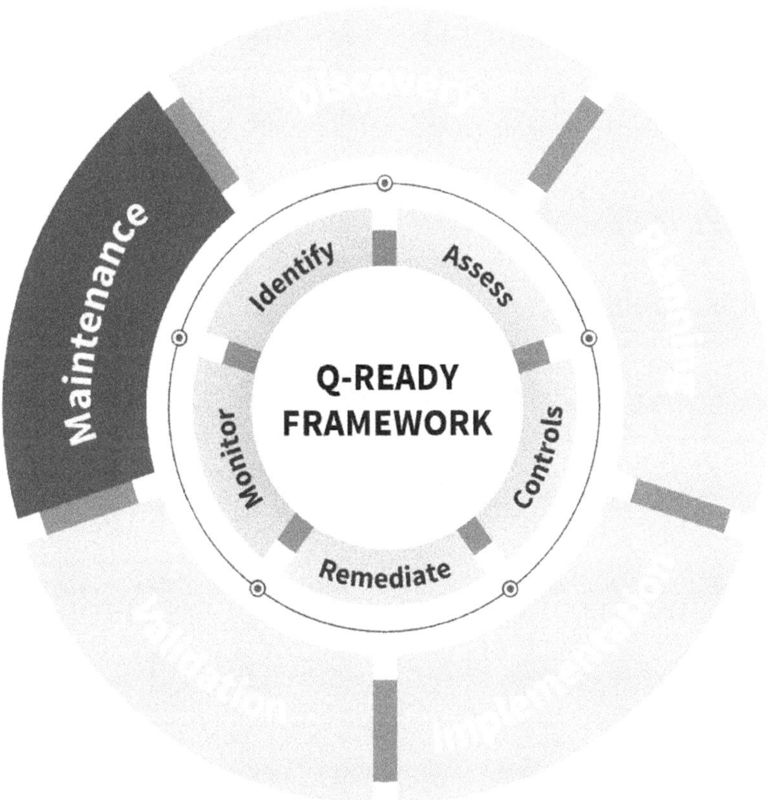

Figure SVI.1 Maintenance phase.

DOI: 10.1201/9781003685760-23

Chapter 17

Maintain crypto-agility

The quantum threat landscape will continue to evolve, standards will shift, and new vulnerabilities will be discovered. To remain secure in this environment, organizations must embrace a posture of continuous adaptation. That means building and maintaining cryptographic systems that can flex as the world around them changes. You should have been embedding crypto-agility into your strategy from the beginning, from early planning and assessment through testing and implementation. If that's been your approach, leveraging those design choices for ongoing maintenance and adaptation should be relatively straightforward. Because crypto-agility has been a recurring theme throughout this book, much of the guidance in this chapter will serve as a review and reinforcement of practices already introduced. This chapter outlines the steps required to maintain a PQC environment over time and how to ensure that agility becomes a built-in capability, rather than an afterthought.

17.1 WHAT MAINTENANCE LOOKS LIKE IN A PQC ENVIRONMENT

A properly maintained cryptographic environment not only preserves what was deployed but also ensures that it remains secure. It actively evolves. Maintenance in this context includes regular algorithm reviews, configuration updates, entropy source validation, certificate management, and compatibility testing.

Many of these tasks are not unique to PQC. What changes are their frequency, sensitivity, and urgency. The novelty of post-quantum algorithms, the rapid pace of academic scrutiny, and the hybrid nature of many deployments will necessitate that cryptographic assumptions be revalidated more frequently and thoroughly than in previous generations.

A basic PQC maintenance schedule might include:

Weekly or biweekly

DOI: 10.1201/9781003685760-24

- Entropy validation checks, especially for quantum RNGs
- Log review for key generation anomalies or certificate errors
- Alerts for crypto events from monitoring tools like IBM Guardium or Sandbox AQ

Monthly

- Review of hybrid TLS session negotiation data for fallback behavior
- Software library updates and patches for crypto toolkits
- Certificate revocation and renewal audits

Quarterly

- Policy reviews and updates to algorithm preferences
- Refresh of the development team's knowledge on PQC changes
- Internal testing of interoperability and regression in staging environments

Annually

- Algorithm deprecation assessments based on NIST and IETF updates
- Vendor roadmap reviews for crypto-agility tooling
- Review of the abstraction layer implementation across apps and services

The exact cadence will depend on your industry, risk appetite, and the maturity of your deployment, but the principle remains the same. You must treat cryptographic maintenance as a living function, not a set-it-and-forget-it activity.

17.2 PREPARING FOR FUTURE STANDARD CHANGES

PQC standards are still solidifying. Even with NIST's recent announcements, additional algorithms are under consideration, and future revisions may alter parameter sets or security assumptions. IETF standards for key exchange and certificate handling are still in draft, and adoption timelines vary by vendor.

This uncertainty requires proactive planning. Do not assume that the algorithm you deploy today will remain the default for the next decade. Instead, architect systems with modular cryptography in mind. Choose libraries that allow you to configure cipher suites easily and update them without rewriting core business logic. Remember, crypto-agility is the ability to rapidly replace, reconfigure, or re-prioritize cryptographic algorithms without a complete system overhaul. It is the foundation of long-term resilience in a post-quantum world.

Abstraction is key. Use cryptographic abstraction layers to decouple the application logic from the cryptographic implementation. For example, instead of hardcoding references to a specific algorithm like ML-KEM or Dilithium, write to an interface that can select the best available algorithm based on policy or configuration.

Popular cryptographic libraries that support this include:

- *BoringSSL and OpenSSL* with post-quantum extensions
- *ISARA Radiate* for hybrid certificate integration and crypto policy control
- *IBM Quantum Remediator* for seamless insertion of quantum-safe cryptographic services into existing networks
- *Sandbox AQ* for centralized control and monitoring of quantum-resilient cryptographic assets

These tools allow organizations to react quickly if an algorithm is deprecated or broken, and to roll out changes with minimal disruption.

17.2.1 Building and maintaining crypto-agility

To maintain crypto-agility, organizations must look beyond the performance of individual algorithms and focus on systemic flexibility. The process starts with how applications are designed. Software must support pluggable cryptographic modules and avoid embedding hardcoded dependencies on specific keys or certificates.

Configuration management becomes a frontline defense. Centralize cryptographic policy control to enable the rollout of new cipher suites or key lengths across environments. This can be done using templates in infrastructure-as-code, version-controlled policy files, or enterprise certificate authorities configured to issue hybrid credentials.

A few examples of crypto-agile design choices:

- Store cryptographic keys in key vaults that support policy-based rotation and revocation
- Use cryptographic gateways or proxies that can terminate and re-encrypt traffic using updatable algorithms
- Deploy code signing services that support hybrid or layered signature verification to ease migration from RSA or ECC

Testing also plays a critical role. Your staging environments should be capable of simulating fallback behavior, cipher suite negotiation, and key lifecycle events. Teams should regularly simulate algorithm swaps to validate that key systems do not fail when cryptographic parameters are updated.

Ultimately, governance must evolve in tandem with technology. PQC working groups should remain active even after the initial migration has been completed. Security leads should monitor developments from NIST, IETF, and quantum research communities. KPIs should include crypto-agility metrics, such as time-to-deploy for a new algorithm or the number of systems supporting algorithm substitution without a rebuild.

17.2.2 Cryptographic Agility Implementation (CAI) Matrix

To support the move to and ongoing maintenance of crypto-agility, NIST's National Cybersecurity Center of Excellence (NCCoE) introduced the Cryptographic Agility Implementation (CAI) Matrix in SP 1800-38B. The CAI Matrix is a self-assessment and maturity model designed to help organizations evaluate and improve their agility across six operational dimensions.

The purpose of the CAI Matrix is to make crypto-agility measurable and quantifiable. Rather than treating agility as a vague aspiration, the matrix provides a structured way to identify strengths, weaknesses, and priority areas for improvement. It aligns directly with the goals of this chapter: to ensure crypto-agility is not only built into your architecture but also sustained through proactive, repeatable, and adaptive practices.

Each dimension in the CAI Matrix represents a key pillar of enterprise readiness for cryptographic change:

17.2.2.1 Awareness

This dimension measures how well stakeholders across the organization understand the implications of cryptographic risks and quantum threats. It evaluates the level of education and visibility at the technical, operational, and executive levels.

To use it: Assess whether teams know which algorithms are in use, whether they're quantum-vulnerable, and how changes might impact systems. For example, a mature organization will have briefings for engineering leads, risk managers, and board-level summaries on PQC timelines.

17.2.2.2 Documentation

This focuses on how well cryptographic assets, configurations, and dependencies are documented and maintained. This includes algorithm inventories, certificate chains, key rotation schedules, and dependency maps.

To use it: Review whether your documentation can answer the question: "Where is RSA still used in our environment?" A low-maturity organization may rely on tribal knowledge, whereas a high-maturity one maintains real-time inventories through Software Bill of Materials (SBOMs) or automated asset discovery.

17.2.2.3 Automation

This dimension gauges the organization's ability to detect, update, and enforce cryptographic configurations automatically. Manual processes are error-prone and slow, while automated tooling accelerates response and reduces risk.

To use it: Look at how cipher suites, certificates, and key lengths are managed. Can changes be pushed through CI/CD pipelines or configuration management platforms, such as Ansible or Terraform? Can expired certs be rotated without human intervention?

17.2.2.4 Responsiveness

Responsiveness measures how quickly and effectively the organization can react to cryptographic vulnerabilities or deprecations. It includes internal coordination, testing pipelines, and change management.

To use it: Simulate a scenario where an algorithm is deprecated, such as the discovery of a new weakness in Dilithium. How long would it take to deploy a replacement across systems? A responsive organization can do this in days, not months.

17.2.2.5 Interdependency

This assesses how well the organization understands and manages its cryptographic supply chain and software dependencies. It focuses on third-party libraries, vendor APIs, and inherited crypto modules.

To use it: Evaluate whether vendors have disclosed their cryptographic roadmaps and whether software bill of materials (SBOMs) include crypto components. Mature organizations ask vendors to prove PQC-readiness and bake those expectations into procurement contracts.

17.2.2.6 Sustainment

Sustainment is about long-term support for crypto-agility. It includes governance, training, tool maintenance, and roadmap integration. This dimension ensures crypto-agility remains an active priority, not a one-time project.

To use it: Establish crypto review cycles and update training for developers. Include cryptographic agility KPIs in quarterly reporting. Ensure that budget is allocated for maintaining scanning tools, certificate authorities, and crypto-libraries over time.

To use the CAI Matrix effectively, assign each dimension a maturity level from 1 (Reactive) to 5 (Strategic). These levels help organizations evaluate where they stand today and where they need to go to achieve sustainable crypto-agility.

- *Level 1: Reactive*
  The organization has little to no visibility into its cryptographic assets or dependencies. Crypto-related issues are addressed only after they cause failures or are flagged by external audits. Responses are manual, ad hoc, and often delayed.
- *Level 2: Aware*
  Basic awareness exists, and some cryptographic assets or risks are tracked informally. There may be pockets of documentation or processes, but they are inconsistent and siloed. Response to vulnerabilities is still mostly manual but somewhat faster.
- *Level 3: Proactive*
  The organization has a working inventory of cryptographic components and some automation in place for tasks like certificate renewal or cipher suite updates. There are established policies, and teams are beginning to standardize crypto management practices.
- *Level 4: Integrated*
  Cryptographic management is embedded into broader IT and security operations. Automated workflows are common, policy enforcement is centralized, and teams coordinate cross-functionally. Vendor management includes PQC-readiness, and testing environments regularly validate crypto agility.
- *Level 5: Strategic*
  Crypto-agility is treated as a long-term strategic capability. The organization anticipates changes in cryptographic standards, participates in industry working groups, and aligns agility efforts with enterprise risk and transformation programs. Metrics are tracked, roadmaps are updated regularly, and agility is sustained through dedicated governance.

For example, Level 1: Reactive organization may lack crypto inventories and rely on manual patching. Level 3: Proactive organization has documented assets and partially automated updates. Level 5: Strategic organization fully automates crypto changes and aligns agility goals with enterprise-wide risk management.

Once scored across all six CAI dimensions (awareness, documentation, automation, responsiveness, interdependency, and sustainment), the matrix highlights gaps and priorities. Organizations can then build a roadmap to mature their capabilities over time, focusing on the areas that offer the highest return in agility, resilience, and operational confidence (Table 17.1).

Table 17.1 CAI Matrix

Dimension	*Current Score*	*Target Score*	*Next Step*
Awareness	2	4	Develop training across departments
Documentation	3	5	Expand to cover all X.509 usage
Automation	1	4	Implement cert lifecycle tooling
Responsiveness	2	4	Simulate deprecation test
Interdependency	2	4	Require crypto SBOM from vendors
Sustainment	1	3	Establish ongoing crypto review

Example

The CAI Matrix helps ensure that the practices you build today can evolve with tomorrow's standards, threats, and algorithms. Combined with architectural modularity, automation, and governance, the CAI Matrix enables teams to not only respond to change but also lead it. In a post-quantum world, adaptability is a form of resilience.

17.3 FUTURE-PROOFING BEYOND PQC

Post-quantum cryptography is a critical milestone, but it is not the endpoint. As quantum technologies progress and cryptanalysis continues to advance, even today's leading PQC algorithms could eventually face compromise. What feels quantum-safe today may be shown to have weaknesses tomorrow, whether through unexpected mathematical breakthroughs, side-channel attacks, or more powerful quantum hardware than originally anticipated. Future-proofing your cryptographic architecture means anticipating change and designing systems that are ready to adapt.

One important complementary technology is Quantum Key Distribution (QKD). As described in Chapter 12, QKD relies on the principles of quantum physics rather than hard math problems to establish secure keys. It offers the strongest form of forward secrecy known today because any attempt to intercept the quantum signal disturbs it in detectable ways. While QKD requires purpose-built hardware and is currently best suited for environments such as financial exchanges, military communications, or government backbones, its relevance is likely to grow. Some organizations may deploy QKD between high-value data centers or across metro fiber networks while relying on PQC for broader client-to-server communications.

The two approaches are not competitors; they are complementary. For example, a company may choose to distribute session keys using QKD between data centers, then use PQC-based encryption for application-level security. Planning now for this convergence, including defining logical separation between transport and application-layer cryptography, helps reduce redesign costs later.

But future-proofing does not stop at selecting a blend of PQC and QKD. There are several additional architectural and operational considerations that can help organizations stay ahead of whatever comes next.

17.3.1 Use cryptographic abstraction layers

One of the most effective ways to prepare for future changes is to abstract your cryptographic logic from your business logic. Rather than embedding algorithm-specific functions like "generate_RSA_key" or "verify_ECC_signature" deep in your application code, design applications to call generic functions exposed by a cryptographic interface. These interfaces can be updated or swapped to support new algorithms without rewriting the entire application stack.

Libraries like BoringSSL, liboqs, and ISARA Radiate offer plug-and-play cryptographic modules that allow developers to update cipher suites via configuration files or environment variables. Centralized control over crypto-policy also enables consistent enforcement of key lengths, algorithms, and hybrid transitions across environments.

17.3.2 Invest in modular cryptographic components

Future-proofing requires hardware and software systems that can evolve independently. Wherever possible, select modular components that support crypto upgrades without replacing the entire system. In embedded environments, this may mean choosing chipsets with dedicated cryptographic accelerators or hardware security modules (HSMs) that support firmware updates. In cloud-native platforms, it might mean using containerized crypto services or service mesh architectures where encryption policies can be managed centrally.

For example, if your gateway supports pluggable crypto modules, you can swap in a new post-quantum key exchange mechanism without redeploying the entire device. Similarly, firmware that uses updatable trust anchors and certificate formats can evolve as standards change without bricking the device.

17.3.3 Embrace hybrid and composite cryptography

The transition to post-quantum standards will not be binary. For years to come, organizations will need to operate in hybrid environments that mix classical and quantum-safe algorithms. This hybrid period allows time for operational tuning, compatibility testing, and policy enforcement, but only if systems are designed to handle multiple algorithm types at once.

Hybrid signatures and composite keys allow systems to validate multiple cryptographic assurances simultaneously. For example, a hybrid certificate might contain both an RSA and a Dilithium signature. If one of those is ever broken, the other can still be trusted. Planning for hybrid operation also allows you to build fallbacks and contingency plans for algorithm deprecation events.

17.3.4 Build cryptographic inventory and lifecycle management into governance

You cannot future-proof what you cannot see. Maintaining a complete and continuously updated cryptographic inventory is a foundational requirement. This involves understanding which applications utilize specific algorithms, identifying the embedded libraries or SDKs, tracking certificate issuance and rotation, and determining where keys are stored or managed throughout the organization.

The inventory work described in Phase 1, Step 1 was not meant to be a one-time activity. It is the beginning of an ongoing discipline. Cryptographic assets must be continuously discovered and cataloged as part of regular maintenance. New services are deployed, software is patched, certificates expire, and cryptographic defaults change with every update. Without constant visibility, even well-governed environments will drift out of alignment with policy.

Automated discovery tools and centralized key management systems are essential for keeping pace with these changes. These tools should feed directly into governance dashboards, configuration management databases, or enterprise asset inventories. Just as critical is lifecycle tracking. Every cryptographic asset should be tagged with metadata, including algorithm type, key size, expiration date, last rotated timestamp, issuance authority, and security classification.

This data must be more than a passive reference. It should actively inform certificate renewal workflows, encryption policy audits, compliance reporting, and deprecation alerts. Governance frameworks should include thresholds and triggers. For example, an expired hybrid certificate or the use of a deprecated cipher suite should generate immediate action. This level of oversight ensures that crypto-related vulnerabilities do not quietly accumulate over time.

17.3.5 Simulate algorithm deprecation scenarios

If one of today's recommended PQC algorithms is broken in the next five years, how quickly could your organization pivot? That question should not be rhetorical. Teams should simulate this scenario by disabling a cryptographic algorithm in test environments and attempting to operate using only the remaining options.

For instance, temporarily disable RSA or ECDSA in your certificate chain and validate whether clients fall back to the PQC option in your hybrid certificate. Remove support for Kyber and verify whether your VPN tunnels still negotiate successfully. These tabletop exercises, or live chaos tests, help build confidence in your crypto-agility and reveal blind spots in configuration or design.

17.3.6 Monitor the standards landscape

The post-quantum ecosystem is still maturing. New standards are being shaped by NIST, IETF, ETSI, and other organizations. The outcome of these discussions will influence how libraries are built, how certificates are issued, and how interoperability is defined.

Designate someone on your team to monitor the standards bodies and update your internal policies accordingly. Vendors that commit to transparency and roadmap alignment with emerging standards should be prioritized in procurement. Staying current with draft RFCs, FIPS publications, and open-source community updates is essential.

Lastly, it is important to understand that no single team owns this responsibility. Crypto-agility touches product development, enterprise IT, security operations, vendor management, and compliance. Legal teams must understand how new algorithms impact contractual terms for data protection. Procurement must evaluate the upgradeability of new equipment. DevOps must be trained in rolling out updated cipher suites across cloud workloads. PQC is only the next chapter, not the final one. By designing for agility, investing in modularity, and committing to continuous visibility, organizations can extend the life of their cryptographic protections well beyond today's standards.

17.4 CONCLUSION

Maintaining crypto-agility allows you to not only stay current but also stay ready for the inevitable changes to come. The reality of post-quantum security is that today's best practices may not hold true tomorrow. Cryptographic algorithms will continue to evolve, vulnerabilities will surface, and new use cases will demand flexibility that cannot be retrofitted after the fact. The organizations that thrive in this environment will be those that treat cryptography not as a static control, but as a dynamic capability.

Agility requires architectural foresight, operational discipline, and continuous governance. It means embracing modular cryptographic frameworks, planning for hybrid and composite environments, and simulating failures before they happen. Crypto-agility becomes part of the organization's resilience posture, touching everything from procurement and product design to patch management and compliance audits.

By investing now in crypto-agile practices, organizations position themselves to move quickly when new algorithms emerge, when standards shift, or when breakthroughs in cryptanalysis require sudden adaptation. Those who build abstraction, automation, and inventory into their cryptographic foundation will gain not only protection from today's threats but also the flexibility to face whatever comes next.

In the following chapter, we turn our attention to one of the most operationally visible components of cryptographic maintenance, certificate lifecycle management. Chapter 18 explores how to monitor certificate validity, automate renewals, and ensure that your hybrid and post-quantum certificates continue to function as intended without disruption or decay.

Chapter 18

Monitor and renew certificates

Certificates play a central role in today's cryptographic systems. They protect web traffic, verify machine identities, control access to APIs, and ensure the integrity of software and firmware updates. When a certificate expires or gets compromised, things can break fast, systems go down, alerts go off, services stop working, and trust is lost. Letting certificate renewals slip through the cracks doesn't just create technical headaches; it opens the door to bigger operational and strategic risks.

For many teams, certificate lifecycle management has long been an afterthought. Certificates are issued, logged, and largely forgotten until they expire. However, the move toward quantum-safe cryptography introduces new challenges. Key sizes are increasing, certificate formats are evolving, and dual-algorithm or hybrid certificates will become more common. The number of machine identities that must be tracked continues to grow across cloud, edge, and containerized environments. As a result, managing certificates is going to take more effort and attention to detail. These changes call for a more mature, ongoing approach. Instead of treating certificate management as a one-off task, it needs to become an automated, policy-based process. Without that shift, your quantum upgrades might not scale the way you need them to, and gaps in visibility could turn into serious security risks.

18.1 WHY CERTIFICATE MONITORING AND RENEWAL MATTER

A certificate expiration is not just a lapse in cryptographic hygiene. It is an outage, a compliance failure, and potentially a breach. In some post-quantum scenarios, this failure can have long-term consequences. If a classical certificate is compromised after quantum adversaries become viable, data encrypted under that certificate can be decrypted retroactively.

More immediately, expired certificates lead to application failures, broken integrations, and loss of customer trust. In regulated industries, they may also trigger audit findings, fines, or contract penalties. These impacts

DOI: 10.1201/9781003685760-25

are amplified in large-scale environments where certificates are used across microservices, CI/CD pipelines, and identity platforms.

For example, if a hybrid certificate used for TLS is allowed to expire, client systems that depend on classical validation paths may begin rejecting connections. If the PQC portion of the certificate is not renewed before the algorithm is deprecated or weakened, encrypted data may be vulnerable to harvest-now-decrypt-later attacks. In the case of firmware signing, an expired or mismanaged post-quantum certificate could result in devices refusing to apply critical updates, or worse, accepting malicious ones that bypass signature validation.

In quantum-ready environments, the number and complexity of certificates will only grow. Hybrid certificates, which combine algorithms like ML-DSA and ECDSA, require new tools and processes for issuance, validation, renewal, and revocation. These cannot be managed manually.

18.2 THE LIFECYCLE OF A CERTIFICATE

Managing a digital certificate involves a series of connected steps that work together to build and maintain trust across your organization's cryptographic systems. From issuing and validating the certificate to deploying, monitoring, renewing, and eventually revoking it, each phase plays a critical role. In a post-quantum world, every one of those steps becomes even more important.

18.2.1 Issuance

Certificate issuance begins with the creation of a Certificate Signing Request (CSR). This request is typically generated on the system or application that needs the certificate. A CSR includes the public key to be certified, along with identifying information such as the domain name, organization, and location. In most environments, tools such as OpenSSL or vendor-specific interfaces are used to generate the Certificate Signing Request (CSR).

For example, a CSR for a web server might be generated using the following command:

```
pgsql
CopyEdit
openssl req -new -newkey rsa:2048 -nodes -keyout server.key
-out server.csr
```

In post-quantum environments, this process becomes more nuanced. A hybrid certificate may require both a classical key (such as ECDSA) and a post-quantum key (such as ML-DSA) to be included in the same Certificate

Signing Request (CSR). As standards evolve, tools like ISARA Radiate and Open Quantum Safe are helping to automate this process.

With the OpenSSL + liboqs fork, you can generate a post-quantum CSR using a quantum-safe algorithm like Dilithium3 as follows:

```
bash
CopyEdit
openssl req -new -newkey dilithium3 -nodes -keyout pq
_server.key -out pq_server.csr -subj "/CN=www.example.com/
O=Example Corp/C=US"
```

This command generates a private key using the Dilithium3 algorithm and creates a corresponding CSR suitable for use with quantum-resistant certificate authorities or internal PKI systems that support PQC. For hybrid CSRs, custom tooling or vendor SDKs such as ISARA Radiate can be used to bundle both classical and post-quantum keys into a single request, depending on your certificate authority's capabilities.

18.2.2 Validation

Once the CSR is submitted to a Certificate Authority (CA), the authority validates the request. This usually involves confirming the requester's identity and ensuring that the domain or resource in question is under their control. In the context of public TLS certificates, this can be achieved through DNS challenge, HTTP file verification, or email-based confirmation.

For hybrid certificates, validation must ensure that both key pairs are properly formed and that the metadata reflects the composite nature of the certificate. Validation engines must be upgraded to parse and evaluate dual-algorithm signatures without error, especially as formats such as X.509 evolve to accommodate new algorithm identifiers.

18.2.3 Deployment

After issuance, the certificate must be deployed to the appropriate systems. This often includes web servers, mail servers, VPN gateways, load balancers, or embedded devices. In DevSecOps environments, certificates may be deployed via CI/CD pipelines using infrastructure-as-code tools such as Terraform, Ansible, or Kubernetes secrets management.

In traditional IT environments, deployment may be manual or handled by middleware that reads certificates from a centralized key vault or management system. Post-quantum deployment introduces new constraints, since key sizes are larger, handshake logic may differ, and endpoint systems may need patches to handle dual-algorithm processing. Testing for compatibility before production rollout is critical.

18.2.4 Monitoring

Once deployed, certificates must be continuously monitored to ensure availability, authenticity, and proper usage. Monitoring tools check certificate expiration dates, detect unexpected changes, and verify whether a certificate has been revoked or tampered with.

Examples of monitoring tools include:

- Venafi Trust Protection Platform
- Keyfactor Command
- AppViewX
- In-house monitoring via scripts using OpenSSL, Cron jobs, and log aggregation tools

PQC-aware monitoring must be able to parse hybrid certificate formats, alert on mismatched key usage, and integrate with key management systems to track the status of both classical and quantum-safe materials. Monitoring should be integrated into your SIEM platform and tied to alerts for anomalies such as early expiration, failed revocation attempts, or validation failures during handshake negotiation.

18.2.5 Renewal

Certificate renewal must occur before the certificate expires to avoid service disruption. In classical environments, renewal can often be automated via Automated Certificate Management Environment or ACME protocols (used by Let's Encrypt and other CAs). In post-quantum environments, renewal may require additional steps to generate new key pairs with updated algorithms or parameters.

Automation is essential. A robust Certificate Lifecycle Management (CLM) platform should rotate keys, regenerate CSRs, validate identities, and redeploy certificates without human intervention. For PQC, this may also include updating hybrid key materials and ensuring compatibility with relying systems that have not yet been upgraded.

18.2.6 Revocation

If a certificate is compromised or no longer trusted, it must be revoked immediately. Revocation can be handled by publishing entries to Certificate Revocation Lists (CRLs) or using the Online Certificate Status Protocol (OCSP). Many organizations also use internal access control lists and key rotation procedures for faster remediation.

In PQC, revocation becomes more complex. A hybrid certificate may need partial or complete revocation depending on which component is compromised. Key management systems must be able to revoke composite identities and ensure that updated certificates are propagated quickly to avoid false trust.

18.2.7 How PQC changes the lifecycle

The introduction of post-quantum cryptography impacts each of these phases. Certificate Signing Requests (CSRs) must support larger key sizes and more complex formats to accommodate post-quantum algorithms, many of which produce significantly longer public keys than traditional RSA or ECC. Validation systems will also need to be updated to recognize and correctly handle unfamiliar algorithms, including those that may not yet be fully supported by standard cryptographic toolkits or existing PKI platforms.

Deployment processes require rigorous testing against updated TLS, VPN, and authentication stacks to ensure compatibility with both classical and quantum-safe configurations. Monitoring must be enhanced to track both classical and quantum-safe materials with equal rigor, particularly in hybrid environments where legacy and PQC algorithms may coexist. This includes validating handshake behavior, key negotiation, and certificate usage across all endpoints.

Renewal cycles may also shorten during the PQC transition period. As cryptanalysis evolves and new vulnerabilities emerge, organizations may choose to limit certificate lifespans to reduce exposure and simplify revocation when needed. Speaking of revocation, the process must become more granular and propagate faster across distributed systems to prevent compromised or deprecated certificates from continuing to grant access.

For all of these reasons, organizations should move toward full automation across every phase of the lifecycle. Manual processes are too slow, too error-prone, and too limited in visibility to keep pace with modern threat models. In the next section, we will examine how dual-algorithm certificates specifically impact lifecycle management practices and why building support for them is an essential step in PQC readiness.

18.2.8 Common certificate use cases and their post-quantum implications

Certificates are embedded in nearly every secure digital interaction, and each use case will need to be reevaluated as PQC becomes standard. The cryptographic mechanisms behind these certificates are foundational to trust, and changes to those mechanisms carry wide-reaching operational implications.

TLS certificates for websites are the most publicly visible use case. They will need to support hybrid handshakes that combine classical and post-quantum key exchange mechanisms. This requires compatibility not only on the server side but also across various platforms, including browsers, mobile apps, and content delivery networks. Organizations should expect to test hybrid TLS configurations with multiple client platforms and ensure their certificate authorities can issue hybrid or post-quantum-only certificates.

Device identity certificates used in IoT, OT, and embedded environments present additional challenges. Many of these devices are resource-constrained and cannot handle large keys or compute-intensive algorithms. PQC schemes, such as Dilithium or Falcon, may require hardware acceleration or delegation to proxy validation services. In some environments, secure gateways or edge devices will need to terminate PQC sessions on behalf of legacy endpoints. This introduces architectural changes that must be accounted for during deployment and lifecycle management.

Code signing certificates are another critical area of focus. As attackers grow more sophisticated, the risk of quantum-enabled forgery becomes real. Code signing certificates will need to adopt PQC algorithms, such as Dilithium or Falcon, or hash-based schemes like LMS or XMSS. Organizations must prepare to update their build pipelines, developer toolchains, and firmware validation procedures to support these algorithms. In regulated industries or high-assurance environments, this transition may require new attestations or FIPS-equivalent validations.

Mutual authentication between APIs or microservices is often overlooked but critically important. In modern architectures, services authenticate each other using mutual TLS (mTLS) and certificate-based trust. Updating certificates for PQC in this context requires careful coordination; rolling out changes to one side of the handshake before the other can result in broken dependencies or service outages. Teams must sequence deployments, validate fallback logic, and build rollback plans to ensure service continuity.

Zero trust architectures further raise the stakes. In these models, trust is continuously verified through strict certificate validation and identity assurance. PQC impacts both identity management and policy enforcement. For example, systems must recognize and validate hybrid certificates, properly interpret expiration or revocation, and manage short-lived certificates for ephemeral workloads. In multi-cloud or hybrid environments, organizations will need to ensure that all identity providers, access brokers, and enforcement points support PQC standards and can interoperate reliably.

As PQC adoption progresses, certificate management will evolve from a background process to a frontline operational concern. Every system that relies on certificates will require updates, testing, and ongoing monitoring. The complexity of this task reinforces the need for crypto-agility and automation across certificate issuance, deployment, and renewal. Waiting until a cryptographic failure disrupts production is not an option – proactive planning and incremental adoption are the only sustainable paths forward.

18.3 MANAGING DUAL-ALGORITHM AND HYBRID CERTIFICATES

Dual-algorithm and Hybrid certificates will become increasingly common during the transition to post-quantum cryptography. These certificates are designed to serve two audiences simultaneously: clients and systems that still rely on classical cryptographic algorithms, such as ECDSA, and those beginning to adopt post-quantum algorithms, such as ML-DSA. By including both in a single digital certificate, organizations can ensure compatibility with today's infrastructure while preparing for tomorrow's threats.

However, not all multi-algorithm certificates are created equal. Let's review the difference between *dual certificates* and *hybrid certificates.*

Dual certificates refer to two separate certificates issued for the same identity: one with a classical algorithm and one with a post-quantum algorithm. They are maintained independently, can be chained to different certificate authorities, and may expire on different schedules.

Hybrid certificates, by contrast, bundle both classical and quantum-safe signatures into a single certificate structure. A hybrid certificate is issued as a composite object, combining both signature schemes into one credential that can be validated by classical and post-quantum clients, depending on their capabilities.

Both models are valid, but they come with trade-offs. Dual certificates are often easier to manage in systems that have not yet adapted to new formats. They fit more easily into legacy chains of trust, where existing tooling may reject hybrid formats. Hybrid certificates, while more elegant and compact, require updated parsing logic and more complex validation handling.

18.3.1 Understanding certificate chains

To understand how these certificates function, it helps to review certificate chains. A certificate chain is a sequence of certificates that link a digital identity to a trusted root certificate authority (CA). At the base of the chain is the root certificate. This is self-signed and distributed by a trusted CA. The root signs an intermediate certificate, which in turn signs the leaf certificate used by the application or device. Each link in the chain confirms the identity of the next, creating a verifiable trust path.

In layperson's terms, think of it like a chain of introductions. A friend introduces you to their colleague, who then introduces you to their manager. If you trust your friend, and each introduction checks out, you trust the final person too. Certificate chains work the same way. You trust the root, and if each step in the chain is signed correctly, you trust the certificate at the end.

In technical terms, the client receives a certificate and validates it by walking up the chain, verifying each signature using the public key of the issuer until it reaches a trusted root in its certificate store.

18.3.1.1 Chaining in dual and hybrid certificates

With dual certificates, you have two separate chains. A client that supports only classical cryptography will follow the chain rooted in a classical CA. In contrast, a post-quantum-aware client will follow the chain rooted in a PQC CA or intermediate capable of issuing quantum-safe signatures. Each chain must be validated independently, and its trust anchors must be present on the client device.

Hybrid certificates typically rely on a single chain but embed multiple cryptographic proofs at each step. The leaf certificate includes both an ECDSA and an ML-DSA signature. Its issuer certificate may also contain hybrid signatures. This means clients can select which cryptographic path to validate depending on their capabilities. However, this flexibility introduces additional validation logic. The client must recognize the hybrid format, parse the correct signature, and confirm its trust in the issuer's corresponding algorithm.

Generating and issuing dual or hybrid certificates requires updated tooling. Most classical CAs and PKI systems were not designed to handle multi-algorithm structures. Organizations will need to upgrade or replace certificate authorities, validation libraries, and management interfaces. Open-source projects, such as Open Quantum Safe, and commercial platforms, like ISARA Radiate, provide hybrid certificate support and development kits to help bridge the gap.

To deploy these certificates effectively, organizations must first ensure that their Certificate Authority (CA) can issue certificates using both classical and post-quantum algorithms. In environments where a single CA does not yet support hybrid issuance, it may be necessary to combine outputs from multiple CAs, one issuing the classical component and another handling the post-quantum component, before constructing the final hybrid certificate.

Next, your certificate lifecycle management (CLM) system must be capable of tracking expiration dates, rotation schedules, and revocation policies for cryptographic components. This dual tracking becomes especially important in hybrid configurations where the post-quantum and classical elements may follow different lifecycles or encounter unique validation requirements.

Infrastructure updates will also be required. Systems must be able to recognize and parse new hybrid formats, including support for these formats in load balancers, gateways, reverse proxies, and client-side libraries.

Failure to recognize or properly process these certificates can result in connection failures or silent downgrades to weaker algorithms.

Finally, hybrid deployments introduce a risk of unintended fallback to classical cryptography. Monitoring this fallback behavior is critical. If systems default to the classical component of a hybrid handshake too frequently, or without appropriate alerting, it can undermine the intended security benefits of PQC. Logging, telemetry, and policy enforcement must be in place to detect and address this behavior in real time.

18.3.2 Fallback risks and vulnerabilities

One of the most significant risks in hybrid certificate deployments is fallback behavior. In many cases, clients will attempt to validate a certificate using the post-quantum algorithm first. If that validation fails, due to missing support, a validation error, or incompatibility, they may silently fall back to verifying the classical signature instead. This approach helps maintain availability, but introduces a critical security trade-off.

If an attacker can manipulate this fallback behavior, they may coerce the client into ignoring the PQC signature and accepting only the classical one. In a post-Q-Day environment, where classical algorithms such as RSA or ECDSA may be compromised, the attacker could forge a valid-looking signature using the classical algorithm, effectively impersonating the system. This is the essence of a downgrade or fallback attack.

To mitigate this risk, security teams must implement multiple safeguards. First, they should ensure that fallback events are monitored and logged, providing visibility into how often and under what conditions fallback occurs. Next, fallback should only be allowed to known, trusted configurations that are explicitly approved. Repeated fallback attempts, especially to unexpected or outdated algorithms, should be treated as potential indicators of malicious activity. Where possible, organizations should adopt a fail-closed posture, meaning that if a post-quantum validation fails, the connection is rejected outright rather than silently defaulting to a less secure classical algorithm.

The core challenge with hybrid certificates lies in balancing security and availability. Hybrid and dual-algorithm certificates were introduced to address this need, but both approaches require trade-offs. For instance, consider a hospital that relies on medical devices with embedded software limited to ECDSA support. Replacing or upgrading the software may be impractical due to regulatory or technical constraints. A hybrid certificate allows the legacy device to continue functioning while newer systems can validate a post-quantum signature. However, if fallback to the classical component becomes the norm rather than the exception, the organization risks believing the system is post-quantum secure when in reality it isn't.

In another example, an enterprise might implement dual certificates, one classical and one post-quantum, and serve each based on client capabilities.

Table 18.1 Dual vs hybrid

Feature	*Dual Certificates*	*Hybrid Certificates*
Compatibility	Higher with legacy systems	Requires newer validation logic
Complexity	Two chains, more manual management	One chain, more parsing complexity
Storage Requirements	Moderate	Higher due to combined key sizes
Performance Impact	Minimal per certificate	Potential for larger cert sizes
Fallback Security Risk	Lower	Higher if improperly configured
Preferred Use Case	Environments with mixed infrastructure	Systems ready for crypto agility

If certificate management is not carefully synchronized and the PQC certificate expires first, quantum-aware clients will begin to fail. Meanwhile, classical clients will continue to function, masking the issue and delaying remediation. These scenarios illustrate why effective fallback management, monitoring, and synchronized lifecycle operations are crucial for securing hybrid and dual-mode environments (Table 18.1).

18.3.2.1 Pros and cons of dual and hybrid certificates

Ultimately, the decision depends on your environment. Hybrid certificates are cleaner and more scalable in systems that can support them. Dual certificates may be safer in highly diverse or legacy-heavy networks where control over clients is limited. Regardless of the approach you choose, treat the certificate as a high-quality cryptographic asset. CLM platforms should be configured to monitor all expiration paths, validate both cryptographic chains, and trigger alerts when one component is nearing failure. Certificates should be regularly tested in both classical and post-quantum clients to ensure compatibility, and fallback behavior should be validated and tightly controlled.

The transition to post-quantum cryptography will not happen overnight. Hybrid and dual certificates provide the bridge, but how you build and maintain that bridge will determine whether you cross safely or fall behind.

18.4 HOW CERTIFICATE LIFECYCLE MANAGEMENT AND KEY MANAGEMENT FIT TOGETHER

Keys and certificates are two sides of the same coin. Certificates bind identities, such as servers, devices, or users, to public keys, while key management ensures that those keys are protected, rotated, and destroyed when they are no longer needed. Without proper key handling, the certificate becomes meaningless. Without an accurate certificate, the key cannot be trusted. The two must move in lockstep.

In a post-quantum context, this interdependence becomes even more critical. Quantum-safe keys, such as those generated from ML-KEM or Dilithium, are larger and sometimes more computationally demanding to use, requiring support for new formats in both the key store and the certificate authority. Managing these assets across hybrid environments, on-premises systems, cloud platforms, and constrained devices introduces new challenges that legacy systems are not designed to handle.

To address this, organizations should take steps to tightly integrate key management systems (KMS) and certificate lifecycle management (CLM) platforms. Integration means more than connecting APIs. It means aligning processes, policies, and ownership models to ensure a seamless flow from key generation to certificate issuance and eventual revocation.

At the heart of every certificate is a public key. When a digital certificate is issued, the corresponding private key remains securely stored, ideally within a hardware security module (HSM) or a cryptographically sound key vault. During authentication or encryption operations, this private key is used to sign data, verify identity, or decrypt information. The public key embedded in the certificate allows clients to confirm that the signed or encrypted data is valid, thereby completing the trust loop.

In traditional certificate chains, each certificate is signed using the private key of the issuer, with the root certificate self-signing its public key. As clients validate a certificate chain, they walk from the leaf certificate up to the trusted root, verifying each signature using the public key of the issuer. If at any point the signature does not match the key, the chain breaks and trust is denied.

In a PQC-enabled environment, the size of keys and signatures increases. For example, a Dilithium-3 public key can be several kilobytes, far larger than an RSA 2048-bit key. This increase affects not only certificate size but also how key pairs are stored, loaded into memory, and backed up. In addition, hybrid certificates may include more than one key and signature, requiring the KMS to associate and manage multiple private keys tied to a single certificate identity.

18.4.1 How to integrate key and certificate management lifecycles

A well-integrated environment synchronizes every stage of the key and certificate lifecycle. Here's how that looks in practice:

18.4.1.1 Key generation and storage

Post-quantum key material should be generated using approved cryptographic libraries (e.g., liboqs or PQClean), ideally within a secure boundary such as a FIPS-validated HSM or a cloud-native key vault like AWS KMS. These vaults must be updated to support post-quantum key formats, and any integration with external certificate authorities should accommodate hybrid key submissions.

18.4.1.2 Certificate issuance

When a certificate signing request (CSR) is created, the associated key must already exist in a managed environment. The CLM platform pulls this public key from the key vault and pairs it with identity metadata such as hostname, role, or organization. The certificate authority then signs the CSR and returns the certificate, which is pushed to endpoints.

18.4.1.3 Monitoring and rotation

Certificate expiration is easy to monitor. Key decay is less obvious. A good integration between KMS and CLM will track both. For example, a key flagged for rotation in the KMS should trigger the issuance of a new certificate in the CLM system. Similarly, if a certificate is revoked, the corresponding key should be locked, expired, or scheduled for deletion. This ensures stale or compromised keys cannot be reused in another context.

18.4.1.4 Revocation and destruction

In the event of compromise or decommissioning, the certificate must be revoked and the associated key destroyed in a coordinated manner. Revocation involves adding the certificate to a CRL or pushing an OCSP update. Key destruction must be verifiable, particularly in regulated environments. Integration between KMS and CLM systems enables a unified audit trail across both events.

Best Practices for Integration

- *Use policy engines to link KMS and CLM workflows*: Configure policies that automatically enforce certificate issuance when a new key is generated, or that prevent certificate renewal if the corresponding key does not meet length, age, or algorithm requirements.
- *Tag and classify key material*: Keys should include metadata such as algorithm type, creation date, cryptographic purpose (e.g., TLS, code signing), associated certificates, and rotation interval. This enables the CLM system to make intelligent decisions based on key properties.
- *Audit and monitor key-certificate associations*: Maintain logs that show which certificates were issued from which keys and when those keys were last rotated or accessed. This visibility is especially critical when managing thousands of keys in a multi-cloud environment.

- *Use modular cryptographic services*: Deploy cryptographic gateways or proxies that can offload complex key and certificate operations, especially in environments where client software cannot be easily updated.
- *Simulate lifecycle events in staging*: Before rolling out new certificate or key formats into production, simulate the full lifecycle in a test environment. Confirm that your systems can generate, deploy, renew, and revoke PQC-based certificates without causing service disruption.

Imagine a financial services provider deploying hybrid certificates to protect API communication. They generate ML-KEM key pairs using AWS KMS extensions and store them in a dedicated post-quantum key vault. When the CLM system, integrated with the AWS API, detects that the current certificate is due to expire, it pulls the corresponding public key and submits a CSR to a quantum-aware CA. Once issued, the certificate is deployed across Kubernetes ingress points and IoT payment terminals. If the key is compromised or fails validation, the system immediately triggers certificate revocation, rotates the key, and pushes a replacement across all endpoints within hours, not days. In this example, the integration between key management and certificate lifecycle tooling ensures continuity of service and the integrity of every cryptographic transaction.

Key management and certificate lifecycle management are not separate disciplines in a post-quantum world. They are interdependent systems that must function as a single, coordinated cryptographic control plane. Integration is the only way to manage the complexity, maintain visibility, and enforce consistent security policies at scale. When done right, every cryptographic operation, whether it's an encrypted transaction, a signed container, or a validated API call, is grounded in a valid, current, and quantum-resilient identity. That is the cornerstone of a trustworthy post-quantum enterprise.

18.5 AUTOMATING CERTIFICATE LIFECYCLE MANAGEMENT

Automation is the only viable strategy for managing certificate lifecycles at scale. In an era of short-lived certificates, dual-algorithm requirements, and increasingly distributed infrastructure, manual certificate management is not only inefficient but also dangerous. Even a single expired or misconfigured certificate can bring down critical applications, disrupt encrypted communications, or trigger compliance violations. At the post-quantum scale, those risks multiply.

Another major driver for increased automation is the CA/Browser Forum's recent decision to shorten the maximum lifespan of SSL/TLS certificates.

Currently set at 398 days, certificate validity will be phased down to just 47 days over the next several years, with full enforcement by March 15, 2029. The transition will occur in three stages: on March 15, 2026, the maximum lifespan will be reduced to 200 days; by March 15, 2027, it will be lowered again to 100 days; and by March 15, 2029, all SSL/TLS certificates must expire within 47 days of issuance.

The primary motivation behind this change is to enhance security by reducing the window of exposure for compromised certificates. The shorter the certificate validity period, the smaller the opportunity for an attacker to exploit a stolen or misissued certificate. This shift also encourages the widespread adoption of automated certificate management practices, as manual renewal at such short intervals is not scalable.

For organizations, this change means that automation is no longer optional. Any environment that issues or consumes SSL/TLS certificates must prepare to rotate them every few weeks by 2029. This fundamentally transforms certificate operations from a periodic task to a continuous, policy-driven automation workflow.

This tightening of certificate lifecycles aligns closely with the demands introduced by post-quantum cryptography. PQC brings new complexities, including dual algorithm stacks, hybrid certificate formats, cryptographic agility requirements, and increased key sizes, all of which further underscore the need for automated management. Organizations already building automation capabilities to comply with the 47-day lifespan should take the opportunity to integrate PQC support into those same workflows.

For instance, when deploying short-lived certificates for web services, it is logical to begin issuing hybrid certificates that contain both classical and quantum-safe keys, such as RSA and ML-KEM, to ensure compatibility with future standards. If development teams are creating CI/CD pipelines that support rapid certificate rotations, they should include logic that enables cryptographic agility now, rather than rewriting those pipelines later to accommodate PQC. Likewise, policy templates in CLM platforms should be structured to include key types, algorithm restrictions, and expiration intervals that reflect the organization's broader cryptographic roadmap.

The upcoming regulatory deadlines effectively serve as a catalyst to accelerate post-quantum readiness. Instead of treating shorter-lived certificates and quantum-resistant algorithms as two separate initiatives, organizations can consolidate both into a unified certificate modernization strategy that supports current and future security requirements.

Certificate Lifecycle Management (CLM) platforms, such as Venafi, KeyFactor, and AppViewX, enable organizations to automate key phases of the certificate lifecycle. This includes automated issuance, expiration tracking, policy enforcement, renewal scheduling, revocation management, and certificate distribution. In large organizations, CLM platforms can manage hundreds of thousands of certificates across cloud, on-premises, and edge environments without human intervention.

To deploy certificate automation effectively, several core elements must be in place. First, you need to inventory your current certificate usage. That includes identifying where certificates are used, which applications depend on them, what types of keys they contain, and which Certificate Authorities (CAs) issued them. If this inventory was built during Phase 1, it must now be integrated into your CLM platform. Automated discovery features in most CLM tools can help update this information on a rolling basis.

Second, you need to define lifecycle policies. For example:

How long should certificates live?
When should they be rotated?
Which algorithms are approved or deprecated?
What naming conventions and metadata must be included in new certificate requests?

These policies should be encoded as templates within the CLM system and enforced automatically. Many platforms allow you to create rules that reject non-compliant CSRs, enforce minimum key sizes, or restrict certain algorithms from being used in production.

Next, integrate CLM capabilities into your development and infrastructure pipelines. That typically means embedding certificate requests into CI/CD workflows using APIs or command-line interfaces. Most CLM tools can be integrated with Kubernetes secrets, Ansible playbooks, or Terraform modules to issue and deploy certificates as part of automated provisioning. This integration ensures that new services automatically receive valid certificates during deployment and that expiring certificates are renewed without downtime.

In post-quantum environments, these processes become increasingly complex. Your automation workflows must support dual-algorithm or hybrid certificates. This means generating and validating both classical and quantum-safe keys, packaging them in supported formats, and deploying them to systems that can recognize both components. ISARA and Open Quantum Safe provide libraries and reference implementations for hybrid certificate generation that can be scripted into CLM workflows.

To maintain operational continuity, automation must go beyond issuance and renewal. Full key rotation, including the regeneration of both private keys and certificates, must be supported. This is especially important in environments that use short-lived certificates or where cryptographic agility is a policy requirement. CLM tools must be able to identify all dependencies on a certificate or key, regenerate secure materials, and push updates to every system that consumes the certificate. For example, if a VPN gateway, load balancer, and application tier all use the same certificate, the automation must ensure all three are updated simultaneously to avoid broken connections.

Monitoring is another critical feature. Your CLM platform should provide dashboards, logs, and alerts that integrate with your Security Operations Center (SOC). Alerts for upcoming certificate expirations, failed renewals, unsupported algorithm use, or unexpected certificate revocations should trigger automated incident response workflows or be escalated to appropriate security teams.

Best practices for automating certificate lifecycle management in a post-quantum world include: Start with hybrid support, even before full PQC deployment, and build in support for hybrid certificates now. This will allow you to begin testing and piloting without disrupting classical systems. Use role-based access control (RBAC); ensure that only authorized services or teams can issue, renew, or revoke certificates. Misuse or accidental issuance can become a vulnerability. Align certificate policies with crypto-agility goals; ensure that your policies define allowed algorithms, transition timelines, and expiration intervals that match your organizational roadmap for PQC migration. Automate revocation and recovery; establish clear policies and automated processes for revoking compromised or outdated certificates and for issuing replacements rapidly. Regularly test automation workflows; run drills where certificates are deliberately revoked or expired, and validate that your automation handles replacement without downtime or error. Centralize logging and audit trails; every certificate action should be logged. These logs should be integrated with your enterprise logging systems and available for compliance reporting.

By approaching certificate automation as an integrated part of your cryptographic maintenance strategy, rather than a separate toolset, you position your organization to scale securely into a post-quantum future. The more seamless and transparent these operations become, the fewer risks you carry as algorithm standards evolve, lifecycles shorten, and cryptographic complexity increases.

18.6 ONGOING MAINTENANCE AND CERTIFICATE GOVERNANCE

Like much of the post-quantum journey, certificate renewal is not a one-time task to be checked off. It is a permanent and central function of ongoing cryptographic hygiene. As outlined in Chapter 17, maintenance in a PQC environment means treating every cryptographic component, whether an algorithm, a key, or a certificate, as dynamic and subject to change. Among all the components, certificate and key lifecycle management will likely represent the most frequent and resource-intensive category of routine upkeep.

To maintain continuity, organizations must build certificate governance directly into their broader PQC maintenance schedule. Weekly monitoring of certificate status, health checks for key usage, and validation of trust chains should be integrated into SOC reporting and daily dashboard routines. Monthly reviews should include forecasting for upcoming expirations, rotation readiness for high-priority keys, and certificate format compliance. Quarterly maintenance windows should reserve time for renewal simulations and revocation rehearsals in non-production environments. These rehearsals serve two purposes: they verify that the system can handle coordinated certificate rollover without disruption, and they keep personnel familiar with failover and replacement procedures.

The information presented in Chapter 17 regarding crypto-agility is directly applicable here. Certificates are the user-facing expression of cryptographic agility. When an algorithm is deprecated, replacing it often begins with certificate renewal. If your abstraction layers and policy management systems are working as designed, a new post-quantum certificate format should be able to replace an older one without rewriting application code or restarting critical services. Maintaining this agility depends on a tightly managed certificate inventory, responsive CLM integration, and clear ownership.

Responsibility for certificate maintenance cannot reside with a single team. While security operations may own monitoring and policy enforcement, platform and infrastructure teams often manage deployment and renewal pipelines. Identity and access management (IAM) teams may oversee issuance and revocation policies, especially for user and machine identities. Compliance officers must ensure that all of these efforts align with regulatory standards, including key rotation and signature validation cadences. In some organizations, this cross-functional responsibility may be formalized through a crypto-governance working group, which regularly meets to review current posture, emerging threats, and planned rollouts.

A clear role definition is essential. For example, CLM administrators should handle configuration, automation, and alerts, while key custodians focus on key vault health, access controls, and usage analytics. DevOps teams should be responsible for implementing certificate and key rotation logic in CI/CD pipelines, ensuring that applications always receive valid and up-to-date materials. Governance and compliance teams must track lifecycle metadata across all certificates and keys, including the algorithm used, expiration date, issuance authority, and associated risk posture.

In practice, this cross-team collaboration will require shared tools, visibility, and urgency. Certificate dashboards must be integrated into enterprise monitoring solutions and be visible across stakeholders. Alerts for expired or invalid certificates should route not only to the SOC but also to the application owners and key custodians. Certificates that fail validation, use deprecated formats, or exhibit unusually short lifespans should trigger automated workflows and real-time escalations. All of this should be governed by clear policies documented as part of a crypto-agility or post-quantum readiness charter.

Revocation events represent the most high-stakes scenarios in certificate maintenance. Whether due to a compromised private key, a deprecated PQC algorithm, or the discovery of a flawed hybrid certificate chain, the response must be fast and coordinated. Ideally, revocation plans are already in place and tested. Mass certificate replacement procedures should be automated where possible, with fallback certificates and alternate validation chains preconfigured. Key rotation and reissuance should happen within hours, not days. Recovery plans should include version-controlled artifacts, emergency issuance procedures, and change approval protocols that are aligned with broader incident response planning.

This shift also places new demands on incident response teams. Traditionally focused on malware outbreaks, privilege escalation, or data exfiltration, IR teams must now develop the expertise to recognize, investigate, and respond to cryptographic events, including failures in certificate validation, unauthorized key use, or signs of algorithm deprecation attacks. As quantum-safe cryptography becomes operationalized, so too must response protocols. IR playbooks will need to include specific procedures for triaging PQC-related incidents, such as identifying whether a certificate failure is due to malicious tampering, misconfiguration, or deprecated algorithms. Response teams must train alongside crypto and platform teams to understand certificate chaining mechanics, fallback negotiation patterns, and the signs of post-quantum exploitation. Integrating certificate lifecycle events into SIEM platforms is only the beginning. IR teams must be empowered with tooling that can trace cryptographic anomalies across services and quickly coordinate with DevOps, IAM, and security engineering to rotate keys, revoke certificates, and restore secure communication. In a PQC-enabled world, cryptographic integrity becomes a frontline security issue, and incident response must evolve to meet it head-on with the same rigor applied to traditional breaches. This means embedding cryptographic event detection into daily SOC operations, refining escalation paths for certificate and key anomalies, and participating in joint exercises that simulate PQC failure scenarios. For example, a tabletop exercise might simulate the sudden deprecation of a hybrid certificate in production, requiring coordinated action across the IR team, DevOps, and CLM administrators. Metrics such as time-to-revoke and time-to-reissue should become part of post-incident analysis. Ultimately, at this stage of your journey, the intersection of cryptography and incident response will no longer be theoretical. As post-quantum systems come online, the IR team must be prepared to treat certificate expiration, key compromise, and algorithmic obsolescence not just as technical failures but as full-blown security events requiring rapid, structured, and collaborative action.

At the end of the day, reporting is what ties everything together. A well-managed certificate environment should give you clear, auditable visibility into the status of every cryptographic asset. Dashboards should display all active certificates, organized by role, algorithm, application, and expiration date. They should flag issues as they happen, whether it's a certificate nearing expiration, a broken validation chain, or a key that hasn't been rotated in a while. It's not enough for these reports to exist; they need to be used. Regular reviews, KPI tracking, and policy updates should all be based on what the system is actually seeing.

By making certificate lifecycle governance part of everyday operations, organizations can keep their cryptographic foundations strong, even as threats continue to evolve. Automation helps scale these efforts, but it's governance that provides accountability. Together, they help ensure that today's systems stay trustworthy over time.

In a post-quantum world, trust is a moving target. Certificates will expire, keys will change, and algorithms will need to be replaced. Still, with the right teams, disciplined workflows, and tools that actually work together, organizations can maintain the trust at the core of their digital infrastructure. Long after the migration is done, ongoing maintenance and solid governance will be what keeps that trust intact.

18.7 CONCLUSION

The journey toward quantum resilience does not end with the selection of algorithms or the rollout of hybrid certificates. It continues through disciplined operational maturity. Chapter 18 underscored that certificate management, once treated as background infrastructure, will now sit at the center of post-quantum trust. It is not enough to know what certificates are issued; you must also know where they are deployed, how they are monitored, when they expire, and how fast you can replace them. More importantly, you must ensure that these processes are institutionalized. As post-quantum cryptography becomes woven into the fabric of your organization, the people responsible for that fabric, security engineers, platform teams, DevOps, IAM specialists, and incident responders must work from a shared set of tools, schedules, expectations, and values. Trust is transitioning from a static credential to a continuous process, and this process must be carefully built, maintained, and governed.

In the next chapter, we turn our attention to the human element of post-quantum readiness. Cryptography does not operate in isolation. It requires people who understand it, organizations that practice it, and leaders who can steer through uncertainty. Chapter 19, "Enhance Organizational Readiness", explores how to build that human foundation. We will look at quantum literacy training for IT and security teams, how to run effective PQC tabletop exercises, and why it is time to appoint a quantum risk owner. The next step involves equipping the organization itself to be agile, aware, and ready for what comes next.

Chapter 19

Enhance organizational readiness

Technology does not secure itself. Even the most robust post-quantum cryptographic implementation will falter if the people managing it are unprepared. Enhancing organizational readiness is more than deploying hybrid certificates or rotating quantum-safe keys. You need to build institutional muscle, train teams to understand new tools, and prepare them to respond to new risks. Then, you must align responsibilities so that PQC doesn't exist in a silo and instead becomes an integral part of everyday operations.

This chapter focuses on three critical capabilities that support that goal: training the workforce, conducting real-world preparedness exercises, and designating clear ownership over quantum risk.

19.1 TRAINING FOR A QUANTUM-AWARE WORKFORCE

Post-quantum cryptography introduces new terminology, tooling, and failure modes that most IT and security teams have never encountered before. Just as important as the technology itself is the ability of your people to use it wisely, recognize when it is failing, and know how to respond. To achieve that, you must build quantum literacy into every layer of your organization.

Quantum literacy training should begin with the teams responsible for designing, deploying, and maintaining cryptographic systems. Security engineers need to understand which algorithms are being phased out and how to implement hybrid or dual-algorithm models safely. Platform teams must learn how to configure systems to accept larger keys, validate hybrid certificates, and maintain crypto-agility through the use of abstraction layers. DevOps teams should know how to integrate PQC libraries into CI/CD pipelines, rotate keys via automation, and use CLM systems effectively. IAM specialists must learn how quantum-safe identity materials interact with authentication workflows, federation protocols, and access tokens. Incident response teams must gain fluency in a new category of risk, cryptographic failures. They need to recognize when a PQC failure has occurred, whether due to algorithmic deprecation, signature validation errors, or

 DOI: 10.1201/9781003685760-26

misuse of fallback mechanisms. Training should include sample scenarios, log analysis exercises, and collaboration with cryptographic engineering leads to ensure that response times remain fast and coordinated.

Even end users should not be left out. While they may not need to understand the difference between ML-KEM and Dilithium, they should be aware of how certificate expirations might impact access, how to respond to trust warnings, and when to report potential cryptographic issues.

A well-rounded training program should begin with an introduction to quantum computing and its impact on classical cryptography. It should also offer a breakdown of PQC algorithms selected by NIST and what makes them secure, helping participants build foundational knowledge. Training should include hands-on labs using OpenSSL with PQC extensions or ISARA Radiate, allowing engineers to experiment in safe environments. Practical exercises in configuring hybrid TLS and testing validation chains help reinforce skills that will be applied in production environments. CI/CD integration should be part of the curriculum, with examples showing how to embed PQC-ready certificates into pipelines and workflows. Teams should learn how to rotate quantum-safe keys with platforms like HashiCorp Vault or AWS KMS, enabling secure key management at scale. Playbooks for responding to PQC certificate or key compromise should be introduced, allowing incident responders to practice and refine procedures. The training should also address the auditing and compliance implications of operating in a post-quantum environment, ensuring that policy teams remain aligned with technical implementation.

A successful workforce development strategy requires not only access to the right training materials but also a clear delineation of roles and responsibilities. Security engineers and cryptographic architects should be responsible for selecting and validating PQC libraries, maintaining crypto-agility frameworks, and designing secure key management practices. DevOps and platform teams should implement, monitor, and update quantum-safe components across cloud and on-prem environments. Compliance officers and internal auditors need to understand the impact of PQC on regulatory obligations, audit scopes, and risk disclosures. Policy and legal teams should develop awareness of evolving standards and regulatory guidance to support contract language, governance policies, and third-party assessments. Each of these roles should have access to role-specific learning paths and resources tailored to their operational focus.

To support this, organizations should create a quantum readiness training roadmap. Begin by establishing baseline competencies by function and then offer tiered education levels. To bring this strategy to life, begin by defining what each functional group must know and create an assessment rubric that reflects their responsibilities. For example, foundational literacy for all staff can be measured through short interactive courses that explain what quantum computing is, why it matters to the organization, and how to spot basic trust failures in applications or communications. These modules should include brief quizzes and scenario-based evaluations to confirm understanding.

For infrastructure and platform teams, assessments should go deeper. Ask participants to walk through practical tasks like updating certificate chains with hybrid algorithms, configuring TLS endpoints to support ML-KEM, or validating key rotation processes using Vault or KMS platforms. Assign lab-based exercises with preconfigured test environments where they can observe how legacy systems respond to new cryptographic parameters. Incorporate review sessions to discuss common misconfigurations and how to address them.

Cryptographic engineers and security architects should undergo rigorous evaluation. This includes troubleshooting broken validation chains, stress-testing hybrid implementations under load, and modeling downgrade attacks in test networks. Assessments can require design reviews of migration plans, critiques of PQC algorithm performance in constrained environments, or evaluation of fallback risks across multiple vendors.

Beyond individual skills, the organization should host integrated tabletop exercises that simulate a cryptographic failure during a certificate rotation or a supply chain compromise involving PQC-incompatible firmware. These simulations help reveal gaps in response coordination, vendor communication, and policy enforcement. Including legal, procurement, and compliance teams ensures that responses are not only technical but holistic, reflecting the full scope of risk.

By building role-specific assessments into your workforce development strategy, you reinforce the shared responsibility model at the heart of quantum readiness. Every function has a role to play, and every team must be equipped to play it well.

There are also a growing number of third-party resources that can support internal learning efforts. The International Institute of Quantum Computing (I2QC) offers a slate of certifications tailored to technical professionals, including the Certified Quantum Practitioner (CQP), which is particularly relevant for cybersecurity leaders preparing to manage quantum risk. More information is available at i2qc.org/certifications. For those looking for a structured academic introduction, the University of Maryland offers UMBC: Introduction to Post-Quantum Cryptography through edX. It is an accessible starting point for technical professionals unfamiliar with PQC fundamentals.

CDW Workforce Development, Sandbox AQ, and academic institutions with quantum security programs all offer curated courses and certifications. However, internal enablement is just as important. Host internal lunch-and-learns, share algorithm updates from NIST, or just set up a lab where teams can experiment without risk. Create a shared glossary to normalize PQC vocabulary across roles. Investing in education ensures that when cryptographic systems evolve, your people are ready to evolve with them.

19.2 TABLETOP EXERCISES AND PLAYBOOKS FOR PQC INCIDENTS

Training is the foundation, but preparedness must be tested. Tabletop exercises bring theory into practice by simulating incidents in a controlled environment. They expose gaps in communication, uncover hidden dependencies, and help teams rehearse coordinated responses before a real crisis emerges. In the context of post-quantum cryptography, these simulations take on greater urgency. The transition to PQC introduces unfamiliar cryptographic tools, longer key sizes, evolving standards, and new failure modes. If your organization is not simulating PQC-related failures, it will not be prepared to respond when they occur under pressure.

A tabletop exercise focused on PQC might center around a scenario such as:

- A hybrid certificate used in production fails post-quantum validation due to an expired or misconfigured quantum signature.
- A new vulnerability is discovered in a post-quantum algorithm, triggering the need to rotate all affected keys and reissue certificates across the environment.
- A system relying on fallback behavior is found to have accepted a forged classical signature during a quantum attack simulation.

Each of these events would involve multiple teams. DevOps would need to verify rollout mechanisms and automation coverage for certificate renewal. IAM teams would assess which machine or user identities were impacted and confirm the scope of the issue. Security engineering would evaluate which systems failed to validate the certificate and whether logs captured relevant anomalies. The incident response team would coordinate communication, mitigation, and external reporting, while compliance teams would begin preparing audit records.

To be effective, tabletop exercises should follow a structured format. A facilitator presents the scenario, outlines time progression, and guides participants through each phase of the incident. Participants respond as they would in a real incident, referencing actual tools, logs, workflows, and personnel. Someone is assigned to document all decisions, questions, and discoveries. The goal is not to "win" the scenario, but to surface confusion, hesitation, or process breakdowns in a low-stakes setting.

Best practices for PQC tabletop exercises begin with focusing on high-risk events that carry broad operational consequences. Incidents such as key rotation failures or invalid hybrid certificate chains should be prioritized, as these represent likely scenarios in the early years of post-quantum adoption and can reveal how well-prepared teams are to respond under pressure. Wherever possible, these exercises should take place in environments that closely mirror production. Using real logs, testing against staging systems, and simulating alerts within your SIEM platform adds authenticity and ensures teams are engaging with tools and data they will encounter during actual events. Participation should be cross-functional. Stakeholders from incident response, DevOps, identity and access management, security engineering, infrastructure, and compliance must be involved to capture the full range of perspectives and responsibilities. Cryptographic incidents touch nearly every layer of the organization, and exercises should reflect that reality. The scope of each exercise should remain manageable. One well-constructed scenario with clearly defined learning objectives will deliver more insight than a sprawling, overly complex simulation. The goal is to build clarity and confidence, rather than overwhelming or confusing participants.

Finally, every tabletop exercise should end with a structured debrief. Teams should reflect on what went well, what fell short, what unexpected challenges arose, and what policies or playbooks need revision. Capturing these insights ensures that each simulation strengthens the organization's readiness for the next real-world cryptographic event. After each tabletop, your team should revise or create playbooks to codify lessons learned.

19.2.1 Playbooks

Playbooks are the documented response plans that transform the lessons from tabletop exercises into structured and repeatable actions. In the context of post-quantum cryptography, these documents must be adapted to address failure modes and scenarios that legacy playbooks were never designed to handle. The aim is to turn simulated decisions into operational steps that can be executed consistently and confidently during an actual incident.

For example, a PQC playbook should outline the steps to detect and confirm cryptographic anomalies. This includes identifying which logs to check, which systems may exhibit validation errors, and what signs might indicate a fallback attack or a failed PQC signature. It should also describe how to disable deprecated or vulnerable algorithms in live environments. This could involve editing TLS configuration files, revoking certificates that rely on the compromised algorithm, or pushing updated cryptographic policies through CI/CD pipelines.

Another key element is guidance on how to revoke and replace certificates associated with compromised keys. This includes coordinating issuance across distributed systems, updating key vaults, propagating new certificates to dependent services, and verifying that deployment has been completed successfully. Playbooks must also provide instructions for cross-functional communication and escalation procedures in the event of algorithmic deprecation, third-party library vulnerabilities, or failures in trust anchors. Finally, each plan should explain how to log and audit these actions, including how to prepare reports for both internal oversight and any required external disclosure.

Every playbook should be built around a specific scenario. It should begin by identifying the triggering event or detection mechanism and clearly defining the roles and responsibilities of each team involved. The playbook also needs to list the systems and tools involved, walk through the response step by step, and call out any points where things need to be verified before moving on. Fallback or fail-safe procedures should be described in case part of the process does not go as planned. The document should also contain a communication plan for both internal coordination and external notification, and set expectations around timelines, including escalation thresholds for delayed resolution.

These playbooks should never be treated as static resources. They need to be validated through regular use. During tabletop exercises and dry-run simulations, the plans should be tested by cross-functional teams and revised as needed to reflect new tools, updated standards, or architectural changes. An annual or even semi-annual walk-through of each critical playbook ensures teams remain fluent in the steps and helps catch issues before they become problems during a real incident.

When writing playbooks, teams should be mindful of several common mistakes. One is relying too heavily on a single expert. Playbooks should be written in an accessible language that any team member can follow, regardless of seniority or role, and they should be stored in a central, version-controlled repository. Another pitfall is drafting documents that are too generic. Playbooks that reference vague procedures are less likely to be followed under pressure. Tailoring them to your actual architecture and team structure increases their utility during high-stress situations. Lastly, teams often overlook access control. Many incidents are delayed because the person on call lacks permissions to access a key vault, revoke a certificate, or trigger a policy update. Access requirements should be clearly defined and tested before a crisis arises.

Change management is critical in this process. Introducing new cryptographic playbooks means changing how teams think about failure. It requires cultural shifts, not just procedural ones. Resistance often comes from the perception that cryptography is "invisible" or "too low-level" to warrant special attention in a crisis. Your job is to shift that mindset.

Behavioral change management can accelerate adoption. Consider gamifying crypto-awareness by assigning team scores during tabletops, offering badges or recognition for cryptographic hygiene, or tracking key performance indicators like certificate renewal time or fallback detection speed. Celebrate successful drills and utilize leadership support to enhance the visibility of cryptographic readiness. Highlight cryptographic lapses during retrospectives, not to blame, but to learn.

This cultural shift is what will ultimately make your post-quantum readiness sustainable. Tabletops and playbooks are training grounds for a new generation of operational security. In a quantum future, your ability to respond quickly, decisively, and with clarity will be the difference between resilience and regret.

19.3 APPOINTING A QUANTUM RISK OWNER

Every organization embarking on the post-quantum journey should designate a single point of responsibility for quantum risk. This role could be the PQC Czar introduced in Chapter 9, who helped guide strategy, maintain the roadmap, coordinate with vendors, and lead early readiness efforts. As systems shift from rollout to routine, this responsibility does not disappear. It simply transitions.

In the maintenance phase, quantum risk becomes a steady-state concern. Although it may no longer dominate daily meetings or project plans, it still requires long-term oversight. The individual in this role may change over time. It could be a senior security architect, a governance leader, or a cryptographic subject matter expert embedded within the security or risk organization. What matters most is not their title, but their ability to act. The quantum risk owner must be empowered to make decisions, track progress, enforce policy, and speak for quantum-related concerns in front of executives.

If you've read my book *The CISO 3.0*, you know that I believe the business should always own the risk. Individual stakeholders should own the asset inventories, threats, and vulnerabilities that roll up into those risks. This philosophy holds true here, even if the title "Quantum Asset, Threat, and Vulnerability Owner" doesn't quite have the same ring to it. So, when we say "Quantum Risk Owner", understand that we mean the person or group of people responsible for managing the quantum-relevant assets, threat models, and known or emerging vulnerabilities that impact an enterprise's cryptographic resilience.

This person must monitor developments from standards bodies like NIST and the IETF. Quantum risk is not static; as algorithms are finalized, updated, or deprecated, the risk owner must keep the organization aligned with those shifts. They must also manage the organization's internal cryptographic roadmap, mapping projected upgrades to broader compliance milestones and operational refresh cycles.

Additionally, this person should chair, or at least contribute meaningfully to, the crypto governance committee or center of excellence. That body, originally established to coordinate migration efforts, now serves as a long-term nerve center for cryptographic decision-making. Whether it's evaluating a new CLM tool or weighing the risk of an emerging side-channel attack, the committee helps ensure decisions remain well-informed and cross-functional.

The quantum risk owner also takes accountability for the health of the cryptographic inventory. They ensure lifecycle automation is functioning correctly and that the organization is always prepared to execute revocation at scale when needed. If certificate chains break or hybrid keys require replacement, this person will not be surprised; they'll already have the playbook tested and ready.

Lastly, this role is responsible for elevating quantum risk metrics to executive leadership. This includes reporting on cryptographic posture to the CISO, risk committees, or compliance leadership. Metrics may include certificate expiration exposure, revocation readiness, algorithm coverage, fallback frequency, or time to remediate for crypto-related incidents.

As responsibility becomes more operationalized, the post-quantum steering committee should evolve into a center of excellence. The group can meet less frequently, but it should not be disbanded. Regular reviews of cryptographic telemetry, policy alignment, vendor readiness, and skills development keep the entire system from falling into complacency. In practical terms, this means formally transitioning PQC responsibilities into the hands of those who will sustain them. Job descriptions should be updated, and performance reviews should include metrics tied to crypto-agility, lifecycle management, and post-quantum risk reduction. Organizational charts should reflect ownership, but most importantly, everyone from engineering to governance should understand that cryptographic security is a permanent, living part of the enterprise's defense posture.

19.4 EMBEDDING PQC INTO THIRD-PARTY RISK MANAGEMENT

The transition to post-quantum cryptography will not happen in isolation. No matter how well-prepared your internal teams are, your organization remains vulnerable if your vendors and partners are not equally ready. This is why post-quantum readiness must be built into third-party risk management.

Procurement teams play a pivotal role in this transformation. They are often the first line of defense when it comes to selecting, renewing, or off-boarding vendors. As such, it is essential that procurement professionals understand the implications of quantum threats and the basic concepts of post-quantum cryptography. They do not need to master the math behind lattice-based algorithms, but they should recognize the difference between a cryptographic claim and a verifiable capability. Knowing what to ask, what to look for, and how to verify those claims will allow them to make more informed decisions.

Vendor onboarding questionnaires should be updated to include explicit questions about post-quantum cryptography. For example: Which cryptographic algorithms does your product or service rely on? Do you support or have a roadmap for PQC-aligned algorithms such as ML-KEM or Dilithium? Are hybrid key exchange or dual certificate chains supported today or planned within the next twelve months?

Contracts should reflect these new expectations. Language can be introduced that requires vendors to maintain a roadmap for PQC compliance, to notify the customer of any known quantum-vulnerable algorithms in use, and to support testing of quantum-safe configurations upon request. Sample contract terms might include:

> Vendor agrees to disclose any reliance on cryptographic algorithms that are known to be vulnerable to quantum attacks as defined by NIST and other governing bodies. Vendor shall provide a documented roadmap to achieve compliance with emerging post-quantum cryptographic standards, including support for NIST-approved algorithms upon availability.

Or:

> The service provider shall support post-quantum hybrid certificate chains (e.g., X.509 with both classical and quantum-safe signature fields) no later than twelve months following the ratification of the corresponding standards.

Service level agreements should also evolve. While uptime and performance remain important, they should be joined by commitments related to cryptographic transparency and adaptability. An SLA might specify timelines for enabling PQC features, turnaround times for updating key exchange methods, or escalation procedures if vulnerabilities are discovered in current implementations.

Checklists can be an invaluable tool in this process. A procurement checklist for PQC readiness might include:

- Disclosure of all cryptographic dependencies
- Timeline for PQC adoption
- Documentation of crypto-agility features
- Support for hybrid or dual-stack implementations
- Participation in NIST PQC testing or early access programs
- Past security audits and cryptographic assessments

Auditing vendor claims will require collaboration between procurement, security, and compliance teams. Marketing brochures are not enough. Ask for technical whitepapers, lab validation reports, or SOC 2 appendices that document cryptographic design. When in doubt, request a demonstration. If a vendor claims to support ML-KEM in production, ask to see the configuration, test vectors, or a test environment.

Embedding PQC into third-party risk management does more than protect against abstract future threats. It establishes accountability today. It sends a clear message to your supply chain that cryptographic resilience is not optional. It also allows you to phase out vendors that cannotor will notadapt. In a world where digital trust is only as strong as the weakest link, this type of due diligence is no longer a nice-to-have. It is an operational necessity.

19.5 CONCLUSION

Enhancing organizational readiness requires more than simply knowing what to do; you also have to be able to do it under pressure, across teams, and with confidence. Technology alone cannot carry the weight of cryptographic resilience. It depends on people, their knowledge, their coordination, and their readiness to respond. This chapter has outlined the practical steps organizations must take to embed PQC into their operational DNA, from training the workforce and conducting live-fire tabletop exercises to appointing and empowering a quantum risk owner who ensures continuity beyond the migration phase.

By investing in training, rehearsing real-world scenarios, and embedding accountability, organizations prepare themselves not just to deploy PQC but to live with it. The next threat may not come from a graduate paper or a government memo. It may come as a Friday afternoon vulnerability disclosure with no patch and only hours to respond. Readiness means having the right people in the right seats, using the right tools, and possessing the foresight to act before trust is lost.

This chapter marks the final step in the final phase of your post-quantum journey. You've laid the groundwork, executed the migration, validated the deployment, and built the maintenance rhythms to keep it going. What comes next is not a new control or checklist; it is reflection. In the final chapter, we'll revisit the path we've taken, highlight key lessons learned, and explore where the road might lead next. The quantum future is not a destination; it is a continuum, and now, you are ready to navigate it.

Chapter 20

The end is just the beginning

20.1 LOOKING BACK ON THE ROAD WE'VE TRAVELED

When we first started this journey, quantum threats felt like a distant concern. They hovered at the edge of cybersecurity conversations, often dismissed as something for the next generation to worry about. As we saw back in Chapter 1, that assumption no longer holds. The age of quantum computing isn't something far off on the horizon. It's already here, growing steadily, and it's beginning to challenge how we think about trust, data, and risk today.

In Chapter 2, we moved from theory to mechanics. We explored how quantum computers process information differently from classical systems and how this fundamental difference leads to unprecedented computational power. Through the lens of Shor's Algorithm, we saw how public key cryptography, particularly RSA and ECC, can be broken, while Grover's Algorithm showed us how even symmetric encryption like AES needs to be re-evaluated. These threats are not distant possibilities but pressing realities, as demonstrated by hands-on experiments conducted on systems like Google's quantum computers and China's Zuchongzhi processor.

Chapter 3 introduced the Mosca Model, a practical way to evaluate how exposed we are. It gave us a framework to weigh how long our data needs to stay protected, how long a migration might take, and how soon quantum decryption could become real. Instead of vague worries, we had something we could actually measure, helping us move from speculation to strategy.

Then came Chapter 4, where we introduced the Q-Ready Framework. This became our map through the quantum transition. It's broken into five key phases: Discovery, Planning, Implementation, Validation, and Maintenance. Each one builds on the last, offering a clear and repeatable structure to guide complex change. The framework gave us not just a direction, but a method to follow with purpose.

Chapters 5 through 7 focused on the Discovery phase. These chapters walked through how to identify where cryptography shows up in your systems, what kind of data it protects, and which assets are most at risk. We

DOI: 10.1201/9781003685760-27

explored the importance of maintaining a solid cryptographic inventory, uncovering certificates, and mapping dependencies. This work set the stage for everything that followed.

Planning took center stage in Chapters 8 through 10. We looked at how to build a migration plan that fits with your business strategy. That included scoping the project, bringing the right stakeholders into the conversation, selecting toolkits like liboqs and OpenSSL, and defining success in terms that matter. Planning wasn't treated as a static document but as a living process shaped by collaboration.

Chapters 11 through 13 brought us into the Implementation phase. These chapters focused on the hard work of phasing out broken algorithms, rolling out hybrid certificates, and integrating post-quantum cryptography into everything from TLS and VPNs to APIs. We dug into the unique challenges of securing firmware, protecting data at rest, and updating embedded systems, while reinforcing the importance of crypto-agility and building defenses in depth.

Then came Validation in Chapters 14 through 16. This phase was about testing what we'd put in place. That included preparing for audits, simulating failures, and making sure everything aligned with standards from NIST and FIPS. The goal here wasn't just to check a box. It was to build confidence that the migration would hold up under pressure.

Chapters 17 through 19 shifted the focus to Maintenance. This is where we explored how to make readiness part of everyday operations. We covered certificate lifecycle management, algorithm agility, ongoing training, real-time monitoring, and policy updates. Post-quantum readiness isn't a one-time milestone. It's a new way of running your security program, and these chapters laid out what that discipline needs to look like going forward.

Now, in Chapter 20, we step back and take stock. What once felt overwhelming has been broken down into a process you can follow. The unknown became something you could plan for. Each chapter added a piece to the puzzle, turning uncertainty into structure and ideas into action.

20.2 KEY LESSONS TO CARRY FORWARD

At its core, this book has been about navigating change, not just technical change, but a change in mindset. The most important lessons we've uncovered weren't related to quantum algorithms or encryption protocols. They were instead strategy, adaptability, and the real meaning of trust in a digital age.

The first major lesson is that quantum risk is no longer abstract. Chapter 1 introduced us to the concept of "Harvest Now, Decrypt Later". This tactic is already in play and highlights how encrypted data can be intercepted today and decrypted years from now with quantum tools. That simple idea reframes our understanding of confidentiality. We are no longer securing data just for today, but for tomorrow's computational capabilities.

Consider the example of a healthcare provider storing genomic data for research. Those records must remain private for decades, often tied to ethical and legal commitments that outlast any individual system. A failure to migrate in time could jeopardize not only compliance but trust in the institution's integrity. This is a potential real-world scenario that every organization with long-lived sensitive data faces.

A second key takeaway is that the migration to post-quantum cryptography is a complex, organization-wide effort. It is not a matter of deploying a patch or swapping out a library. As Chapter 8 demonstrated, it demands a programmatic approach that includes governance, stakeholder alignment, timeline coordination, and careful resource planning. One global logistics company we consulted with discovered over a hundred distinct cryptographic systems across its environment, many embedded in legacy industrial control systems. Replacing these systems will require a multiyear roadmap, vendor partnerships, and a realignment of security and IT priorities. The project won't just change code; it will have to change culture.

This brings us to another critical insight, which is that crypto-agility is not just a technical feature; it's an organizational virtue. Chapter 13 made clear that the post-quantum future will not be static. Standards will evolve, and adversaries will adapt. Organizations that survive will be the ones that can adjust. Crypto-agility is now table stakes for long-term resilience.

Fourth, visibility is non-negotiable. You cannot secure what you do not understand. Chapters 5 through 7 focused heavily on cryptographic discovery, and for good reason. Many of the organizations I've consulted underestimated their crypto footprint by an order of magnitude. Secrets were hidden in old source code, certificate chains were misconfigured, and legacy systems relied on vulnerable protocols nobody had touched in years. A team that thought it had a dozen certificate authorities uncovered over a hundred. This is why continuous cryptographic inventory and assessment must become a standard operating practice, not a one-off audit.

The fifth lesson is about risk. The Mosca Model, introduced in Chapter 3, gave us a powerful way to measure exposure. It taught us that the problem isn't just when Q-Day arrives. It's about whether your timeline to migrate is shorter than the time left before encryption fails. If your systems take five years to migrate and your data needs to stay protected for ten, then the window for action is already closing. One financial institution ran this model against its own systems and realized its exposure would outlive its migration timeline by nearly a decade. That insight forced a wholesale reprioritization of its cryptographic transition.

Finally, we learned that success in this journey is not about achieving perfection but rather making steady, strategic progress. The Q-Ready Framework exists to support that progress. Whether you are starting with an inventory, designing a test lab, or pushing new certificates into production, what matters is forward movement. You don't need to boil the ocean; you just need to take the next meaningful step.

So, what are the most important lessons to carry with you? Quantum risk is here and growing. Migration is not an IT project; it is a business transformation. Crypto-agility will define the winners. Visibility drives everything. Readiness is measurable, and the best time to begin was yesterday. The second-best time is now.

Together, these lessons form more than a checklist. They tell a story of what it means to lead through uncertainty, to prepare without panic, and to preserve trust in a world where the ground is shifting beneath our feet. The quantum era is coming, but the wisdom from this journey will serve you well, not just in post-quantum readiness, but in every security challenge that lies ahead.

20.3 PREPARING FOR WHAT'S NEXT

If the past chapters have prepared you for what must be done now, this final section is about what comes after. Q-Day is not the end of the story. In the wake of Q-Day, we can expect a sweeping shift across global IT systems. Algorithms such as RSA, ECC, and DH will no longer be relied upon for trust or confidentiality. Their replacements, drawn from NIST's post-quantum cryptography standardization process, like CRYSTALS-Kyber for key encapsulation and CRYSTALS-Dilithium for signatures, will become foundational to new deployments. Hybrid models that combine classical and quantum-safe algorithms will act as transitional bridges, allowing systems to validate both legacy and next-generation cryptographic proofs. This coexistence may persist for a decade or more, depending on adoption rates and the longevity of embedded systems. However, even these new algorithms may not be the end of the story. There is a good chance that some post-quantum cryptographic algorithms won't hold up indefinitely or that advancements in quantum computing will render them obsolete sooner than expected. At the same time, quantum computing may unlock new methods of encryption altogether, potentially even protocols that leverage quantum entanglement or multi-party computation to achieve forms of secrecy we can scarcely imagine today. That is why crypto-agility is so crucial: the ability to pivot to new cryptographic standards rapidly will determine who stays secure and who gets left behind.

Looking ahead, we may see future algorithms that harness complex mathematical constructs, such as supersingular isogeny graphs or module lattices, in more efficient ways, delivering both compact key sizes and strong resistance to side-channel attacks. Some researchers are already experimenting with quantum-enhanced cryptographic protocols, systems that use the quantum state itself as a kind of signature or proof of authenticity, making forgery nearly impossible. Others imagine a world where cryptographic security is not just algorithmic but entangled, where trust is physically encoded at the quantum level.

But cryptography won't be the only area of transformation. Quantum computing itself will usher in changes across a wide array of technologies. Edge computing, already vital for latency-sensitive applications, will likely pair with quantum-enhanced models to perform localized quantum-assisted decision-making. Imagine logistics operations where quantum optimization algorithms, running on edge nodes, calculate ideal delivery routes in real time, based on shifting constraints.

In the realm of blockchain and decentralized ledgers, Q-Day could pose an existential threat to systems relying on public key signatures for identity and immutability. This will force a reengineering of smart contracts and wallet mechanisms, and possibly drive the adoption of quantum-resistant consensus algorithms. Some forward-looking projects are already exploring lattice-based or hash-based signature schemes, preparing for a future where blockchain continues, but under different cryptographic assumptions. For cryptocurrencies like Bitcoin, the implications are particularly stark. Bitcoin's security model depends on the elliptic curve digital signature algorithm (ECDSA), which secures wallets and transaction authorizations. Once large-scale quantum computers become capable of running Shor's algorithm, an attacker could derive private keys from public addresses exposed in the blockchain, allowing them to steal funds, forge transactions, or disrupt the network's integrity. While addresses that have never been used remain secure (since their public keys are not visible), any address that has signed a transaction becomes vulnerable after Q-Day. This has prompted some in the cryptocurrency community to advocate for preemptive key rotation, address obfuscation, or even hard forks that introduce post-quantum cryptographic primitives. Without proactive mitigation, Q-Day could lead to the rapid erosion of trust in major blockchain networks and a catastrophic compromise of the value stored across millions of wallets.

The Metaverse, which promises immersive, persistent digital environments, will face novel challenges and opportunities in a post-quantum world. The massive authentication, asset ownership, and secure interaction requirements of these virtual spaces will need cryptographic agility to safeguard identity and value. Quantum-secure identity frameworks may underpin avatars, digital property, and transactional integrity within these extended realities. Without them, Q-Day could open the door to digital theft at scale. For example, if virtual real estate or in-game items are tied to blockchain-based tokens signed with classical cryptography, a quantum-capable attacker could extract private keys from exposed public keys and transfer those assets to their own wallet, effectively stealing digital land, exclusive NFTs, or high-value gaming assets. In a world where virtual goods carry real monetary value, the erosion of cryptographic trust could trigger not just in-game chaos, but also real-world legal and economic disputes.

Biotechnology, too, stands to be reshaped. The fusion of quantum computing with bioinformatics will unlock insights previously unreachable, predictive modeling of protein folding, genetic mutation analysis, and drug synthesis pathways. These capabilities, when paired with cryptographically assured data provenance, could redefine clinical research, patient privacy, and genomic IP protection. However, Q-Day could also introduce profound risks, especially for emerging technologies such as computer-brain interfaces (CBIs). These systems, which directly link neural activity with digital networks, rely on secure communication channels and trusted device authentication. A quantum-enabled adversary could compromise the encryption protecting brain-machine data, intercepting or altering neural input and output in real time. This opens the door to alarming scenarios, from unauthorized access to brain-controlled prosthetics or communication devices to the manipulation of sensory input or even cognitive influence. Ensuring post-quantum protections in CBIs won't just be a matter of data integrity; it will be a matter of human safety and autonomy.

Then there's the future of AI. Quantum computing may dramatically accelerate AI model training, compressing what takes weeks into minutes. With it, the need for trustworthy inference and verifiable model outputs will only intensify. Post-quantum cryptography could ensure that AI decisions can be audited, authenticated, and securely distributed, especially in sensitive sectors like defense, finance, and healthcare. The implications, however, go further when considering generative and agentic AI systems, models that not only generate content but also take autonomous action, make decisions, or interact with external systems on behalf of humans.

In a post-quantum world, the integrity of these AI agents will become a high-value target. Without strong quantum-resistant signatures, malicious actors could forge agent credentials, spoof command origins, or hijack decision chains in distributed AI systems. For example, an agentic AI used in autonomous logistics could be tricked into rerouting sensitive shipments or altering procurement decisions if cryptographic controls are compromised.

Generative AI models that issue or verify legal documents, financial transactions, or medical reports will need to prove provenance and authenticity at every step. Quantum-safe digital signatures will become essential to ensure that outputs cannot be tampered with or falsely attributed. Without these safeguards, deepfakes and fabricated content may be indistinguishable from verified outputs, eroding trust in even the most legitimate systems.

Moreover, as AI models themselves become intellectual property assets, ensuring that weights, prompts, and outputs remain protected from theft or unauthorized duplication will be critical. Post-quantum protections will be needed to secure AI training data, verify model origin, and enforce usage licenses in decentralized environments. In effect, Q-Day could force a complete rethinking of how we secure, govern, and trust the actions of increasingly autonomous AI systems.

At a broader level, we can expect quantum computing to challenge even the structure of the internet itself. New forms of encryption, transmission, and validation may give rise to quantum-native protocols. These might include quantum key distribution networks for unbreakable communication links, or entirely new layers of infrastructure where classical and quantum systems operate side by side.

Q-Day may also reshape our relationship with time, identity, and memory in digital environments. With quantum capabilities, the real-time simulation of complex systems, such as climate, traffic, markets, and ecosystems, could move from aspirational to operational. Long-standing challenges, such as real-time urban optimization, personalized medicine, and predictive infrastructure maintenance, could be solved not just faster but also differently. When paired with next-generation AI, these advances could give rise to sentient agents that co-develop solutions with humans in quantum-enhanced collaborative loops.

Yet the promise comes with significant risk. Q-Day could compromise the secure data pipelines that emerging technologies depend on. Systems built on assumptions of trusted encryption and immutable communication could be exposed to interception, manipulation, or outright failure. The more advanced and interconnected our infrastructure becomes, the more devastating the consequences of cryptographic collapse. Trust in data provenance, secure model training, distributed control, and inter-system coordination could all be called into question if quantum-readiness is not built into the foundation.

The very interconnectedness that powers scientific and technological progress becomes a liability if post-quantum safeguards are not in place. Without a quantum-resilient foundation, many of the advances on the horizon could become high-risk vulnerabilities in a world where cryptographic certainty no longer exists.

All of this underscores the reality that Q-Day is not an endpoint; it is a threshold. A frontier beyond which our current assumptions no longer hold, but with the right preparation, it can also be the beginning of an era defined by resilience, reinvention, and remarkable potential. The choices you make now, the foundations you lay, and the agility you foster will shape not just how you endure the quantum shift, but how you thrive in what comes next. Q-Day doesn't just threaten what we have; it offers a rare opportunity to reimagine what's possible.

20.4 FINAL WORDS OF GUIDANCE

Congratulations. If you've made it this far, you've not only completed this book, but you've also stepped into a new era of cybersecurity leadership. This is more than just the end of a reading journey; it's the beginning of a strategic, operational, and philosophical shift in how we think about digital trust.

You now understand the quantum threat, its timeline, and the technologies poised to replace vulnerable cryptographic systems. You've walked through frameworks for readiness, seen real-world use cases, and learned how to lead your organization toward resilience. This knowledge puts you ahead of the curve, but only if you act on it.

So here's the challenge: begin. Take the first concrete step toward post-quantum readiness. Start where you are, inventory what you have, and prioritize what matters most. Use the frameworks and models presented here to guide your decisions. You don't have to be perfect, but you do have to be proactive. Build an inventory, schedule a stakeholder workshop, start a test lab, and talk to your vendors. Share what you've learned with your team and your peers. Transformation only happens when insight becomes implementation.

You are now an ambassador of quantum resilience. Others will look to you for clarity, direction, and leadership. Embrace that role. Champion the shift, and if you need help bringing these ideas to life inside your organization, know that support is available. If you have questions, want to go deeper, or are looking for guidance tailored to your environment, I invite you to reach out directly. You can contact me at theciso30.com. Whether it's consulting, collaboration, or conversation, I'm here to help you navigate the next phase.

Thank you for taking this journey. Now go lead the way.

Index

D

Q

R

S

T

U

V

W

Z

For Product Safety Concerns and Information please contact our EU
representative GPSR@taylorandfrancis.com
Taylor & Francis Verlag GmbH, Kaufingerstraße 24, 80331 München, Germany

www.ingramcontent.com/pod-product-compliance
Ingram Content Group UK Ltd.
Pitfield, Milton Keynes, MK11 3LW, UK
UKHW022218190926
475702UK00003B/417

* 9 7 8 1 0 4 1 1 6 6 6 8 9 *